METRICS
AT WORK

METRICS AT WORK

JOURNALISM AND THE CONTESTED MEANING OF ALGORITHMS

Angèle Christin

PRINCETON UNIVERSITY PRESS

PRINCETON AND OXFORD

Published by Princeton University Press
41 William Street, Princeton, New Jersey 08540
6 Oxford Street, Woodstock, Oxfordshire OX20 1TR

press.princeton.edu

First paperback printing, 2022
Paperback ISBN 9780691234458

The Library of Congress has cataloged the cloth edition of this book as follows:

Names: Christin, Angèle, author.
Title: Metrics at work : journalism and the contested meaning of algorithms / Angèle Christin.
Description: Princeton : Princeton University Press, 2020. | Includes bibliographical references and index.
Identifiers: LCCN 2019044937 (print) | LCCN 2019044938 (ebook) | ISBN 9780691175232 (hardback) | ISBN 9780691200002 (ebook)
Subjects: LCSH: Web usage mining in journalism—United States. | Web usage mining in journalism—France. | Journalism—Technological innovations—United States. | Journalism—Technological innovations—France.
Classification: LCC PN4784.W43 C47 2020 (print) | LCC PN4784.W43 (ebook) | DDC 070.4/30285—dc23
LC record available at https://lccn.loc.gov/2019044937
LC ebook record available at https://lccn.loc.gov/2019044938

British Library Cataloging-in-Publication Data is available

Editorial: Meagan Levinson and Jacqueline Delaney
Production Editorial: Kathleen Cioffi
Text and Cover Design: Leslie Flis
Production: Erin Suydam
Publicity: Kathryn Stevens and Kate Hensley

This book has been composed in Sabon LT Std text with Helvetica Neue LT Std display

CONTENTS

••••••••••••

ACKNOWLEDGMENTS

This book would not exist without all the journalists, editors, and blog-gers who generously agreed to talk to me. My gratitude especially goes to the editors-in-chief of the websites who opened the doors of their news-rooms to an enthusiastic ethnographer, perhaps without fully realizing that they would have to contend with my questions for years to come. I hope that they will recognize their experiences and words in this book.

I thank all of my colleagues in the Department of Communication at Stanford University for their intellectual community and for making it possible for me to finish this manuscript in spite of the demands of early parenthood and busy campus life. Particular thanks to Fred Turner for his mentorship and invaluable feedback on several versions of this man-uscript, and Jay Hamilton for his crucial support and advice. I am also indebted to the Journalism faculty and John S. Knight Journalism Fellow-ship group for their suggestions over the years, with special gratitude to Janine Zacharia, Dawn Garcia, and JSK fellows Frédéric Filloux, Alina Fichter, and Cécile Prieur.

This book draws on my dissertation work, conducted in the Sociology Department at Princeton University and at the Ecole des hautes études en sciences sociales. I am eternally grateful to my chairs, Kim Lane Scheppele and Florence Weber, as well as to my committee members, Viviana Zelizer and Paul DiMaggio, for their guidance, unwavering support, and opti-mism through all the stages of this work. I remember my cross-Atlantic dissertation defense with great fondness and thank the French and Amer-ican members of the jury for their insightful comments, which helped me through the revision process from dissertation to book: Didier Fassin, Michael Schudson, Philippe Steiner, Janet Vertesi, and Bob Wuthnow.

Seen from Silicon Valley, my two years of post-doc life in New York have acquired an aura of sophisticated intellectual urbanity. This would not have been possible without the amazing mentorship of danah boyd at the Data & Society Research Institute and Jeff Goldfarb at The New School for Social Research. At the New School, Virág Molnár and Rachel Sherman warmly welcomed me in the Sociology Department. My year at Data & Society was an exhilarating experience—thanks to all the fellows and staff for making this place what it is, with a special note to Alex Rosen-blat, Madeleine Clare Elish, Robyn Caplan, Karen Levy, Mimi Onuoha, Natasha Singer, Zara Rahman, Julia Ticona, and of course danah boyd for, well, everything—they'll know what I mean. None of this would have been possible without the support of several institutions during these years of transition: the Porter Ogden Jacobus Honorific Fellowship (Princeton University), the Josephine DeKarman Foundation, the Andrew W. Mellon Foundation, the Fondation Maison des Sciences de l'Homme, and the Fernand Braudel IFER Postdoctoral Fellowship.

As in web newsrooms, much collective work has gone into bringing this work to its current shape. I am incredibly grateful to the colleagues and friends who have read large chunks or the entirety of this manuscript. I feel very fortunate to have gotten terrific feedback from Mike Ananny, Jenna Burrell, Paul Edwards, and Dan Kreiss through a book workshop organized by Fred Turner at Stanford University. At ASA, Dan Menchik generously organized a second workshop with an equally wonderful crew: major thanks to Clayton Childress, Mariana Craciun, Alison Gerber, Steve Hoffman, Jennifer Lena, Omar Lizardo, Terry McDonnell, Vanina Lechziner, Sida Liu, Aaron Panofsky, Benjamin Shestakovsky, Julia Ticona, and Janet Vertesi for helping me improve this book. Our discussion—and the "writing like a dude" joke that came out of it—will remain a highlight of what collaborative work should look like. I also warmly thank my fellow book writers Morgan Ames, Beth Bechky, Philippa Chong, and David Pedulla for our chapter swaps. Our exchanges kept me going over the years. At Stanford, I feel lucky to have found superb intellectual partners across campus to provide feedback on this project. These include Michael Bernstein, Mark Granovetter, Jeff Hancock, Pam Hinds, Tomás Jiménez, Woody Powell, Francisco Ramirez, Byron Reeves, Mitchell Stevens, Forrest Stuart, Melissa Valentine, as well as graduate students Sanna Ali, Janna Huang, Anna Gibson, Andreas Katsanevas, Becca Lewis, Nika Mavrody, Ayinwi Muma, Jeff Nagy, and Sheng Zou. Particular thanks to Anna for her statistical skills, and to Sanna for the whirlwind of references that she put into shape. Across the bay, Marion Fourcade, Neil Fligstein, and Heather Haveman provided extremely helpful counsel at different stages of the process. Alec Glassford and Yanni Vardi conducted different iterations of the web crawls used for the quantitative part of the analysis. Isabella Furth copyedited the manuscript. Leah Horgan turned my amateurish sketches into sophisticated graphs.

This book would not exist without the editorial team at Princeton University Press who made it happen. All my gratitude goes to Meagan Levinson, Jacqueline Delaney, Theresa Liu, and the rest of their team. Several anonymous reviewers provided insightful and constructive feedback on the manuscript—the book is much better thanks to them.

These acknowledgments would not be complete without mentioning the many friends and colleagues in the United States, France, and many other places who have been my intellectual "compagnons de route" over the past decade: Fabien Accominotti, Guillermina Altomonte, Kalinka Alvarez, Chris Anderson, Michel Anteby, Sofya Aptekar, Beth Bechky, Sarah Beytelmann, Juliana Bidadanure, Agnès Blasselle, Sarah Brayne, Marianne Blanchard, Taina Bucher, Clayton Childress, Philippe Coulangeon, Olivier Donnat, Florence Eloy, Meghan Flaherty, Elsa Forner-Ordioni, Vicky Fouka, Léonie Hénaut, Shubha Herlekar, Kate Kellogg, Pierre-Antoine Kremp, Marci Kwon, Michèle Lamont, Alice Leduc, Jeffrey Lane, Jenn Lena, Gwénaëlle Mainsant, Grégoire Mallard, Cristina Mora, Ekédi Mpondo-Dika, Toussaint Nothias, Aurélie Ouss, Peter Pesic, Caitlin Petre, Aurélie Pinto, Ronny Regev, Rania Salem, Stephanie Schacht, Hana Shepherd, Kyla Thomas, Raphaëlle Théry, Julia Ticona, and Steve Vallas. Thank you to my parents Pierre Christin and Florence Fouquier, who followed my intellectual and geographical adventures with patience, sometimes amusement, and love always.

I dedicate this book to my son Félix and my husband Andrei Pesic, the greatest joys of my life.

PROLOGUE

••••••••••••••

Paris, January 2012. 9 a.m.

The shape of a city changes more quickly than the mortal heart, wrote Baudelaire. The northeast of Paris is certainly no exception. In the rapidly gentrifying neighborhood of Belleville, North African delis and old-fashioned sports bars are being replaced by pour-over coffee shops, pop-up restaurants, and municipally sponsored tech incubators like the white building where the *LaPlace* office was located.

Three journalists were having a cigarette and a cup of coffee downstairs, making snarky comments about the latest press announcement of then-President Nicolas Sarkozy and discussing where they would have lunch later that day. After a couple of jokes, someone buzzed me in and I climbed to the second floor, where I entered the asymmetrical open space of the newsroom: six large tables with a dozen journalists checking their Twitter feeds. The newsroom was quietly buzzing. Later, journalists would start their newsroom banter, pitching their ideas to colleagues, bickering with editors about headlines, and commenting on each other's articles.

At 10:30 a.m., a copy editor shouted to Clément, one of the interns: "Your article is out!" The first piece of the day, about a bullying scandal in an elite Parisian university, had just been published on the homepage of the website. The rhythm of interactions suddenly accelerated in the newsroom. Editors and copy editors congregated around one of their computer screens and looked together at traffic numbers to check how the article was doing, ready to change the headline if readers were not clicking enough. At his desk, Clément tweeted the piece and started typing furiously, replying to the many reactions that his article provoked on Twitter. A couple of hours later, the article had attracted tens of thousands of visitors.

Throughout the day, staff writers came to congratulate Clément on his piece. The collective energy of the room was palpable. A journalist in the political section who had also published an article that morning lamented: "You're getting all the attention … my article will never get more than 10,000 clicks!" Another one joked: "Guys, our morale correlates with the number of visitors … should we worry?" People chuckled and went back to their screens.

New York, October 2012. 10:30 a.m.

The noise of Lower Manhattan receded when I turned onto one of the quiet, tree-lined streets of the West Village. I signed in at the front desk of a nondescript office building. An elevator took me up, and sleek glass doors announced the offices of *TheNotebook*. I entered a large open space, with gray cubicles, wall-to-wall carpeting, and closed individual offices along the walls. In each cubicle were a couple of workstations, grouped more or less by section: culture here, politics there.

The place was quiet. Most of the senior writers were not in the office that day—they worked remotely. Myra, one of the copy editors, started to edit a short piece about the television series *Top of the Lake*. She checked for typos and added hyperlinks for all the DVDs, CDs, and books that appeared in the article and were sold on Amazon. "It's a big stream of revenue," she sighed. In between two articles, Myra looked at the internal group chat tool. She laughed at a picture of people wearing panda costumes: "It's a running joke here…. Our editor hates pandas, so we keep sending him pictures of pandas…. We like to be serious about silly things and silly about serious things," she mused, "That's the feel of *TheNotebook*."

Several meetings structured the day. In the 11:30 a.m. editorial meeting, journalists pitched their ideas. During the 3:30 p.m. meeting, editors decided on the headlines of the articles that were scheduled to be published the next day. Unlike the Parisian journalists, staffers at *TheNotebook* did not make plans to get lunch outside between meetings: most people brought in sandwiches or salads and continued to work at their desks.

Josh, the social media editor, scrutinized several charts on his screen. "The article on 'binders full of women' did really well on social…. Twelve percent of the readers come from Facebook, with Twitter, 20 percent total…. That's good. I mean, we knew it was going to do well. It was embarrassing for Romney, a lot of people noticed it, people tweeted about it. Traffic … there's no science about it. When something stands out, we know it's going to work."

In my field notebook, I wrote: "Weird. Traffic here is technical, not emotional like at *LaPlace*. Why?"

• • •

Clicks, likes, and shares are part of the background noise of our digital lives. Most of us see traffic-related metrics throughout the day, through social networking sites, apps, and other platforms that send notifications to our screens. Digital metrics have become so ubiquitous that we often take them for granted. Yet this does not mean that we always interpret them in the same way. In some cases, metrics can become deeply wrapped up in our affective lives, changing how we feel about others and about ourselves. In other cases, we keep metrics at a distance, treating them as technical indicators that can easily be manipulated. Depending on the context, we put metrics to distinct uses; we value them differently and project different kinds of meanings onto them.

In this book, I analyze how people react to digital metrics and why this matters. I focus on the case of journalism, a field that has been dramatically transformed by online technologies. *Metrics at Work* examines the role of audience analytics in the lives of web journalists working for two websites, one in Paris and the other in New York. The two sites had much in common: they shared similar editorial goals, used the same technological tools, and even had the same furniture. Over time, they both faced growing pressure to attract more traffic.

For four years, I followed journalists and editors as they struggled to maintain editorial quality while receiving massive flows of quantitative data about the preferences of their readers, the popularity of their articles, and the reactions of their followers. Even though they relied on similar metrics to assess their audiences, web journalists in New York and Paris still defined their journalistic roles and responsibilities to their algorithmic publics in strikingly different ways, with important consequences for the kinds of news they published. This book analyzes why this happened, and what it means about the reproduction of cultural difference at a time of technological convergence.

METRICS
AT WORK

Introduction

We live in a world of data. Our work, as well as how we stay informed and interact with others, increasingly takes place online. Our activities on the internet generate a tremendous amount of information about our social networks, financial records, shopping preferences, and geographical movements, all of which are recorded, stored, and analyzed by the very websites we spend time on. Our data is valuable. In what is sometimes compared to a new "oil rush," companies gather and mine this information to determine algorithmically what we see when we browse the web. Think of Google, which personalizes its results based on our search histories, or Facebook, whose newsfeed decides which friends and brands are relevant for us. Our online histories overwhelmingly shape our future options in the brave new world of digital platforms.[1]

It is not only as individual consumers that we are being tracked, quantified, and analyzed. It is also as workers and employees. In domains as varied as healthcare, finance, education, insurance, transportation, advertising, or criminal justice, organizations now draw on a trove of digital data to monitor what their employees are doing. This is particularly true for the people who create the online content that we consume every day. For many "digital laborers," as these workers are sometimes called, work has become inextricably intertwined with the platforms that put them in touch with potential clients and the metrics used to assess their outputs—whether in terms of clicks, rankings, or stars. Even workers who used to be protected from quantitative evaluation are now confronted with a flurry of data assessing their daily performance.[2]

Of course, the impetus to put numbers on things, people, and ideas is not new. The current avalanche of digital metrics is only the latest wave in a much longer history. From the birth of public statistics in seventeenth-century Europe to the ruthless system of slave accounting on American plantations in the nineteenth century, the rise of Taylorism in the 1930s, or the growth of cost-benefit analysis in the 1980s, there have been multiple waves of quantification—the transformation of qualities into quantities—of the social world. Yet the scale, granularity, and circulation of data accelerated dramatically with the development of ubiquitous computing and the automated collection of individual information that came with it.[3]

In this book, I examine how this multiplication of digital metrics, analytics, and algorithms is reconfiguring work practices and professional identities. I focus on the case of journalism, a field that has been profoundly changed by digital technologies. When we think of journalism, images of paper-filled newsrooms and reporters conducting interviews with notebooks and pencils often come to mind. Yet newsrooms do not look much like this today: from group chats to social media platforms and content management systems, digital tools are omnipresent in the gathering, production, and diffusion of information on the web. The business models of news organizations are also rapidly evolving. As people started accessing information on the internet, the demand for print advertising plummeted. News organizations began relying on online advertising and digital subscriptions as their primary source of revenue. In parallel, a new market emerged for "web analytics," or software programs tracking the behavior and preferences of internet users. Editors and journalists are now provided with a constant stream of data about their audience. They receive increasingly detailed information, often in real time, about the number of visitors, comments, likes, and tweets that their articles attract. What began as tools to track reader behavior and optimize news placement gradually turned into a means to measure workers' performance: many newsrooms now consider traffic metrics when deciding on hiring, promotions, and layoffs.[4]

To date, most practitioners and scholars have judged the increasing importance of web analytics to be a negative development for online news. Media experts criticize the frantic rhythm of real-time information on news websites; they describe journalists as mindlessly running on a "hamster wheel" of continuous updates, tweets, and blog posts.[5] They condemn "clickbait" articles as degrading the provision of quality information, and frequently hold the short news cycle responsible for the disappearance—or at least lesser prominence—of "shoe leather" reporting and investigative journalism.[6] These criticisms increased after Donald Trump's election in 2016: people blamed news organizations, along with cable television, for their continuous coverage of Trump's provocations, which provided him with a free platform in the name of attracting more page views. According to these commentators, it is the traffic-oriented business models of online news organizations, together with their reliance on algorithmically fueled social media platforms, that bear the responsibility for everything that went wrong in the public sphere.[7]

Contrary to the idea that digital metrics have solely negative consequences on news production, in this book I examine how metrics are discussed, contested, and put to a variety of uses. I argue that metrics are transforming journalism in unintended and sometimes paradoxical ways by comparing web newsrooms in the United States and France, two countries with markedly different journalistic traditions, relations to the market, and regimes of state regulation.[8] Between 2011 and 2015, I conducted in-depth ethnographic fieldwork at offices of news websites in New York and Paris. During that time, I followed web journalists and editors in their daily work. I sat with them and asked them about their careers and compensation. I observed how they made sense of traffic numbers and tried to understand their relationships with their online audiences.

Based on this ethnographic material, I find that the chase for clicks took strikingly different shapes in the United States and France, with significant consequences for the kind of news being published. Contrary to the idea that the digital transition necessarily leads to a standardization and impoverishment of journalistic production, I document how American and French journalists reproduced cultural differences at a time of economic and technological convergence. Beyond the case of journalism, the book provides a new framework for understanding the contested meaning of digital metrics and what they entail for work practices and professional identities in the algorithmic age.

Algorithms as Contested Symbolic Resources

Over the past decade, multiple overlapping terms have emerged to describe the complex technologies of quantification that sustain the digital ecosystem, including "big data," "metrics," "analytics," and "algorithms."[9] *Metrics at Work* focuses on the effects of algorithms and metrics on news production. "Algorithms" can be defined as sequences of logical operations providing step-by-step instructions for computers to act on data. In practice, algorithms are typically software programs that perform specific computational tasks.[10] "Digital metrics" and "analytics" (I use the terms interchangeably) refer to the quantitative outputs provided by algorithmic software programs for the benefit of online users. Digital metrics are typically displayed through data visualizations such as dashboards, rankings, lists, graphs, and maps.[11]

To date, much of the coverage of algorithms and digital metrics has split between technological utopianism and dire warnings. On the optimistic side, advocates tout the benefits of using "smart statistics" to make more informed, efficient, and objective decisions. In Silicon Valley and elsewhere, many praise the higher intelligence and formidable computational capabilities of algorithms in order to address long-standing social issues, from disease prevention to crime prediction. Computer scientists and engineers are not naïve: they agree that algorithms are far from perfect. Yet they strongly believe that the issues affecting algorithmic systems are primarily technical. As these systems become more sophisticated, advocates argue, the remaining issues will be fixed. It is only a matter of time before algorithms can help create a better world.[12]

Pessimists fundamentally disagree with this analysis. For them, algorithms are first and foremost social constructions with problematic political effects. Thus, critics analyze the discriminatory impact of algorithms, emphasizing how computational technologies can reproduce and even reinforce social and racial inequalities because of the training data and models they are built on. They criticize the lack of transparency of machine-learning algorithms, which they compare to "black boxes" that amplify the lack of accountability and power imbalance of existing political and commercial institutions. They argue that algorithms function as a form of surveillance—a subtle but deeply asymmetrical type of control that gives us the illusion of choice while monitoring us from a distance. For critical scholars, algorithmic systems are worrisome because they hide discriminatory outcomes under a patina of efficiency and objectivity that make biases even more difficult to address.[13]

These discussions between advocates and critics raise essential questions about the good and bad effects of "smart machines" in the contemporary world.[14] Yet the current debate remains too limited. In particular, existing discussions often take the efficacy and power of algorithms for granted: they tend to pay more attention to how algorithmic instruments are constructed rather than study how they are implemented in the social world. In the process, they underestimate the role of users and their practices in shaping the effects of algorithms—what I have called "algorithms in practice."[15] Whether focusing on the technical potential of computational tools, or criticizing the "tyranny" of metrics and algorithms, advocates and critics err on the side of technological determinism, attributing changes in society to changes in technology.[16]

Metrics at Work is not about the tyranny of metrics, even though metrics are ubiquitous in the world of web journalism. Instead of technological determinism, I conceptualize digital metrics as symbolic resources that can be negotiated, contested, and used in different ways depending on their institutional context. Metrics always come with a symbolic potential. As such, they can accomplish much more than the increased efficiency sought by their proponents or the discrimination and surveillance diagnosed by their critics. Like other complex symbols—ideas, art, values—metrics are never *just* metrics: they always stand for something larger.[17] Metrics can reorganize social worlds around them, bending themselves to many different kinds of relational activities. Such a perspective provides a much richer view of metrics than the deterministic approach.[18] In particular, focusing on the strategic uses of metrics reveals significant gaps between the intended and actual effects of technologies of quantification: people always find ways to manipulate or transform digital metrics in order to fit local priorities, as I examine in the case of journalism.[19]

Web Newsrooms between Editorial and Click-Based Evaluation

In this book, I analyze how journalists use and make sense of audience metrics. I find that metrics are highly contested symbols in most newsrooms, where they are intertwined in broader debates about journalistic quality and the role of publics in the digital age.[20]

First, metrics become mobilized within two competing modes of evaluation. On the one hand, web journalists argue that the primary criteria for assessing journalistic excellence concern the internal qualities of one's articles: being a good journalist means writing articles that document something new about the world. Key terms in this view include original reporting, fact checking, innovative angles, and earning the respect of fellow journalists. I call this set of justifications the *editorial* mode of evaluation. On the other hand, many writers—occasionally even the same people who evoke the editorial definition—also describe their work in quantitative terms. For them, being a web journalist is primarily about maximizing diffusion and promoting one's content by creating a "buzz," "going viral," or "trending" on social media platforms. In this view, the worth of an article depends primarily on its online popularity, which is primarily measured through web analytics. This constitutes the *click-based* mode of evaluation.[21]

In an ideal world, all good articles in terms of editorial content should score well in terms of clicks; conversely, all popular articles should have a strong editorial value. Yet this is rarely the case. As web journalists know all too well, editorial and a click-based evaluation often clash. An in-depth investigation of state corruption in Syria may score high on the editorial scale but will probably attract fewer clicks than a piece about Kim Kardashian, which in turn may not have high editorial value, even if it is entertaining to read. By making different categories of articles commensurable on a single, quantitative scale, clicks have transformed hierarchies in web newsrooms: many sections that have little prestige from an editorial perspective receive a new visibility because of their high traffic numbers. Hence, most journalists in New York and Paris experience an acute sense of conflict between editorial and click-based definitions of their work.[22]

It is worth noting that the tension between editorial and commercial evaluation is not new in the media world. As a French editor-in-chief once told me: "An editor cannot always act as he would prefer. He is often obliged to bow to the wishes of the public in unimportant matters." He was quoting from a play written by Henrik Ibsen in 1882.[23] Clicks are, in some ways, merely the latest instantiation of the economic pressures that have shaped journalistic production for the past century and a half. The chase for clicks—and the obsession with traffic numbers that comes with it—is part of the longer trend of already commercially oriented journalistic fields towards market forces and corporate logics.[24]

Yet web analytics differ from previous manifestations of market pressures because of their individualizing focus. Contrary to circulation figures for print newspapers or audience ratings for television, analytics software programs provide fine-grained data about the popularity of each writer and each article in a given newsroom. Clicks not only individualize market forces, they also function as profoundly ambiguous symbolic objects in the digital world that web journalists inhabit. This is because metrics are never *just* metrics: they always represent something else. In web journalism, I argue that clicks stand for the complex and contested entities that I call algorithmic publics. These publics in turn take on strikingly different meanings in the United States and France.

Algorithmic Publics in the United States and France

Digital workers operate in an increasingly globalized and connected environment: they use the same technological tools, share the same platforms, and face comparable business constraints around the globe. This applies to journalists: in newsrooms across the world, staff writers and editors work on the same brands of laptops, use the same social media platforms, sit on the same types of chairs, and look at the same web analytics software programs.

Such similarities raise important questions about the relationship between global forces and local cultures. Are cultural differences being effaced in the digital age? To date, two main perspectives have emerged in studies of offline phenomena. The "Americanization" or "McDonaldization" approach answers in the affirmative: local cultural specificities and media representations are being destroyed by the cultural imperialism of the United States. In contrast, the "hybridization" perspective answers negatively, focusing instead on the appropriations and "bricolages" between different cultural forms that take place on the ground.[25] To investigate what is changing with online technologies, one needs comparative and transnational studies of digital phenomena across national contexts. Yet most existing research on digital work focuses on the United States. From analyses of early blogs to the study of online marketplaces, "methodological nationalism," as it has been called, still reigns in the study of digital technologies.[26]

Here, I rely instead on a comparative perspective to examine the effects of digital metrics on news production in the United States and France. To compare the structures, norms, and histories of journalism in the two countries, I use the concept of national journalistic fields. In the framework of sociologist Pierre Bourdieu, fields are configurations of positions—and sites of tension over what the field is about—that possess some degree of autonomy from the broader social structure. Thus, journalistic fields are structured by an autonomous logic (e.g., the quest for professionalism and prestige) on one hand, and a heteronomous logic (e.g., commercial pressures or political constraints) on the other hand.[27]

As media scholars often emphasize, the tension between professionalism, market forces, and political approval is always central in journalistic fields.[28] Yet there is variation between countries in the level and kind of heteronomy at stake. Nowhere is this clearer than when comparing U.S. and French journalism. Throughout the nineteenth and twentieth centuries, journalists in the United States and France developed strikingly different definitions of their professional autonomy, relationships to market forces, and norms about their public role. In the United States, journalism underwent an early professionalization process and faced strong market pressures beginning in the nineteenth century. In contrast, in France, journalism was long protected from market forces by the state. It became professionalized later, and remained driven to a greater extent by civic goals. Starting in the 1980s, journalists in both countries experienced growing market and financial pressures, leading to heated debates about the role of audience preferences in news production.[29]

Writing about print newsrooms, communication scholar James Carey described the public as the "god term of journalism ... , its totem and talisman."[30] As is the case for many talismans, however, the perception of the public among journalists has always been ambiguous. From the definition of the press as the "fourth estate" to the belief in the virtues of "watchdog" journalism, publicity has long been praised as the lodestar for American journalism, in print and online.[31] Similarly, in France, journalists have long defined themselves as "intellectuals" in charge of shaping public opinion. Yet journalists in both countries traditionally avoided paying attention to the actual preferences of their audience. Research in print newsrooms showed that journalists in the two countries typically ignored the opinions of their readers: they dismissed letters to the editors as "insane," refused to read marketing reports, and relied instead on idealized representations of their audience.[32]

Given the multiplication of analytics in web newsrooms, one might expect a rationalization of the relationship between journalists and their publics.[33] Yet in spite of the increasingly fine-grained data they receive, I found that journalists still could not reliably predict what would be popular: in online news, as in other sectors of intellectual and artistic production, "all hits are flukes."[34] Overall, traffic analytics always stand in for broader and more elusive entities—what I call *algorithmic publics*, publics that are mediated *and* represented in web newsrooms through computational software programs. Web analytics mediate the relationship between journalists and their publics, materializing these online collectives through dashboards, metrics, and dials on their computer screens. When journalists look at digital metrics, they see in one place the complex and distributed communities of online readers that come from Facebook, Twitter, Google, and other algorithmic platforms.[35]

These algorithmic publics in turn remained deeply ambiguous objects in the web newsrooms I studied. In New York, journalists primarily interpreted audience metrics as indicators of market pressures: they understood the publics these numbers stood for as fragmented and commodified readers—as "eyeballs" that could be counted, targeted, and priced.[36] In contrast, journalists in Paris understood audience metrics as a complex signal of a writer's relevance in the public sphere. This came with an ambivalent understanding of algorithmic publics as collective entities that had both commercial value and civic potential. As we will see, such representations were shaped by the longer history of the national journalistic field within which web journalists were embedded; they also came with important ramifications on the news being produced in the United States and France.

Comparing *TheNotebook* and *LaPlace*

In this book, I focus on two news websites: *TheNotebook* in New York and *LaPlace* in Paris. The two publications have much in common. The journalists who founded both websites believed that they could take advantage of the internet to transform journalism. They had big ideas, eager funders, and an enthusiastic staff of writers dedicated to the cause. During their first years of existence, they attracted praise and prizes, including prestigious journalism awards. Editors from the two websites also knew each other: the French editors consciously imitated the U.S. website when developing their website, and the publications had an informal editorial partnership for a while. Both sites relied from the beginning on advertising as their main source of revenue. Over time, they realized that they needed to attract more traffic in order to survive in an increasingly competitive market. This led them to rely heavily on analytics and audience metrics for editorial and managerial decisions.

Between 2011 and 2015, I followed the journalists and editors of *TheNotebook* and *LaPlace* as their editorial dreams were confronted by new realities in the market for online news. Moving back and forth between New York, close to my PhD program, and Paris, where I was born and grew up, I conducted more than a hundred semi-structured interviews with journalists, in English and in French. I asked them questions about their careers, their writing routines, their relationships with their colleagues, what they thought of their readers, how much money they made, and what it meant for them to be journalists at that point in time. I also conducted ethnographic observations in order to better understand their professional practices and to contrast what they told me during the interviews about their work with what I saw when I spent time with them.[37] I spent several days per week in the newsrooms, sitting in the middle of open-space offices and following their online and offline activities. I kept track of their traffic numbers and asked them how they made sense of those metrics. I attended the conferences where they were speaking, read the articles they published, joined their coffee breaks and lunches, and observed some of their romances and clashes on Twitter and in real life. In parallel, I collected quantitative data about the content they published online.

TheNotebook and *LaPlace* occupy a hybrid position in the world of online news: founded by print journalists, they operate exclusively online. This provides a rare opportunity to examine the transition from print to web journalism in the two countries. While *TheNotebook* and *LaPlace* are at the center of the story told in this book, they are only a part of the larger digital news ecosystem in New York and Paris that I studied for this project. In addition to these two websites, I examined so-called legacy news organizations (news organizations founded before the advent of the internet), traffic-driven news aggregators, and specialized websites.

The methodological appendix of this book presents the data collection process and includes more information about why I chose the websites, how I got access, and how I gathered a mix of online and offline data for this analysis.

A note about anonymization: readers may have noticed that the names of the publications and journalists studied in this book have been changed. They may wonder why the author would bother with anonymization in such a name-driven industry. I realize that anonymization may appear frustrating, or worse, pointless. Ethnographers have noted the difficulty of anonymizing prominent political figures, intellectuals, and one-of-a-kind institutions. One could add that anonymizing news organizations and writers whose main ambition is to be visible online is an even more fruitless exercise.[38] And yet, there are important reasons for doing so. Anonymization provides a layer of confidentiality protecting the organizations and individuals who agreed to participate in this project, give me detailed accounts of their conflicts with their superiors, and tell me about their salaries, all under the condition of confidentiality. I am respecting my promise here. I use pseudonyms and have also removed or changed pieces of information that would have immediately revealed the unique features of the individuals and organizations under consideration.

In spite of these efforts, some readers will be able to identify the names of the journalists and publications. I think that they should try to forget those names as much as possible. One benefit of anonymity is to enable us to think in analytic terms instead of relying on vague reputations. It forces us to focus on organizational features and field-level processes instead of brand names and knee-jerk reactions when trying to understand when and why online publications act the way they do. Such a careful approach is essential to understand why news websites are struggling in the digital economy and to come up with new ideas about what can be done about it.

The Argument

Based on this material, *Metrics at Work* documents a process of difference within convergence. On the convergence side, I show that in spite of their different locations, *TheNotebook* and *LaPlace* went through strikingly similar phases over time as the market for online news became more competitive. At first, they had high editorial ambitions and low expectations of making a profit. At about the same time, however, the two newsrooms entered the chase for clicks. Editors and journalists then started using the same analytics tools, developed similar traffic-related expertise, and relied on the same editorial formats to attract more page views. Over the years, both *TheNotebook* and *LaPlace* became characterized by an acute tension between editorial and click-based definitions of journalism.

In spite of this process of convergence, *TheNotebook* and *LaPlace* also developed strikingly different uses and understanding of audience metrics. At *TheNotebook*, web analytics were understood as unambiguous signals of market forces. Editors relied upon them to make decisions about the editorial line of the website; however, the staff at *TheNotebook* understood traffic as a technical game—one that was important economically but did not affect their professional identity, which in turn depended primarily on their professional reputation among their peers. In contrast, everybody at *LaPlace*, editors and journalists alike, displayed deeply conflicted feelings with respect to traffic numbers. Though they criticized clicks as indicators of market pressures hostile to their journalistic mission, editors and journalists also fixated on metrics in their daily work, interpreting them as signs of their professional value and relevance as public intellectuals.

To make sense of these differences between *TheNotebook* and *LaPlace*, I rely on the concepts of *bureaucratic* and *disciplinary* power. In the New York newsroom, a strong division of labor, hierarchical stratification, and clear symbolic boundaries between click-based and editorial evaluation prevailed—a structure in line with previous definitions of bureaucratic firms. In contrast, the Parisian newsroom relied on a flatter hierarchy, weak specialization, and fuzzy internal boundaries to organize its production process, keeping click-based and editorial goals constantly intertwined. Journalists internalized pressures to be productive and "disciplined" themselves to get more clicks—a process that resembles previous definitions of how disciplinary power operates.[39] The relationship with the websites' audiences, the production of news, compensation systems, and even the careers of the journalists and bloggers working for the two websites were affected by the distinct infrastructures put in place to manage the tension between click-based and editorial priorities.

Metrics at Work analyzes these differences using a multilevel theoretical framework. I find that the internal cultures of the hybrid websites I studied were shaped by the distinct trajectories and structures of their national journalistic fields.[40] The editors and journalists who founded the two websites—many of whom had spent most of their careers working for print newsrooms before starting these digital projects—reproduced what they knew best when trying to figure out the dilemmas of online news production. At *TheNotebook*, journalists drew on a long tradition of professionalization, peer evaluation, and a marked separation between marketing and editorial functions when organizing their digital production process. As a result, the New York newsroom developed a bureaucratic system for handling traffic concerns, keeping them strictly separate from editorial goals. By keeping traffic metrics at bay, the journalists reinforced an understanding of their algorithmic publics as fragmented, commodified, and irrelevant for professional evaluation.

In contrast, the French editors and journalists did not develop such compartmentalized organizational forms. Instead, they inherited an understanding of journalism as a form of intellectual production geared towards the public sphere. In addition to monetized eyeballs, the French journalists conceptualized their publics as a civic collective endowed with political will—a unitary, durable, and authoritative entity whose opinions mattered.[41] Consequently, they took traffic metrics to heart, interpreting them both as commercial signals *and* as indicators of a civic public. This meaning of metrics, together with the relative absence of division of labor in the Parisian newsroom, resulted in a disciplinary system in which journalists internalized the pressure to maximize traffic. These different priorities percolated through the editorial production and compensation practices of the two organizations, affecting the journalists' professional identities and the kind of news published by the two websites.

Overall, these findings show how digital metrics can be put to strikingly different uses depending on their institutional contexts—here, the national settings, professional fields, and organizational structures in which journalists were embedded. In the process, *Metrics at Work* reveals how cultural difference can be reproduced at a time of economic and technological convergence. Digital metrics and software programs spread across national borders, usually with the ambition to provide one-size-fits-all solutions. Yet what happens on the ground often differs from these grand intentions as people find ways of putting metrics to work.

Book Outline

The book is structured into six chapters. The first chapter provides the structural and historical background for the rest of the analysis, retracing the distinct relationships and quantitative modes of representation that developed between journalists and their publics over the course of the past

century and a half. It relates these developments to the different trajectories of the journalistic field in the United States and France.

The second chapter turns to the early days of online news, before
profit, traffic, and metrics-based imperatives became key concerns. It focuses on the first years of *TheNotebook* and *LaPlace*, two publications
that started as innovative, playful, and collaborative editorial projects.
Even though they shared similar utopian beliefs, they also had distinct
political and editorial identities. In particular, in spite of its explicit imitation of *TheNotebook*'s editorial project, the French website was more
countercultural, participatory, and politically engaged than its U.S. counterpart from the start.

The third chapter examines how the two websites entered the chase
for traffic. At about the same time, *TheNotebook* and *LaPlace* realized
that they needed to attract more online readers to survive. In spite of their
distinct political and editorial identities, they developed the same editorial and organizational strategies to increase their traffic over time: publishing more, faster, and tracking the behavior of their online readers
more closely than ever before. Both websites started experiencing an acute
tension between editorial and click-based modes of evaluation, which
affected the kind of content they published.

The fourth chapter focuses on the uses and interpretation of web analytics at *TheNotebook* and *LaPlace*. The two publications used the same
software programs to track the preferences of their online readers, but
they made sense of the metrics provided by these programs in strikingly
different ways. In New York, traffic soon became an imperative for the
top editors in charge of managing the publication, whereas staff writers
refused to embrace the tyranny of metrics. In contrast, journalists in Paris
were simultaneously deeply critical of traffic numbers *and* obsessed with
clicks. This chapter shows how metrics do more than function as market
indicators: they also reveal the journalists' representations of their algorithmic publics.

The fifth and sixth chapters explore the consequences of these distinct
understandings of metrics on two key aspects of the daily life of news
organizations: editorial production and compensation systems. In the fifth
chapter, I analyze the editorial routines associated with online news production. Though both *TheNotebook* and *LaPlace* faced a similar tension
between "fast" and "slow" news, they handled it differently: in one case
a strong division of labor prevailed, whereas in the other porous boundaries and versatility dominated. Building on the previous chapters, I contrast the bureaucratic and disciplinary dynamics that structured the daily

life of *TheNotebook* and *LaPlace* respectively. These differences reveal distinct strategies for handling the tension between click-based and editorial modes of evaluation.

The sixth chapter explores the ramifications of these conflicting systems of evaluation by turning to the thorny question of compensation. *TheNotebook* and *LaPlace* faced the same dilemma: how to get people to work without enough money to pay all contributors a decent wage. In both places, traffic became an important criterion for deciding whom to pay, and how much to pay them. Yet the two organizations relied on distinct strategies to decide how much to pay their flexible workers. The chapter examines how this affected the identities and careers of freelance journalists in the two countries. It analyzes why, overall, American journalists were less conflicted about using metrics-related criteria than their French counterparts.

In the conclusion, I examine the implications of this work for further studies of digital metrics beyond the case of journalism. At a time when nearly every domain is affected by analytics and algorithms, *Metrics at Work* provides an overview of what kinds of changes we might expect—and what should not be taken for granted—whenever metrics take over.

From Circulation Numbers to Web Analytics

Journalists and Their Readers in the United States and France

I first encountered the software program Chartbeat during one of my early days at *LaPlace*. It was a tense period for the news website, which had just been acquired by a larger media company; the journalists were cautious. During their many cigarette breaks, they devised complex strategies to get what they wanted from "the bosses" (*les chefs*). I was not invited to join them during these breaks. In fact, I was not told much at that point. When I asked the journalists who were storming in and out of the newsroom questions about the sale, most responded to me with cursory declarations about the freedom of the press. More often than not, I was left to my own devices in a half-empty newsroom. In these meditative moments, I had to find a place where I could sit and observe the journalists without being too conspicuous. Soon the copyediting desk emerged as the safest corner in the open-space office; at least one of the two copy editors was always there, correcting and publishing articles online, in constant contact with the editors and staff writers. I gratefully sat at their table, relieved to have found an unobtrusive way to spend time in the newsroom.

Chartbeat had come up in passing during several of my interviews, but until that point I had not focused on it; it was one of the multiple new technical terms that I was learning during my first months of fieldwork. It was only when I sat with the copy editors in the semi-deserted office that I first looked carefully at the software program. The copy editors kept Chartbeat open on one of their double computer screens, along with their Twitter deck, the Gmail chat program they used to converse with other journalists, their Word documents with "track changes" mode on, and the CMS (content management system) with which they published articles on the website.

A static image (Figure 1.1) cannot give a complete measure of Chartbeat's mesmerizing qualities. Its busy screen changes every few seconds, lending it the appearance of being alive. Numbers move constantly, accelerating and decelerating without warning. The position of the articles in

Figure 1.1. Screenshot of Chartbeat. Retrieved from https://chartbeat.com /demo/#_ on August 22, 2017.

the rankings changes rapidly, up and down, left and right, tracking the pieces that are "trending" and those that have not attracted the readers' interest. The speedometer-like icon on the top left shows the number of concurrent visitors currently on the website. For each article, the Chartbeat dashboard provides data about the number of visits, the numbers of likes and tweets on social media platforms, the average time spent on each page, and the geolocation of the readers, comparing these numbers with equivalent data from the previous weeks and months. Articles with low numbers of readers seem to hide ashamedly at the bottom of the page, whereas popular articles move up, and up again, until they reach the top of the charts. The upward movement of successful articles fills the observer with a sense of joy and excitement: the outside world likes the piece! Online readers are clicking!

Chartbeat is a powerful device. The more time I spent in web newsrooms, the more I became accustomed to its ubiquitous presence. All the newsrooms I studied in New York and Paris relied on Chartbeat; many used additional analytics programs to complement it. Over time, the dashboard lost its novelty for me. Yet some of the magic of this first encounter persisted. Editors on the French side gave me the access codes to the program. Months after the end of the in-depth phase of my fieldwork, I still regularly checked Chartbeat out of sheer curiosity, comparing the popularity of different articles and imagining how the journalists were making sense of it.

Even as an external observer, I could feel the addictive quality of Chartbeat. How would I react if I were a web journalist who wrote and published articles every day? Like them, I might describe Chartbeat as the "crack cocaine" of online news. Like them, I might compare the real-time dashboard to the "flickering lights" of an addictive slot machine, or to a weapon triggering a "race to the bottom" between newsrooms.[1] Like one of them, I might write that:

> Every time I sat down to work, I surreptitiously peeked at it—as I did when I woke up in the morning, and a few minutes later when I brushed my teeth, and again later in the day as I stood at the urinal. Sometimes, I would just stare at its gyrations, neglecting the article I was editing or ignoring the person seated across from me. My master was Chartbeat, a site that provides writers, editors, and their bosses with a real-time accounting of web traffic, showing the flickering readership of each and every article.... Like a manager standing over the assembly line with a stopwatch, Chartbeat and its ilk now hover over the newsroom.[2]

This fascination with Chartbeat comes in part from what it represents. The program provides a quantitative visualization of the distributed audience visiting a news website at any given moment. Its dashboard gives a sense of the ongoing, decentralized, and large-scale online dialogue taking place between journalists and their online readers. It resembles what Karin Knorr-Cetina and Urs Bruegger analyze as the "appresentational work" of computer screens—what they call "scopic systems"—in highly mediated workplaces. As they write in their study of financial traders, "the screen 'appresents' the market: it brings the territorially distant and invisible 'near' to participants." Similarly, analytics software programs like Chartbeat "appresent" the demand side of online news: they put online readers and their clicks at the very center of web newsrooms, in front of journalists, throughout their daily routines.[3]

• • •

But before the existence of digital technologies that could represent readers as moving numbers on a screen, print journalists already had a relationship with their publics. They already received data about their readers. And they already had ideas about who their ideal readers would be. This chapter offers a comparative genealogy of how the relationship between journalists and their readers evolved in the United States and France over the past century and a half and how this history shapes current interpretations and debates about web analytics.[4]

Journalism as a field, as an industry, and as a form of public expression, has taken different paths in the United States and France. As early as the late nineteenth century, journalists in the two countries had a strong sense of how and why their writing styles differed.[5] Yet the differences between the United States and France went further than style alone: the balance between commercial and civic forces also differed profoundly between the two countries. As a result, journalists on each side of the Atlantic made sense of their publics in strikingly different ways. Drawing on this historical material, I argue that it is impossible to separate the question of publics—and, relatedly, of how journalists interpret audience data—from the broader and conflicting forces that shape journalistic fields: commercial pressures on the one hand and civic ambitions on the other.

Sensationalism versus Professionalism: American Journalism in the 1890s

In the United States, a mass newspaper market developed in the 1830s with the "penny press." From the start, the newspaper industry was based on what economists call a dual-product marketplace: newspapers sold editorial content to readers first, and their readers' attention to advertisers second. As advertising in newspapers grew, the press turned into a profitable industry attracting large amounts of capital. Many newspapers gradually abandoned the most visible forms of political and party-affiliated partisanship. By the end of the nineteenth century, the mass newspaper market had become highly competitive.[6]

In parallel, some journalists played an active role in shaping public debates. At the peak of the Progressive Era, reform-minded writers—often grouped under the umbrella term of "muckrakers"—documented and challenged the human toll of industrialization, detailing the abuses stemming from unbridled capitalism in the pages of magazines and newspapers. From Ida M. Tarbell's excoriation of the Standard Oil monopoly to Upton Sinclair's writings on the meatpacking industry and Ida B. Wells' coverage of racism and lynching in the South, muckrakers put the factual orientation of journalistic writing at the service of a progressive and sometimes openly political agenda.[7]

Such reform-minded investigative articles came with an explicit desire to change public opinion. Circulation figures—then the main metric assessing the commercial reach of a newspaper—were often mobilized as a signal that reporting had captured public attention. For instance, Nellie Bly's series on psychiatric hospitals was widely credited as having significantly increased the *New York World*'s circulation numbers. Politicians cared about these large numbers, and increasingly recognized muckraker writers as an important force to be reckoned with. Yet—and, as we will see, contrary to what took place in France at about the same time—the way that American muckrakers engaged in the public debate was not based on their intellectual or political prestige. Instead, many of them emphasized their individual moral responsibility in addressing abuse and injustice: as Christians, as educated people, and as active members of their communities, they saw it as an ethical duty to get involved.[8]

Over time, lines became increasingly blurred between the reform-minded investigative articles inspired by the muckraking tradition and what came to be known as the "yellow press": sensationalist and self-aggrandizing newspapers featuring lurid headlines, factual approximations, and melodramatic prose. Yellow newspapers regularly published muckraking articles, but also featured attention-grabbing "tabloid" stories about crimes, wars, corruption, and scandals.[9] As journalism scholar Michael Schudson argued, the growing popularity of the yellow press marked the beginning of a conflict between distinct paradigms defining journalistic production. Yellow newspapers relied on a "news as stories" paradigm emphasizing the entertainment value and enjoyability of journalistic articles. To entertain their blue-collar and immigrant readers, yellow newspapers used the original "clickbait," so to speak: they featured illustrations and cartoons, relied on simple words and narratives, and prominently published what we would now call "lifestyle" content, such as etiquette and consumption-oriented articles. In contrast, the "news as information" paradigm emphasized verifiability, impartiality, and trustworthiness. In the words of Adolph Ochs, owner and publisher of *The New York Times* after 1896: "It will be my earnest aim that *The New York Times* give the news, all the news, in concise and attractive form, in language that is parliamentary in good society; ... to make the columns of *The New York Times* a forum for the consideration of all questions of public importance, and to that end to invite intelligent discussion from all shades of opinion."[10] To distinguish itself from its mass circulation competitors, the *Times* sought to appeal to a narrower but more affluent audience—the educated middle and upper-middle class.

Over time, American journalism underwent a professionalization process that further strengthened the "news as information" paradigm and its emphasis on accuracy and impartiality. A new mythology emerged contrasting the social characteristics of "old reporters"—uneducated, ignorant, and often drunk—and "new reporters"—younger, sober, idealistic, and highly trained. Journalism programs, schools, awards, and associations multiplied during the first decades of the twentieth century. Journalists by then were relying more consistently on specific editorial formats: they conducted interviews and relied on reporting techniques; newspapers were often criticized when they did not stick to "facts." The number of full-time journalistic jobs in the United States also increased, together with the average salary of journalists, which turned the press into an appealing option for college-educated young men from the middle class. This impetus towards professionalization accelerated during and after the First World War, when journalists actively sought to distinguish themselves from their competitors in the public relations industry.[11]

In the first decades of the twentieth century, the number of publications boomed, together with the number of companies interested in advertising their products and services in the pages of newspapers. News organizations and marketers began to gather more information about their audiences in order to convince advertisers to buy space in their pages. Newspapers and magazines developed customer surveys, asking readers about their socio-demographic characteristics, preferences in news, and consuming habits. Marketing departments began to sell advertisers specific segments of their audiences based on income, location, age, or gender.[12] These developments spurred new worries about the influence of capital, competition, and advertising pressures in the media. In *Public Opinion* (1922) and *The Phantom Public* (1925), writer and reporter Walter Lippman criticized the commercial orientation of newspapers, which he argued left journalists able to cover topics only superficially, while readers lacked the knowledge and critical skills necessary to truly participate in public affairs.[13]

By the 1920s and 1930s, the field of journalism in the United States was already structured by two equally strong and conflicting forces: market pressures and professionalization. Mainstream journalists had different options at their disposal to assert their newfound importance. They could have taken the muckraking road of politically informed engagement and produced sensational stories geared towards civic reform and the shaping of public opinion. Instead, they took the path of professionalization, relying on the norms of objectivity, factuality, and collegial control to legitimate their status. This changed the meanings journalists gave to audience measurements. Instead of being a signal of one's relevance in the public sphere, as they had been for the muckrakers, newspapers' circulation figures primarily became a signal of commercial success. As the field became more professionalized, many journalists stopped following audience numbers altogether, focusing instead on writing "good copy" and getting the respect of fellow journalists. At that point, American journalists could be said to care more about the opinion of their peers than about the public at large.[14]

French Journalists and the Birth of the "Intellectuals"

In France, a mass newspaper market developed in the last decades of the nineteenth century, after the passage of a law protecting the freedom of the press in 1881. The impulse behind the law was to engineer a well-read and educated public that would be able to make informed political decisions.[15] Economic growth and industrialization also brought new capital and workers to Paris, turning it into a financial and industrial center in addition to a political and cultural one. A wide range of newspapers and magazines were launched, from mass circulation newspapers to highly politicized pamphlets (feuilles) and literary magazines. As in the United States and other parts of Europe, reading mass circulation newspapers became a daily ritual for a large part of the French population, forming "imagined communities"—to borrow the expression of political scientist Benedict Anderson—at the local and national level.[16]

In the 1880s and 1990s, this expansion enabled a growing number of journalists to make a living from their writing. Yet being a full-time publiciste—as journalists then called themselves—was far from easy.[17] Consequently, many journalists used their newspaper connections to further their careers not in journalism but in literature or politics instead. Boundaries between journalists and novelists were then highly porous: reporters often wrote best-selling novels; best-selling fiction writers also regularly contributed to newspapers. On the political side, the back and forth was no less fluid. Journalists took advantage of their reputations as publicistes to negotiate administrative or elected positions. Conversely, politicians frequently launched newspapers to publicize their views.[18]

Unsurprisingly, newspapers' coverage reflected these porous boundaries between journalism, literature, and politics. French writers valued a vivid writing style that featured lengthy descriptions and psychological speculation. They criticized the rise of journalistic techniques that had become mainstream in the United States several decades before, such as interviews and reporting.[19] Instead, the literary quality of articles was paramount, especially for prestigious formats such as *grands reportages* (long-form investigative stories), *chroniques* (often about inequalities, exposing what came to be called the "social question"), and literary criticism. Most newspapers and magazines also saw it as their role to be politically contentious.[20]

This political engagement reached new heights with the Dreyfus Affair. Alfred Dreyfus, a Jewish artillery officer, was sentenced to life imprisonment in 1894 for allegedly spying on the French Army. In the last decade of the nineteenth century, journalists, writers, politicians, and a large swath of the French population took sides in proclaiming his innocence or guilt, becoming either *Dreyfusards* or *Anti-Dreyfusards*. The press turned into a primary medium for public communication: major developments in the case were announced in the pages of newspapers. Though most of the mass circulation publications were anti-Dreyfus, many famous pro-Dreyfus editorials were also published in newspapers, most notably Emile Zola's "J'accuse," featured in *L'Aurore* on January 12, 1898.[21]

In the process, a new category of actors emerged: the *intellectuels*. These men and women of culture—writers, journalists, academics, politicians, etc.—were conscious of their role as engaged producers and consumers of civic opinions. Newspapers became essential platforms in the construction, coordination, and publicization of this new group, which was largely pro-Dreyfus. The *intellectuels* gathered petitions, letters to the editor, and pieces of evidence that they published in newspapers and magazines. As contemporary observers noted, newspapers then effectively stood for public opinion itself.[22]

The Dreyfus Affair marked a turning point for French journalists, who overwhelmingly embraced a public role based on intellectual prestige, civic engagement, and contentious position-takings. Contrary to the American case, the French journalistic field remained weakly autonomous and relatively unprofessionalized, with no clear boundaries distinguishing journalists from writers, politicians, or even academics. French journalists did not create specific codes of ethics, training programs, or related professional strategies to promote and solidify their occupational identity. Instead, they saw it as their role to participate—alongside others—in the public debate.[23]

This continued after the censorship of the First World War. Journalists created unions to negotiate better labor conditions, but these did not come with a markedly collegial or procedural professional ethos. If anything, the legitimacy of the press decreased throughout the 1920s and

1930s following a string of corruption scandals that revealed the involvement of publishers in cases of insider trading and payment for favorable coverage. Critics denounced the "abominable venality of the press" and problematic role of *financiers*' money in shaping newspaper coverage.[24]

Over time, French editors and journalists developed an ambivalent understanding of commercial success, high circulation figures, and other manifestations of popularity. On the one hand, they saw circulation figures and other types of reader feedback (letters to the editors, petitions, and so on) as a signal of their relevance and impact in shaping public opinion. On the other hand, they criticized such feedback as a vile manifestation of commercial goals. These values shaped the relationship between journalists and their readers for the rest of the twentieth century.[25]

American Journalism from the Wall of Separation to Audience Segmentation

After the Second World War, U.S. newspapers and magazines entered a period of confident optimism: in the words of media scholar Daniel Hallin, this was an era of "high modernism" for American journalism. Journalists saw themselves as the very incarnation of democracy at a time of Cold War politics. The idea that journalistic coverage should be factual and impartial had by then become a matter of course in professional associations' ethical codes; the ideal of objectivity also reigned supreme in the curricula of journalism programs, which were multiplying on college campuses.[26]

As in other sectors, this modernist ideology was the result of heated debates that had begun in the 1930s about the proper role of the media in democratic societies. As Victor Pickard explains, the settlement that emerged was marked by three defining assumptions: that the American media should be self-regulated (through professional norms and associations); that journalists should practice social responsibility (a vague and elusive term); and that media organizations should be protected by a negative freedom of the press (e.g., "freedom from" government interference instead of "freedom to" feature diverse viewpoints). The resulting paradigm resolutely favored the interests of corporations, while also supporting a liberal political consensus shaped by Cold War politics.[27]

This emphasis on business interests and self-regulation came with important repercussions for news organizations. Over time, American publishers put in place specific institutional forms to protect journalistic autonomy. First among these protections was the creation of physical and symbolic "walls of separation" between editorial and marketing departments. This was based on the idea that a publisher's political preferences or commercial concerns should not—and would not—infringe on editorial decisions. Editorial offices had to be "sanctuarized" and kept separate from marketing departments. In his classic 1960s study of *CBS*, *NBC*, *Newsweek*, and *Time*, sociologist Herbert Gans noted that "editorial and business departments operate independently of each other." Newsrooms also functioned in a highly specialized fashion, with both vertical divisions (strong hierarchies between editors and staff writers) and horizontal divisions (thematic sections and "beats"). These organizational structures turned editorial positions into specialized ones, depending on one's hierarchical status and "beat" (politics, local news, sports, and so on).[28]

This paradigm of self-regulation also affected the relationship between journalists and their readers. Following the rise of audience research in the motion picture industry, radio, and television during and after the Second World War, the marketing departments of newspapers and magazines began to gather detailed information about their audiences through systematic circulation assessments and reader surveys.[29] Yet most editorial departments did not take this information seriously into account when deciding what to cover and how. In the words of Gans, print journalists at the time had "little knowledge about the audience and rejected feedback from it.... Instead, they filmed and wrote for their superiors and for themselves, assuming that what interested them would interest the audience."[30]

Whereas muckrakers had made a sustained effort to participate personally in the public debate, by the 1950s and 1960s, most mainstream journalists refrained from such a posture. Instead, they developed an occupational identity defined by the ideal of objectivity, the hierarchies of editorial departments, and the wall of separation. This paradigm of press freedom came with an abstract and distanced relationship between journalists and their readers: journalists wrote most directly for their peers, their sources, and their superiors, not for the public at large. As historian Robert Darnton recalled from his days as a newspaperman at the *New York Times* in the 1960s,

> We really wrote for one another. Our primary reference group was spread around us in the newsroom, or "the snake pit," as some called it. We knew that no one would jump on our stories as quickly as our colleagues; for reporters make the most voracious readers, and they have to win their status anew each day as they expose themselves before their peers in print.[31]

As in other fields of intellectual and cultural production, journalists then primarily determined professional excellence by relying on the opinions of other journalists, conveyed through informal feedback, imitation by other newspapers, and professional awards to assess editorial quality. In the process, they kept audience feedback at bay. When explicitly asked about their readers, observers noted that journalists relied on "idealized" or "fantasized" representations, mentioning family members or invoking abstract figures of ideal readers. Actual reader feedback in the form of letters to the editor was ignored and often dismissed as "crazy" or unrepresentative—especially when this feedback was critical or negative.[32]

By the 1970s and 1980s, the economics of media production were changing. Advertising revenues increased exponentially, in part because of the multiplication of metropolitan region newspaper monopolies, turning the media industry into a highly lucrative business. By the end of the 1980s, the annual profits of newspapers companies like the New York Times Company and the Washington Post Company were ten times higher than they had been in 1975. The 1970s and 1980s brought waves of mergers and acquisitions, a rapid increase in newspaper chain ownership, and a multiplication of media behemoths—including Gannett, Knight-Ridder, and News Corp—making double-digit profits year after year.[33]

Somewhat paradoxically, though, media executives began to worry about the future of the industry. Even though the U.S. population was growing, newspapers' circulation was stagnant. Young people in particular seemed to be less interested in reading newspapers than the preceding generation. For an industry that privileged growth almost as much as actual profits, this was bad news. Though the media were more profitable than ever before, analysts predicted a gloomy future.[34] Within news organizations, these anxious forebodings led to a reorganization of the relationship between media companies and their audiences. Whereas journalists had previously assumed a kind of benign neglect towards their readers, the 1980s saw a new rise in marketing and audience research. Like Nielsen for television and Arbitron/Nielsen Audio for radio, multiple marketing companies and bureaus—the Alliance for Audited Media, BPA Worldwide, Simmons DataStream, Scarborough Research, and others—developed new types of audience metrics, measuring and categorizing readers' preferences into highly detailed segments.

The image of the audience that emerged from such studies was complex and often contradictory. Based on this data, however, news organizations arrived at the following interpretations: readers, they concluded, had a short attention span and a poor memory. They preferred entertainment to public interest stories and wanted "news you can use," such as local information, lifestyle pieces, cooking recipes, and other "how to" articles. In spite of the reluctance and criticisms of many journalists, managers began to reorganize newsrooms following in the footsteps of Gannett's *USA Today*: they turned to "market-driven journalism" that explicitly sought to attract and retain certain valued audience segments.[35]

Was this reorganization of news production around audience-led imperatives all bad? On the one hand, information certainly became more democratized: mainstream newspapers had new incentives to publish more diverse articles, including coverage of topics such as sex, gender, race, and inequality, which they did not cover much until then.[36] On the other hand, these new incentives tilted the news balance towards entertainment and away from public interest stories. In the words of Mark Fowler, chair of the Federal Communications Commission (FCC) under Ronald Reagan, by 1982, "the public's interest ... defines the public interest."[37] This rhetorical amalgamation of the civic needs of a democratic public and the actual preferences of an audience monetized for commercial purposes helped justify the consolidation and financialization of the U.S. media throughout the 1980s and 1990s.

In the process, the dominant conceptualization of the audience in the U.S. journalistic field changed. From the earlier high modern era's abstract conception of ideal newsreaders, mainstream media organizations moved in the 1980s towards a commercialized, individualistic, and consumer-oriented definition of their readers. It is important to note, however, that there were then other definitions of the role of journalists in the public arena—including the politically-engaged messages of publications connected to the countercultural, civil rights, and feminist movements, as well as the participatory culture promoted by initiatives in "public journalism." Some of these innovations eventually made their way into mainstream media; others remained at the margins of the journalistic field.[38]

French Newspapers, the State, and the Public

In France, the journalistic field took a different path following the Second World War. After the liberation, the state played an essential role in structuring the media landscape, with lasting effects on the organization of French journalism. In 1944, Charles de Gaulle's postliberation government forbade most newspapers from reopening: out of the 206 daily newspapers that were publishing in 1939, only 28 were allowed to resume operations. For the new public officials—many of whom had been members of the Resistance—the for-profit orientation of most newspapers, together with the political preferences of their wealthy publishers, were to blame for the press's collaboration with the Nazis.[39]

Consequently, the new regime engaged in intense regulatory efforts to protect the media from commercial interference. In 1949, all radio and television channels were nationalized and put under the control of a regulatory agency. The state also controlled the price, circulation, and paper allowance of newspapers. When former Resistance member Hubert Beuve-Méry founded *Le Monde* in 1944, it was at the explicit invitation of Charles de Gaulle, who wanted a "newspaper of prestige" for the "national interest."[40] Along similar lines, the government promoted the creation of a public news agency to gather reliable information, strengthened the system of public subsidies to the press, and consolidated the legal framework regulating journalistic work that had been put in place in 1935.[41] At the same time, newspapers continued to claim their involvement in public affairs and, often, their political affiliations. This tradition of a politically engaged press endured all the way to the post-May 1968 era.[42]

In parallel, journalism slowly became more professionalized. Journalism schools were created, and the social and educational background of journalists changed during the economic boom of the *Trente Glorieuses:* journalism became a more attractive profession for middle-class men and women with postsecondary education.[43] As in the United States, a new paradigm of self-regulation gradually came to define the daily operations of French news organizations. In the French context, however, this did not involve a "wall of separation" between marketing and editorial departments, nor did it entail a retreat from intervention in the public debate. As journalism scholar Jean Padioleau noted, French newspapers then often presented themselves as "national monuments" that were more public than private, in contrast with the economic orientation of American newspapers.

In many newspapers, self-regulation was enforced by the creation of representative bodies that voiced the concerns of journalists (*sociétés de journalistes*). Such bodies were originally put in place to protect journalistic autonomy from commercial and political interference. Over time, they acquired significant negotiating power, often vetoing the nomination of top editors and managers through strikes and protests.[44] Thus, top editors typically occupied uneasy positions balancing between the *sociétés de journalistes* and the demands of the newspaper's management. Their legitimacy within newsrooms usually stemmed from their journalistic career and intellectual prestige rather than their economic and managerial skills. As a result, editors maintained a complicated moral standing within many French news organizations.[45]

Throughout these changes, the relationship between journalists and their readers retained its ambivalence. Overall, French journalists kept a distanced attitude towards their readers, considering that trying to please their audience would threaten their independence and lower the quality of their news coverage. In the words of *Le Monde*'s top editors in the 1970s: "We are in the dark: no one here or anywhere at the newspaper knows who our readers are. Anyway, even if we knew, we wouldn't make our newspaper based on it. It is made according to what journalists think should be done. We refuse to follow a commercial policy that would affect our editorial department."[46]

Yet French journalists also remained far more concerned with their public aura and intellectual prestige than their American counterparts. This was in part due to the low specialization of French newsrooms, as well as to the higher legitimacy of editorials and opinion pieces among staff writers: many journalists still felt responsible for guiding public opinion and enlightening their readers about the central political ideas and events of the day.[47] This public mission to "educate, guide, and train the masses," in Padioleau's words, could take different avenues depending on the publication. For instance, at centrist newspapers like *Le Monde*, the writing style of journalists was often compared to the didactic tone of primary school teachers.[48] In contrast, at the alternative, politically engaged newspapers and magazines that emerged after the student movement of May 1968, journalists saw it as their civic duty to give voice to the powerless and to criticize the government's actions.[49]

In the 1980s, similar to what occurred in the United States, commercial pressures on news production increased. Advertising, which had remained relatively low compared to circulation revenues, took off. After François Mitterrand became president in 1981, the government ended the public monopoly on radio channels and television stations. Large media conglomerates emerged, together with for-profit television and radio channels. This growing competition was accompanied by new anxieties about circulation figures. Media executives, observing what U.S. newspapers were doing, came to the same conclusions as their counterparts across the Atlantic and started relying more heavily on audience research. French observers sometimes describe the 1980s and 1990s as "the money years" (*les années fric*). In the case of the journalistic field, that meant a rapid increase in privatization and concentration.[50]

Yet it is important to add that this process of marketization remained limited compared to the United States. For instance, the French regulatory framework was updated in 1986 to include restrictions on public stock ownership of media companies and foreign investment in the media sector, which constrained the rise of multinational corporations. Consequently, few French newspapers were chain-owned or acquired by publicly traded corporations; this stood in contrast to the United States, where many newspapers were acquired by public companies in the 1980s and 1990s. Similarly, French public subsidies to the press stayed high, averaging about 10 percent of total press revenues, which had no equivalent on the American side. Last but not least, advertising remained modest in French newspapers. For instance, in the early 2000s, only 39 percent of French newspapers' revenues came from advertising, compared to 87 percent in the United States. Thus, one should not overestimate the similarities between the U.S. and French press during those years.[51]

Figure 1.2 summarizes the dominant definitions of the public that emerged in the U.S. and French journalistic fields over the course of a century, between the 1880s and the 1990s. It compares how journalists conceptualized their public role along two dimensions: first, the relative weight of commercial versus civic definitions, and second, the overall level of attention that news organizations and journalists devoted to their readers. Until the 1980s, the American journalistic field relied on a more commercial definition of readers, a process largely driven by the strong market pressures that shaped news coverage in the United States throughout the second half of the twentieth century. In contrast, from the Dreyfus Affair onwards, the definition of the public that dominated the French journalistic field was more civic, in part because French journalists saw it as their role to guide and shape public opinion.

Online News and the Turn to Online Tracking

Starting in the 1990s, the transition to online news reconfigured journalistic production on both sides of the Atlantic. Following the diffusion of broadband internet in the 1990s, the U.S. journalistic field began a slow transition to digital media. After several videotext attempts, in which newspapers experimented with computer-like delivery of news content to

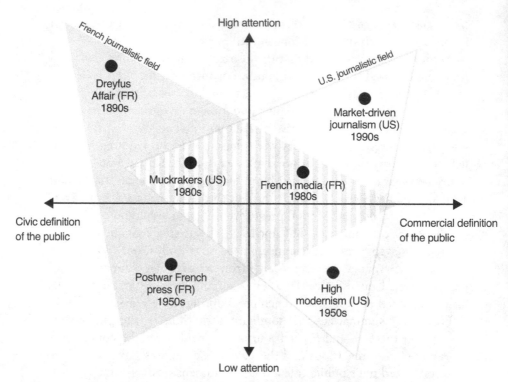

Figure 1.2. Journalists and their readers in the United States and France, 1880s–1990s.

their readers, newspapers paid closer attention to the World Wide Web. They usually began with "shovelware" strategies in which they simply cut and pasted (or shoveled) content online from their print publication. In parallel, individual journalists started taking advantage of the participatory capabilities of the internet. Whereas the early years of blogging had been marked by relatively intimate forms of personal expression inspired by diaries and personal journals, the blogosphere took a political and news-oriented direction with the development of blogging platforms in the second half of the 1990s. Writers, journalists, activists, and politicians opened blogs on which they shared news, updates, and opinion pieces, often with the explicit purpose of shaping the public agenda on questions they felt strongly about. News websites followed, featuring blogs on their homepages and opening commenting sections for more participation from and interactions with online readers.[52]

At the same time, the media industry entered an economic maelstrom. Classified advertising was moving online, to Craigslist and other websites, punching a major hole in the advertising revenues of print newspapers.

As the inventory (or amount of advertising space) of online publishers grew and became more diverse, the decline of newspapers' advertising revenues accelerated, falling by more than half—from $63.5 billion to $23 billion—between 2000 and 2013. After decades of stagnation, the circulation figures of daily newspapers also began to decline, from about 62 million total in the early 1990s down to 55 million in 2000, 50 million in 2007, and 40 million in 2014. At print publications, budget and staff cuts were instituted to meet the demands of shareholders and private equity investors to maintain high profit margins. Over 23,000 newspaper positions were lost in the United States between 1989 and 2015; an additional 38,000 magazine jobs disappeared between 2009 and 2014. In France, as we saw, news companies were less reliant on advertising revenues, but media executives still foresaw the same early signals as in the United States, including decreasing newspaper circulation figures and a decline in print advertising revenues—a 30 percent drop between 2008 and 2012.[53]

How could news organizations compensate for their losses? Over the course of the 2000s, many developed a hybrid system based on a mix of free access, digital subscriptions, and online advertising revenues. This system in turn led to the adoption of more encompassing forms of audience tracking than ever before in the history of American media. From the start, media companies had trouble selling the new digital medium to advertisers. Marketers soon asked online publishers to provide them with more information about internet users. In particular, they wanted data on users' web browsing histories (which websites they visited, how long they stayed on each page, which links they clicked on, which searches they made, and so on) in order to engage in behavioral targeting.

Online news publishers offered little resistance to these new demands of advertisers. They could deliver this information thanks to an innovation that made it possible to take consumer surveillance to a new level: "cookies," or early tracking software that stored detailed information about internet users' behavior based on a website's server data. Drawing on these "dragnet" technologies, as journalist Julia Angwin called them, news organizations started collecting fine-grained data about their readers.[54] Online publishers used this information to set the rate for their inventories, both in direct negotiations with advertisers and when selling space on real-time bidding platforms or "ad exchanges." They augmented traditional exposure-based metrics ("cost per mille" or CPM, based on the number of readers exposed to a given advertisement) with a new array of engagement-based metrics ("cost per action" or CPA, based on the numbers of readers who click on a given advertisement). In the words of media scholar Joseph Turow, news organizations "had little choice. Having rather quickly decided that their audiences would not pay for their online content, they looked to media planners and their clients for long-term survival."[55]

The Bazaar of Web Analytics

This is where we are today. As a consequence of these new demands from advertisers, online news publishers turned to online tracking in order to survive. Broadly defined, the terms "web metrics" or "analytics" include all data used to analyze and optimize web usage. Common examples of analytics include number of page views, unique visitors, comments, and average time spent by readers on a given webpage. Other metrics relate to audience engagement on social networking sites, such as numbers of "likes," "tweets," "shares," and posts on Facebook, Twitter, Instagram, and so on.

According to scholar Shoshana Zuboff, this arsenal of metrics is part of the "parasitic logic" of "surveillance capitalism," this "new economic order that claims human experience as free raw material for hidden commercial practices of extraction, prediction, and sales." Zuboff laments the success of this "coup from above," which enabled technology and media corporations to monetize our behavioral data with little resistance. Yet a closer look at the market for web analytics reveals that it is rife with contradictions, overlaps, and inconsistencies—an ecosystem that seems closer to the complex and nonstandardized exchanges of bazaar economies analyzed by anthropologist Clifford Geertz than to the rationalized surveillance order envisaged by Zuboff.[56]

To be sure, the market for web analytics is flourishing: multiple companies now offer suites of software programs that gather, mine, and help visualize web metrics. Yet these programs' outputs do not necessarily present coherent measurements; in fact, they often contradict each other.[57] This is in part because they use different methods and kinds of data—most importantly panel-based and server-based data—for measuring online traffic. Traditionally, media companies in radio and television relied on panel-based data, gathered and compiled by firms such as Nielsen and Comscore, which adapted their methods to assess online news consumption. They recruit people to participate in their panels, installing metering software programs on participants' home computers to track their activity, and then weight the results to approximate the socio-demographic characteristics of the national population. The resulting data includes detailed information about the socio-demographic characteristics of users, which is useful for marketing purposes, but comes with limitations. For instance, it does not usually track what people do on computers other than their home computers.[58]

In contrast, server-based data is based on internet traffic to a particular server or website. When a reader visits a website, their computer is tracked by cookies and related technologies storing data about the reader's browsing history, on that site and others. One of the main advantages of server-based data, which is provided by companies such as Google Analytics (now part of Google Marketing Platform), Quantcast, and Omniture, is its level of detail about the behavior of the readers: how they came to the website, how they navigated through the different pages, the time they spent on the site, even their scrolling patterns on a given page. But it also has limitations: individuals who use several computers can be counted more than once, and nonhuman visits ("bots" or "spiders") are also likely to be included in the count. All in all, less than 60 percent of web traffic is considered to be human; the rest comes from bots.[59]

In spite of the well-known unreliability of web metrics, media organizations' marketing departments relied on an increasingly detailed mix of panel-based and server-based data to construct a quantitative portrait of their audience over the course of the 1990s and 2000s. Yet editors and journalists largely ignored such data until the development of a new wave of analytics software products explicitly designed for editorial rather than marketing departments. These programs—with names such as Chartbeat, Parse.ly, or SocialFlow—were designed with an ambitious goal: to close the gap between journalists and their readers, transforming the criteria that journalists have to consider when deciding what to write. This was made clear in the corporate mission statement of Chartbeat, the real-time analytics program introduced at the beginning of this chapter, which was created in New York in 2009:

> We are leaders of the real-time revolution. We partner with doers—editors, writers, marketers, developers—to deliver the data they need, when they need it. Our real-time information gives these front-line teams instantly understandable data on their users' emergent behavior. It ends the command-and-control setup where higher-ups dictate tactical moves that the front-line should make. Instead, it empowers the front-line to be autonomous.[60]

In the bazaar of web metrics, the ambition of Chartbeat was nothing short of a "revolution": it aimed to transform the journalists' relation to their public by offering a detailed dashboard featuring granular data about the behavior and preferences of online users. Chartbeat's dashboard showed many metrics that could be of interest to editors and journalists, such as the number of concurrent visitors on the website, its evolution over time, the number of "likes" on Facebook, the "tweets" on Twitter, and the number of times an article was emailed. It also listed the sources of traffic, the average time spent on the website, and the location of the readers. As of 2018, Chartbeat was one of the most widely used real-time analytics programs in online news. The program recorded the activity of about 50,000 websites in sixty countries (including France), tracking more than 50 billion page views per months. About 80 percent of the largest publishers in the United States used it.[61]

In the process of "engaging" audiences, tracking and analytics software programs provided new representations—or "appresentations," in Knorr-Cetina and Bruegger's words—of online publics as fragmented entities possessing a fixed set of preferences and socio-demographic characteristics that could be monitored and acted upon, with or without their consent. Such representations certainly stemmed from the technical features and values of the new system of "surveillance capitalism" analyzed by Zuboff, but they were also shaped by the previous stages and values that defined the U.S. journalistic field throughout the twentieth century, as we saw earlier in this chapter. Over time, these representations of online audiences made their way into editorial departments. Understandably, most journalists and journalism scholars analyzed the growing role of web analytics in newsrooms as an encroachment of market forces on editorial autonomy.[62] Because Chartbeat offers a quantitative, commercial, and fragmented representation of the public's interest, analysts argued that it resulted in a "dumbing down" of news content in line with the market-driven imperatives that have shaped news production in the United States for the past forty years.[63]

As we will see, however, the specific definitions of online audiences embedded in analytics dashboards do not always translate into similar representations among the editors and staff writers who use the tools. In many cases, gaps emerged between the intended and the actual uses of web analytics in newsrooms. This came with unexpected consequences for the connection between journalists and their algorithmic publics.[64]

Conclusion

Journalists have always maintained a complex relationship with their publics. Depending on the time, place, and medium, they have oscillated between commercial and civic conceptions of who their readers are and why they matter.

These differences are particularly salient when comparing how journalists make sense of audience data in the United States and France. In the United States, the early professionalization of the journalistic field was accompanied by a retreat from explicitly political agendas, whereas in France journalists continued to see themselves as intellectuals in charge of guiding public opinion. Throughout the twentieth century, mainstream American print journalists largely neglected audience data, which they saw as an encroachment of commercial concerns on their editorial autonomy. In contrast, French journalists developed a more ambivalent understanding of public success, which they both criticized as a form of market pressure and valued as a signal of recognition in the public sphere.

Starting in the 1980s, news organizations in the two countries experienced a process of convergence, with more commercial definitions of their readers gaining ground. Both in the United States and France, the rise of online tracking and the development of fine grained behavioral analytics further promoted an individualized and commodified representation of online readers. At the same time, however, utopian ideals were emerging about the rise of a networked public sphere where journalists and publics could interact as equals. This new idealized relationship between journalists and their readers is at the center of the early years of *TheNotebook* and *LaPlace*.

CHAPTER 2

Utopian Beginnings

A Tale of Two Websites

The internet may have a short history, but it is already full of surprising twists. From the early days of the cyberpunk movement and the techno-utopianism of *Wired* to the global empires of Google, Facebook, Amazon, and Apple, the digital landscape has witnessed major evolutions over the past twenty years.[1] Online news is an important part of this story. In the 1990s, many of the journalists who started writing online considered the internet a new frontier—a place where they could fix what they found problematic in traditional media. They thought that they had found uncharted territory where they could reinvent the news.

As in the nineteenth century, the metaphor of the frontier came with specific political and ideological underpinnings: web journalists—mostly young, white, male, and educated—saw themselves as digital pioneers opening new spaces for democratization.[2] They gave optimistic accounts of the positive effects of digital technologies and peer production on public debate. The World Wide Web had a revolutionary potential, they said: by lowering the transaction costs associated with the circulation of news, it could democratize and open up the public. In the words of Clay Shirky, internet guru and author of *Here Comes Everybody*, "netizens" would share information for free in the era of "mass amateurization," relying on the "wisdom of crowds" to sort through the news of the day. A new relationship between news organizations and their audiences seemed possible.[3]

Contrary to the paradigm of a fragmented, forgetful, and commodified audience that had dominated the American news media since the 1980s, advocates of peer production saw in the internet a unique opportunity to redefine the respective roles of writers and readers in the "networked public sphere."[4] As journalism scholar and blogger Jay Rosen argued in an influential address to print journalists:

> You don't own the eyeballs. You don't own the press, which is now divided
> into pro and amateur zones. You don't control production on the new platform, which isn't one-way. There's a new balance of power between you and

us. The people formerly known as the audience are simply *the public* made realer, less fictional, more able, less predictable. You should welcome that, media people. But whether you do or not we want you to know we're here.[5]

The development of the blogosphere came with a radical reconceptualization of the journalist's role in the public debate. Instead of delivering a neatly packaged, "objective," and factual message to a distant and passive audience, journalists were asked to mingle with their online, active, and empowered "communities." They were asked to do so as equals, as fellow netizens with their own emotions and opinions. As had been the case during the Muckraker era and related periods of increased attention to civic initiatives in the journalistic field, U.S. journalists in the 1990s were explicitly encouraged to play an active role in the construction of new forms of public debate.

For the first time, however, they were asked to do so not from a position of intellectual authority, but as coordinators and facilitators of a chorus of equally legitimate voices, all connected through the new communicative capabilities of digital platforms.[6] These conceptions of the radical political capabilities of the internet in turn drew on a longer political tradition. As communication scholar Fred Turner explains, the development of microcomputing and online technologies in Silicon Valley was connected from the start to the bohemian, decentralized, and anti-hierarchical ideals of the counterculture. Twenty years later, such ideals found a new application in the journalistic field. Yet the realities of digital innovation turned out to be messier than many internet enthusiasts had envisaged.[7]

This chapter examines the practices associated with experimentation on the web by comparing the early years of *TheNotebook*, in New York, and *LaPlace*, in Paris. Far from a simplistic story in which early utopian ideals were betrayed for monetary gain, I retrace the hopes, doubts, and stumbles that characterized the beginnings of the two stand-alone news websites. *TheNotebook* and *LaPlace* started with ambitious ideas for transforming journalistic production on the web. In Paris, *LaPlace*'s founders explicitly imitated *TheNotebook*, which they deeply admired. The first couple of years were playful and innovative, generating new relationships with online publics and low expectations for making a profit. Audience metrics were, during this early phase, noticeably absent. Instead, online readers were mobilized through participatory initiatives that aimed to disrupt the unilateral flow of information between journalists and their publics. In spite of these similarities, innovation in New York and Paris took different shapes. From the beginning, *TheNotebook* was a pragmatic endeavor: the team's focus was editorial innovation and the founders prided themselves on their business acumen. In contrast, the French newsroom was a more socially and politically engaged project from the start: the Parisian journalists wanted nothing short of a countercultural revolution in news-making. By comparing the identities of the two organizations before metrics entered the picture, this chapter sets the stage for how news websites later handled the chase for clicks.

East Coast Journalists Meet the World Wide Web

TheNotebook started as John's pet project. John, a prominent East Coast journalist and editor, had a prestigious reputation in the early 1990s: he wrote a widely read column for a liberal political magazine and hosted a political debate show on a popular television channel. At the time, John explained, "I was on [television], every night. I'd had about enough of that.... I, like every other magazine journalist, wanted to start a magazine." John had begun writing nonfiction during his undergraduate years at Harvard. Twenty years later, John had a plan: he wanted to create a magazine that would "intelligently summarize the news" instead of focusing on soft content, which in his view had taken over traditional publications.[8]

TheNotebook was originally supposed to be a print magazine, not a website. When John started meeting with potential investors, however, he realized that they were more interested in the nascent internet than in his print project. In the enthusiasm that came in the 1990s with the diffusion of broadband internet, firms and venture capitalists were ready to invest large amounts of money on the World Wide Web. John reminisced: "Everyone had heard of the internet, and nobody understood it, including me. I thought, if you go to someone and say, 'I want to start a magazine,' they'll say, 'Come back with $40 million, or something like that, and we'll start a magazine.' But if you said, 'I want to start an internet magazine,' they'd throw money at you. I decided I would try and do that."[9]

Being a pragmatic man, John reframed his project as an online magazine, even though he had no specific expertise in digital technologies. TechCorp, a multinational technology company, was interested and proposed to hire John to develop it. In addition to John's online magazine—a miniscule part of their budget given the large size of their operations—TechCorp was starting other media projects, online and offline. John did not hesitate for long. He accepted and moved to the company's headquarters on the West Coast.

John vividly described the confusion of his first days at TechCorp: "I went out there. It was unclear what I was going to do.... I think at that time, if you said the word 'internet,' people freaked out. Everyone was trying to figure out what they were going to do with it and throwing a lot of money at the wall, see what stuck." Far from media gurus' grand proclamations about the world-changing potential of the digital revolution, people were mostly confused about the actual capabilities of the new medium. What would an online magazine look like? John thought hard about it during his first months at TechCorp and drafted a memo summarizing his preliminary ideas. Ten years later, he bemusedly recalled his first plan:

> My original idea, believe it or not, was a publication that you would download and print out once a week. It would have been an inferior version of a print magazine—a bunch of pages stapled together (if you had a stapler nearby). By the time *TheNotebook* was launched, we had moved beyond that primitive once-a-week notion. I remember, with some embarrassment, the eureka moment when it dawned on me that an online magazine doesn't have to publish an entire issue at once. Pretty soon, I even figured out that you didn't need to have "issues" at all.[10]

In many ways, this is a typical internet story. People first planned to use parts of the technology for a specific purpose before stumbling into something else and coming up with a new practice. Take the case of email, which emerged as an unintended consequence of the ARPANET project. In addition to accessing each other's macro-computers, the scientists who were part of the network soon discovered that they could use ARPANET to send messages to each other about sci-fi novels and local restaurants; email was born. Similarly, John and his colleagues originally thought of the internet as an inexpensive distribution channel rather than a new medium. Like other early online actors, it took them several months to realize that a web magazine did not have to be a weekly publication: it could, in fact, be updated as often as desired.[11]

The project then moved forward quickly. John asked several friends and colleagues to join him. Most of them only had a vague idea of what the internet was about but welcomed the opportunity to do something new. Sam, who started as a staff writer, remembered his first impressions:

> I came to *TheNotebook* before it launched, in the mid-1990s. John was a journalist hero of mine. The internet ... I didn't know anything about it. I had actually never been on the web before coming to *TheNotebook*. I was young and had nothing to lose. Why not go there? I had been working for

a local paper. I was kind of bored. So I was looking for a change of some sort. And the people at *TheNotebook* were just super people.

Esther, a culture editor who was hired at the same time, confirmed: "I've always liked starting things, and it wasn't only starting a new magazine but starting a new form. John presented it to me as a grand experiment.... Well, it just seemed very exciting!" About fifteen full-time journalists and editors joined John for *TheNotebook*'s experiment. Some of the writers moved to the West Coast; others stayed in New York and Washington, D.C. Most of them were prominent intellectual figures from the East Coast magazine world. They had degrees from Ivy League universities and saw themselves as writers, not news buffs—and certainly not "geeks," as the new internet crowd started to be known.

In fact, the relationship between the Ivy League–educated writers and TechCorp's computer programmers was not immediately productive, as John recalled: "I found the engineers who worked for *TheNotebook* very nice people, but they were spoiled rotten. You could never get what you wanted from them. They got very angry at me when I said, 'Why can't we do "X"?' This was after I realized that we had to reinvent the form to some extent. We couldn't put it out and let people print it out. We were constantly stumbling over things related to their being engineers rather than writers." "It wasn't the best marriage of talent," as another writer from that time diplomatically put it.[12]

"The Voice of Email"

After several months of back and forth between the editors and the programmers, *TheNotebook* was finally launched in the mid-1990s. Writers and editors moved to luxuriously appointed offices and started publishing news articles about politics, culture, history, and international news, among other beats. Many praised the nonhierarchical and innovative atmosphere of the newsroom during these early years. Sean, a writer who had his first position out of college at *TheNotebook* in the 1990s, remembered: "I loved it because people were so smart and funny.... It was a very non-hierarchical structure. I could make any joke I wanted, or write any way I wanted, or be as sharp or biting as I wanted ... and they liked it!"[13]

Online competition was then almost nonexistent: the journalists of *TheNotebook* were mostly hoping to compete with prestigious print magazines, as Aaron, a writer at the time, recalled: "We wrote for our own perceived audience, which, you know, we thought of as an audience ... similar to the *New Yorker*, the *New Republic*, the *Atlantic*. The competition was in that game.... We just happened to be online." As in other web newsrooms from that period, the design of the magazine remained largely determined by print routines during its first years of operation.[14] In Esther's words:

> At the beginning the design was very imitative of a print magazine. We had pages, we had a table of contents, clicking through was sort of laborious. And we also had a printed issue! We would select and print the highlights and send it to a small list of influential subscribers.... The idea was that if we wanted to have, as they called it, "policy significance," we had to be printed, because people were not reading magazines on the web yet.

Editors and journalists gradually started to experiment with new interactive formats inspired by the blogosphere. Readers were encouraged to participate, through prompts ("What did you think of this article?") and invitations to chat with editors and writers. The publication also put in place a commenting system where readers could post their feedback.

Yet readers' comments soon became controversial within the newsroom. As Esther, the culture editor, explained: "It was overwhelmingly underwhelming, and uncurated. It was a combination of very intelligent, educated responses and nutty, anti-Semitic, and racist stuff. When I read these things I feel that there is a lot of resentment. *Ressentiment* would be a better word ... and hostility towards journalists. They think they know better."

Journalists were taken aback by the perceived lack of respect from online readers. As one of *TheNotebook*'s editors explained: "I do find it surprising how little automatic respect ... posters have for the writers: They think the writers are no different from any poster. This I found—after many years as a journalist—quite shocking. I believed we had some credibility, some trustworthiness. Wrong." Like many other journalists at the time, the New York–based writers were experiencing the contradictions of participatory platforms: they wanted to hear from their readers, but had trouble dealing with the offensive comments and lack of respect they perceived from online commenters. As a result, journalists avoided reading the comments altogether.[15]

More successful was the adoption of the casual writing style of the blogosphere. For instance, one of Esther's main initiatives as the culture editor of *TheNotebook* was the creation of a book club: "We tried to come up with more and more features that were blog-like. We had this book club.... We thought that we had invented a new form of criticism. It was spontaneous and it was like talking to people, it wasn't like the angst of writing. We just let ourselves go. There was no limit and we could do what we wanted. I found that kind of spontaneous writing very fun." Journalists were creating a new writing style, less formal than the usual magazine style. They experimented with formats and tones that imitated conversations between people. Over time, the editorial line of *TheNotebook* crystallized around a witty and conversational take on current events. As Sam, a staff writer who later became editor-in-chief, told me:

> There is a tone in web journalism, and a way of writing with direct address, a conversational, very "you-oriented" tone, which *TheNotebook* took on very early. That was our voice.... It's not written down *to* a reader, it's a conversation *with* the reader [*his emphasis*], it's as though you're speaking to them. It's the voice of email, that's the way people write emails. *TheNotebook*'s competitive advantage in the world is a quality advantage. When you get to *TheNotebook*, the things you see will be smarter, funnier, more provocative than what you get elsewhere. Our advantage is that we are, like, smartypants.

Over the years, many readers and critics characterized the editorial line of *TheNotebook* as "contrarian," because of the writers' casual and witty style and their provocative takes on the subjects of the day. Jane, a former assistant editor, concurred: "Every piece is supposed to have an idea. And hopefully the idea is a bit unusual. *TheNotebook* is caricatured as being contrarian.... But certainly, if something was presented with a contrarian idea that was great! Yeah, when they zig we zag. So, I guess you could characterize it as 'you think this, but you're wrong,' or 'everybody thinks this, so they're all wrong.' That can be a lot of fun." It soon became clear that the main editorial innovation of the magazine was not so much to cover new topics or provide in-depth commentary of political issues, which had been John's original plan. Instead, *TheNotebook* developed an editorial identity of its own based on its spontaneous tone and casual writing style, sometimes described as the "voice of email."

Charity Kid or Real Business?

At about the same time as *TheNotebook* found its voice online, journalists and editors began to worry about the future of the site. Advertising revenues were low. The publication was far from being profitable. From the start, it had been understood that *TheNotebook* would be losing money for several years before starting to make a profit. But things did not go exactly as planned.

John's original idea, which he had sold to TechCorp, was to have readers access the publication for free for a couple of years and then, having secured a loyal readership, create a paywall and monetize content. Following the plan, a paywall was created in 1998. But only 30,000 out of the 400,000 monthly readers subscribed—an extremely low number compared to what everybody had expected. John realized his mistake, backpedaled, and a year later the paywall was removed. After that, TechCorp continued to finance the online magazine, but editors and journalists felt that *TheNotebook* was no longer one of TechCorp's priorities. According to Sam, the early 2000s were marked by a feeling of doom:

> *TheNotebook* cost millions of dollars to run every year.... And the revenue was maybe 10% or 20% of that. It wasn't really a business. TechCorp was making so much money and we were so prestigious that they didn't care. They were making billions and billions of profit and *TheNotebook* was only a few million dollars, so it didn't matter, especially if *TheNotebook* gave them good publicity. But after 1998, TechCorp cut back their investments in online content. *TheNotebook* was the only one sitting there. We became totally irrelevant to the enterprise. They were perfectly nice to us, but they never tried to make it a business. Between 1999 and 2004, it was depressing because they weren't investing in us. There was no sense that we could try new things, there was no plan.

The founding team of writers started leaving the ship for more promising venues. Esther went to work for the *New York Times* book section in 2001. John himself resigned in 2002 and started working for the *Los Angeles Times*. Those who stayed were worried about the future of the publication. They wondered about the profitability of the website and worried that TechCorp would stop paying the bills. It was therefore not a surprise for the remaining staff when TechCorp sold *TheNotebook* to a large media company, Newspapers Inc., in 2004. Though the specifics of the deal were kept secret, experts estimated the transaction to be worth between $15 and $20 million. Most of *TheNotebook*'s journalists and editors were happy about the sale. Newspaper Inc., after all, had been in the media business for many years; it already owned several print and digital publications. Like Sam, many found that it was a more natural home for *TheNotebook* than TechCorp:

> It was only when Newspapers Inc. bought us that we began to become a real business. Truthfully, no one really liked the way TechCorp was handling it.

We didn't want to be the charity kid, we wanted to be a real business. It's not sustainable to be somebody's toy. We always had the idea that we had to be a great magazine that also supports itself. As a journalist, it is important to be independent from the whim of rich people. So it's nice to have a rich owner who's going to lose money on you but it's much better to show that the work you do sustains itself on a market. And then you don't have to compromise your standards; you can do the journalism that you want to do. And that's what we've been doing.

Like many print editors in the United States before him, Sam emphasized the importance of being a "sustainable" business in order to keep an independent editorial line. In keeping with the paradigm of self-regulation that emerged in the American journalistic field during the era of high modernism, he equated commercial success and journalistic autonomy.[16] Yet becoming a "real business" under the umbrella of Newspapers Inc. came with new responsibilities that eventually affected the editorial line of the website. I will return to these evolutions after examining the early years of *LaPlace*, a news magazine *à la française*.

LaPlace: A Collective and Participatory Adventure

In Paris, not far from the Place de la République on the Right Bank, a dozen journalists started meeting in 2007 in André's kitchen once a week. Regardless of age or status, the journalists who attended these early meetings talked until late at night, drinking and smoking together. For many of these participants—even those who later became critical of *LaPlace*—these discussions transformed their vision of journalism.

How did it start? In the early 2000s, Philippe, Eric, André, and Adrien were mid-career journalists who worked for the same left-leaning daily French newspaper. Philippe was then the chief of the newspaper's Washington bureau; Eric was its correspondent in New York; André was the Beijing correspondent before becoming deputy editor-in-chief; and Adrien was a senior editor at the newspaper. The four journalists were prominent writers whose careers had overlapped at different points in time. Philippe, Eric, and Adrien had done their undergraduate studies at Sciences Po Paris, and Philippe and Adrien had both attended journalism schools. Philippe and Eric overlapped for a year in the United States, while André worked with Adrien in Paris.

Without being close friends, the four journalists belonged to the small world of elite print Parisian newspapers—which was then overwhelmingly white, educated, and male. They shared a strong interest in digital media, which they had discovered during their time abroad. During his time as a correspondent in the United States, Philippe wrote a blog, which Eric later took over when he replaced Philippe on the East Coast. André had run a popular blog for many years that analyzed international politics, whereas Adrien had created an activist blog devoted to drug policy and legalization. After many years working for print newspapers, they all enjoyed the stylistic freedom of the blogosphere, its casual writing style, and its emphasis on first-person narratives, which were prohibited in newspapers articles at that time. Yet the journalists' real epiphany came from their encounters with online readers.

Most of us today are so accustomed to the interactivity of social media that it takes an effort to realize how shocking it may have been for Philippe, André, and their colleagues to start chatting with strangers at the very beginning of web 2.0—or the "social" web, as it came to be called. All of them recounted the endless discussions that took place in the comments sections of their blogs. They would disagree, argue, and discuss facts and angles with their readers, regardless of anyone's credentials or journalistic experience. This would have been unimaginable within the hierarchical structure of print newspapers. In André's recollections: "With the blogs we had real encounters with readers, people who were telling me, 'I disagree, and by the way I know more about this than you do.' It was wonderful." For the first time, the four journalists felt that they could learn things from their readers. Though they did not use these terms, they shared the beliefs of many of the "peer production" scholars that the internet would contribute to the emergence of a new public sphere, less hierarchical and more inclusive than ever before.[17]

The four journalists avidly followed the developments of the English-language blogosphere, which they found more vibrant than the French one. Philippe, who later became *LaPlace*'s editor-in-chief, remembered his excitement when he moved to the United States to start his position as a foreign correspondent on the East Coast:

> When I arrived in the United States ... I really discovered the internet there. Of course I was using it before, but there I started surfing a lot, I saw what was going on, websites such as *TheNotebook* or *Talking Points Memo*. Everything new, everything counter-intuitive was there. And the blogosphere was very rich in the U.S., they even had conservative blogs. It was very lively, people talked to each other. In France that was less the case. I participated in the beginnings of a website, *TPM Cafe*, with Josh Marshall.... I remember, he worked in a Starbucks—he would lock his laptop to the table so that he could grab a coffee once in a while! I loved it.[18]

Everything about the American blogosphere enchanted Philippe—from the freedom of being able to work in a Starbucks to the liveliness of the exchanges between conservative and liberal bloggers. When he returned to Paris in 2006, Philippe was disappointed: "In Paris, I became the editor of the editorial and op-ed section. I wasn't happy. It was very traditional.... I tried to put things online, but it didn't really work out. I was bored."[19]

Creating a Website, Imitating *TheNotebook*

Back in Paris, Philippe, André, Eric, and Adrien soon began to think about creating a news site together. When defining their editorial project and business plan, the four journalists explicitly wanted to replicate and improve on the innovations that they had witnessed in the United States. They drew on the novelty of the blogosphere and the prestige of American journalism to sell their project to French investors. In an email sent in 2006 to a potential investor, the four founders explained what they had in mind for the website, which they called "Project X."

Email sent by Philippe to a potential investor
December 1, 2006
Subject: The X project roughly summarized

Dear [friend],
As I briefly mentioned on Thursday, we are thinking of launching a news site/online magazine. It would be exciting, original, and playful. It would be an (or "the"?) online reference for news, news analysis, and debates. It would rely on the participation of internet users.
There is nothing like this in France, in contrast to the United States (The Notebook.com as well as Huffington.com [sic], TPM Cafe)....
The idea is to break out from the current model based on production and reception (breaking news, print articles posted online) and to create a community of "addicts" instead.
The website would encourage everything that print newspapers currently forbid: first-person journalism, unrepentant subjectivity, original angles, humor. It would respond to the strong demand for participation in the public debate....

Waiting to hear from you,
Philippe

Among the different projects they mentioned, *TheNotebook* was a particular source of inspiration. The French journalists admired the editorial line of the website, which they read every day. Philippe and Adrien also knew journalists at *TheNotebook*, including Sam, who was at that point a section editor. They wanted to imitate *TheNotebook*'s witty editorial style and its business model based on advertising revenue. After the website was created, *LaPlace* replicated specific formats that *TheNotebook* had developed, such as a column dedicated to simple explanations of complicated phenomena. Between 2007 and 2009, the French journalists went a step further and negotiated an editorial partnership between *TheNotebook* and *LaPlace*. Philippe even travelled to the East Coast for the occasion:

> We had a partnership with *TheNotebook* for a while, because I knew the editor-in-chief, Sam. I even went to visit their newsroom! I have a video of it.... I had a tiny video camera, I entered their newsroom during the editorial meeting. I wanted to show their newsroom to the staff here at *LaPlace*. At the beginning we had an agreement, we could translate some of their articles and put them on our website ... and they could do the same. They never did it. We did it quite a lot.

Taking a step back, this is a clear case of transnational circulation of form and content between the United States and France. Between 2007 and 2009, *LaPlace* published more than fifty articles translated from *TheNotebook* that were translated into French. When they did so, they featured *TheNotebook*'s logo at the top and bottom of the webpage. *TheNotebook* never translated a single article from *LaPlace*, however, which gives a sense of the relative asymmetry between the two websites.[20] On the American side, the partnership was considered to be a highly informal affair, as Sam recalled:

> I met Philippe through a friend. He said he was starting *LaPlace* and we set this kind of casual partnership, it was probably during the first year that the site was up. I don't even remember what it was ... it was very casual. We let them run our stories, they would tell us when they had something.... There was no money, no investment or anything.... My French is much worse than it used to be 20 years ago. Once in a while I go to their website and check, "oh, what's going on." But I don't follow what they do closely.

For a long time, the United States has served as a model and a reservoir of ideas to imitate in other parts of the world. From Hollywood movies to McDonald's or the Chicago school of economics, institutional entrepreneurs have imported cultural forms originating in the United States to other countries. In most cases, this process of transnational import/export comes with a double effect. First, the people in charge of these importations draw on the prestige associated with cultural and industrial production in the United States to increase their own status in the national field where they operate. This is what Yves Dezalay and Bryant Garth call "international strategies," or "the ways that national actors seek to use foreign capital, such as resources, degrees, contacts, legitimacy, and expertises ... to build their power at home." Second, in the process of importing such ideas and organizational forms to fields with different characteristics, importers usually have to work as cultural translators in order to adapt and adjust the ideas and products to their new context.[21]

This is precisely what happened here. *LaPlace*'s founders drew on two main forms of international legitimacy in order to support their project and attract French funders. First, they capitalized on the prestige and history of American journalism, which French journalists have observed closely since the nineteenth century, as we saw in the previous chapter. Second, they relied on the "buzz" associated with online innovation on the West Coast (Silicon Valley) and East Coast (Silicon Alley). In the process, however, they had to transform *TheNotebook*'s editorial and commercial recipes in order to make them fit the French context. In the words of Philippe: "Translating American articles for a French audience is not easy. They are too long.... And it didn't work well in French, their pieces had to be completely rewritten." It took a lot of work from the Parisian journalists to make the articles written in the United States relevant for their readers. The exchange ceased after a couple of years, when *The-Notebook* created a partnership with another French publication.

When I started my fieldwork at *LaPlace*, three years later, most staffers and editors still read *TheNotebook* every day and emphasized strong feelings of similarity with the American publication. In the meantime, however, *LaPlace* had developed an editorial and political line of its own.

Experimental Startup or Anti-Hierarchical Utopia?

After months of discussions and negotiations, Philippe, André, Eric, and Adrien had gathered enough money to start the website. They provided most of the initial capital themselves: one million euros, which came from their own savings as well as from the unemployment subsidies they had received after quitting their newspaper.[22] They also relied on several external investors, mostly friends and acquaintances. The founders then started hiring. As at *TheNotebook*, many of the people they contacted immediately accepted. Gabriella, *LaPlace*'s first managing editor, recalled her feelings at the time: "I was a freelance journalist in New York. When Philippe and Eric were based in the United States, we were good friends. We kept talking about the future of the press, about online news. I was interested in the experimental part of launching of a news website—the exploration, the search for a new model, the hesitations. I figured that it would be interesting."

After meeting at André's place for several months, the four founders, Gabriella, and a handful of journalists moved into a new office space. They hired several computer programmers who developed the website using open-source software, a logical choice given the founders' anti-establishment ideology and their then-limited financial means. Unlike the glamorous offices of *TheNotebook*, *LaPlace*'s setup was artisanal: the journalists and programmers helped the funders unpack and assemble the furniture that would be used in the office. Once the office space was installed and the website running, *LaPlace*'s editorial line soon developed around two central pillars: a left-leaning stance and a participatory approach.

Compared to *TheNotebook*, which in spite of its position on the liberal side of the spectrum prided itself on being nonpartisan, *LaPlace* was politically engaged from the start. It is not a coincidence that *LaPlace* was created during the rise to power of the conservative presidential candidate Nicolas Sarkozy. *LaPlace*'s founders and journalists wanted to use the website as a political platform against Sarkozy, and over time, the website became well known for several scoops implicating him. It also published highly critical coverage of his party, often relying on inside jokes and a satirical writing style that compared politicians to comic book characters (for instance, "the Daltons," villains in the classic French comic books *Lucky Luke*) or providing irreverent descriptions of the palace wars taking place at the Elysée.

LaPlace also adopted a decidedly participatory approach. The journalists developed the idea of "information with multiple voices," which included the journalists but also (as the official description of the website put it) "experts and internet users." Even the name of the publication stemmed from this participatory ideal. As the founders wrote, "we wanted a name that was a synonym for circulation, encounters, life, and café terraces." Blogs and user-generated content became an essential part of the editorial project. The readers, affectionately nicknamed "the neighbors," were encouraged to participate in the daily life of the newsroom: they could follow the editorial meetings and provide suggestions about topics that should be covered. Readers were also invited to write first-person "testimonies" (*témoignages*) about significant events in their lives that connected with the news of the day.

As at *TheNotebook*, there were aggressive and provocative "trolls" from the beginning. Some of them were ferocious in their critique of the website's editorial line. For example, a recurring commenter who took the pseudonym "*LaPlace* Gutter" harshly criticized the website on a daily basis, insulting the journalists in each comment. The journalists did not particularly enjoy it. As Alexandre, one of the staffers, explained, "The comments are usually annoying. There is a lot of trolling involved, people who come to mess around, some of them are very negative, they post insults every day.... It's depressing. But when they ask actual questions, I answer." Like Alexandre the founders and journalists also saw it as their responsibility to keep interacting with online readers, foul-mouthed as they were. In the words of Gael, the assistant editor: "The commenters are very critical, very politicized, often offensive.... It's true that they can drag the discussion down, but it's also a gold mine, the information they're giving us.... Here we all have to interact with online readers."

All of this felt new. Most of the people who worked for *LaPlace* during these first years felt that they were changing journalism in a meaningful way. Jean, a former staffer, remembered the energy and excitement he felt at the time:

> For a couple of months, we were inventing something new every single day. We didn't know how it was going to turn out. We were only ten people in the team when we really started.... We were creating a new media! We really wanted to be an independent website, we didn't want to follow the agenda of the other media. We wanted to mix videos, sound clips, everything. I knew how to use a camera: two weeks later I was teaching André how to use a camera! André is really somebody in journalism. It was great, I was a beginner but I could bring something specific to all these very skilled people. We had no weekends, nothing was planned, there was no morning meeting—we were only ten, underpaid, working all the time, 24/7.

The journalists who were part of the group were developing what they described as a new, irreverent approach to journalism: a casual writing style, multimedia articles, innovative angles, and a different way of interacting with their community of readers. They were mixing political and tabloid topics, crossing the lines between news and magazine reporting.

They were also active in promoting independent and quality journalism on the web: with several other independent news sites, *LaPlace*'s journalists organized a union for the advancement of independent journalism on the internet (Syndicat de la Presse Indépendante d'Information en Ligne, or SPIIL).[23]

During these years, the journalists were working long hours, in an unstructured way. Most of the original team of staffers had received shares in the company, but they were paid very little—and sometimes not at all. Most of them stayed because of the strong personal and emotional connections that they found at *LaPlace*. There were a variety of social ties within the team: family ties, friendship and romantic ties, but also relations of admiration and even adulation, according to the former managing editor, Gabriella: "The first employees came to *LaPlace* and worked for free for a while because they were fans of Philippe and André. And it's really because they were fans and because they saw the founders as gurus that they could work 70 hours per week.... I remember, for a month or two, I would come to editorial meetings with my newborn daughter, then I would go back home and work from there. So it had good sides as well.... It was a mix of a start-up and a family."

This experimental atmosphere was largely due to the lack of financial means, the small team, and the new media used—what the staffers often called the "start-up" aspect of the enterprise. Yet the left-leaning and countercultural ideology of the founders also played a role in the process. In addition to renovating journalism, the founders wanted to transform the social organization of the newsroom, following their post-May 1968 convictions. André, founder and chairman, had been a Maoist in his youth and may have retained some of the anti-hierarchical ideology of this period—he certainly joked about it. Philippe, the editor-in-chief, also explained:

> I was very influenced by the free radios [*radios libres*, i.e., pirate radios that were created in the 1970s to subvert the French state's monopoly on radio networks]. It's something that I've been trying to recreate since.... There was so much freedom! It was a new media, we could have the style we wanted, we could invite the audience to participate. I belong to the generation of the orphans of May '68—I was born too late.... With the free radios, we had the same spirit of counterculture, we cared about freedom and we were trying to experiment.... That's my matrix.

In contrast to the early years of *TheNotebook*, which was from the start a profit-oriented project backed by the large financial and technical means of TechCorp, and in spite of its explicit imitation of the New York website, *LaPlace* was characterized by an experimental, countercultural, and left-leaning ideology. Several decades later and in a different environment, the French journalists revived the utopian spirit of the beginnings of the internet in Silicon Valley. Yet those lighthearted years of *TheNotebook* and *LaPlace* did not last long. In both cases, though for different reasons, the two websites faced strong pressures to become profitable in a market that was becoming highly competitive.

Conclusion

The early years of *TheNotebook* and *LaPlace* were an optimistic period when audience metrics and economic constraints were notably absent. On both sides of the Atlantic, the websites' beginnings were marked by entrepreneurialism, a climate of playful innovation, and what sociologist Randall Collins calls high "emotional energy": journalists felt that they were part of a project larger than their own individual interests; there was a palpable excitement in the two newsrooms about what they were doing. In both cases, journalists developed novel forms of interactivity and adopted a more casual writing style (see Table 2.1).[24]

Table 2.1. The Early Years of *TheNotebook* and *LaPlace*

Structural similarities	
Created by print journalists Focus on news, politics, culture, and technology High editorial ambitions; award-winning publications Interactivity and casual writing style Income from online advertising Not profitable	
Built-in convergence	
LaPlace consciously imitated *TheNotebook* from the start Editorial partnership between 2007 and 2009	
Early differences	
TheNotebook:	*LaPlace*:
Funding from a technology company Politically centrist Classic workplace dynamics Limited participatory content	Independent website Politically left "Fan club" with "gurus" More participatory content

In spite of this built-in imitation and the similarities between *The-Notebook* and *LaPlace*, there were also important differences between the two organizations. Over time, the two newsrooms developed different organizational styles, in line with the dominant structures and trajectories of their national journalistic fields discussed in chapter 1. Indeed, despite the positive feelings of "fun" and experimentation, *TheNotebook* was a professionalized and commercial initiative from the start: people were paid, staffers worked in well-appointed offices, and the boundaries between journalists and their readers were never abolished. In contrast, *LaPlace*'s left-leaning engagement and countercultural project shaped how they related to their online community, which was invited to participate in the production of information. The staffers were unpaid or poorly paid for years at a time, meeting in the kitchen of one of the founders, and behaving more like a "fan club" or a social movement than like a company. This utopian atmosphere continued to inform the editorial line of the Parisian site in the following years, when it launched into the chase for clicks. Paradoxically, as we will see, the countercultural beliefs at *LaPlace* translated into a much more problematic environment than *The-Notebook*'s matter-of-fact approach, especially after metrics entered the picture.

CHAPTER 3

Entering the Chase for Clicks

Transatlantic Convergences

Markets and industries are sometimes dramatically reconfigured around new measurements of value and success.[1] This is what happened in online news around 2008 when, during the Great Recession, news websites entered the chase for traffic. Faced with strong pressures to make a profit, editors and staff writers in New York and Paris searched desperately for techniques that would magically attract more readers to their webpages. They began surveilling and imitating their competitors. Eventually, they adopted the same strategies to stay afloat financially: publishing more, faster, and paying closer attention to the technical underpinnings of traffic maximization, all of which laid the ground for the implementation of web analytics. In spite of the different organizational cultures and national contexts of the two websites, a process of convergence took place: a similar tension emerged in the two newsrooms between what I call an "editorial" and a "click-based" mode of evaluation. This chapter shows how media organizations located thousands of miles apart ended up making similar editorial decisions when they entered the chase for clicks.

TheNotebook: An "Old New Media" in a Competitive Landscape

In the previous chapter, we left *TheNotebook* in 2004, when TechCorp sold the magazine to Newspapers Inc. At that point, Newspapers Inc. was a publicly traded company whose owners had kept a majority of the shares and owned several major publications, including a daily newspaper and a prestigious print magazine, as well as a profitable publishing company unrelated to news production. *TheNotebook* was expected to be the flagship site of Newspapers Inc.'s digital presence. The website then seemed to be on a steeply ascending trajectory: it had just received a national award for its online coverage; John had been named "Editor of the Year" by a prominent journalism review for his work at *TheNotebook*; the publication employed around thirty staffers and attracted 5 million unique visitors per month, which was more than the 4.5 million monthly visitors that the online version of the main newspaper owned by Newspapers Inc. received. *TheNotebook* had even been profitable for a time, indicating that it could be getting close to making a profit on a regular basis.

Yet things did not quite turn out as planned. Several issues arose in the years following the sale. First, it took time for the digital economy to recover from the 2001–2002 dot-com crash, which reverberated in the advertising sector. After the 2008 financial crisis, online advertising rates continued to stagnate: in 2010, the average CPM (cost per mille) for ad views at news sites was still a disappointing $7—a low number given the predictions of the early years. This made it harder for news organizations to reach financial equilibrium with a business model based only on advertising revenues.[2]

Digital competition was also changing. News websites with large amounts of capital and aggressive traffic maximization techniques were launched over the course of the 2000s: *Gawker* was created in 2003, the *Huffington Post* in 2005, *BuzzFeed* in 2006, *Business Insider* in 2009. All of these sites encroached on *TheNotebook*'s share of traffic and advertising, in part because they were good at promoting their content on social media platforms, which had started to expand exponentially. Facebook, launched in 2004, attracted 360 million monthly users by 2009. Twitter, created in 2006, had 54 million users by 2010. By 2012, 49 percent of U.S. adults reported getting at least some of their news through social media platforms (this number went up to 68 percent in 2018). Aggregation-based news sites like the *Huffington Post* and *BuzzFeed* quickly adapted to these new rules of the digital game by developing innovative techniques to promote their content and maximize its visibility on Facebook and Twitter.[3]

These changes transformed *TheNotebook*'s intellectual and commercial environment—or, in Bourdieu's terms, the field in which it competed. Unlike the early days of the publication, the upper management was now unclear about who their main competitors were: traditional publications such as the *Atlantic*, the *New Yorker* or the *New York Times*, or new rivals such as the *Huffington Post* and *Gawker*? Staffers who worked at *TheNotebook* in the late 2000s mentioned that an Orwellian kind of "doublespeak" came to dominate the newsroom. As former assistant editor Jane explained: "We would have these conversations where we would say, 'OK, who are our competitors? Are we competing with *Gawker*, are we trying to compete with the *Huffington Post*?' And then the editors would go, 'Oh no no no no no, we're not competing with the *Huffington Post* and *Gawker*, we're a different sort of magazine, that's not what we're trying to do.' And then thirty seconds later, they would be talking about how great the *Huffington Post* traffic was.... I mean, this would happen all the time!" Indeed, in 2013, when I asked him about the competitors of the website, Sam—who was by this time *TheNotebook*'s editor-in-chief—was still somewhat unsure:

> Our main competitors are the *Atlantic, Gawker* maybe.... But not really. And then tons of other places, the *Guardian*, the *New York Times*, the *Huffington Post, Business Insider*.... Everyone's a competitor. The *Huffington Post* is in a completely different business, they're doing something completely different, they're amazing.... I'm sure that they have advertising that we would love to have, and they have readers that we would love to have, but we're not in the same set anymore. I'm not saying that everything they do is bad, but their basic business is this quick aggregation, quick recapitulation of the news, and that's not our business. Our business is analysis, understanding, it's something richer than that.

Compared to the early days of *TheNotebook*, the boundaries of the field had changed: everybody had become a competitor. Faced with this rapidly evolving landscape, the website had turned, in the eyes of many media experts, into an example of "old new media," not agile enough to compete with these new actors. These changing perceptions took a toll on the website's revenues: advertisers were less interested in buying space on *TheNotebook*, which could not promise the same traffic growth rate as some of its newer competitors. The survival of the website felt at stake. *TheNotebook*'s editors decided to act on what seemed like the only option at their immediate disposal: they entered the chase for clicks.

Publishing More, Publishing Faster

TheNotebook developed a dizzying array of techniques to "capitalize on traffic," as the expression then went among New York journalists. A first path was to increase exponentially the amount of content posted online: the number of articles published every year on *TheNotebook* more than doubled between 2008 and 2012, according to its top editors. As one editor sheepishly put it, "there has been this expansion in what we do, just ... publishing more, doing a lot more." Yet multiplying the amount of published content risked either spending more money or letting the quality of the articles drop dramatically. The editors relied on several strategies to address this conundrum, each of which was problematic.

First, they developed new partnerships or agreements with other organizations that agreed to share a certain amount of content for free. The most visible and durable collaborations included a non-profit foundation, a state university, and a news agency, as well as a political figure who also hosted a television show. Though these partnerships did increase the amount of content published on the site, they were not ideal either. Not unlike what we saw at *LaPlace* earlier, *TheNotebook*'s editors realized that a website cannot feature a great deal of content that is not primarily designed for its own publication, because partnership pieces were frequently at odds with *TheNotebook*'s editorial focus and tone.

A second option was inspired by the success of one of *TheNotebook*'s rivals, Gawker Media, which by then had launched multiple sub-sites (*Jezebel, Gizmodo, Gawker, Kotaku, io9*, etc.). For a while, *TheNotebook* followed suit, creating several topic-specific sites, including one about gender and women-related questions, one about the economy, and one about African-American topics. The rationale behind this was to attract advertisers interested in these specific customer segments. Of the multiple sub-sites created over the years, however, only one survived. Jane remembered the confusion and failures that marked this period:

> *TheNotebook* tried to imitate the *Gawker* model, spinning out.... *Gawker* is very smart about spending money, and the editors at *TheNotebook* wanted to do the same thing. Their initial mission from Newspapers Inc. was to create one or two new sites a year. Yeah. They created a women's site, a video site, a business site, a Black interest site.... The idea was that they had some editors, freelancers, maybe one or two staff writers. But they put virtually no money into design or backend stuff so these sites were just really clunky. They all failed within two years.

A third strategy to get more content was to hire new people. As Sam, the editor-in-chief, told me, "We brought in some young people, some highly energetic new writers who are super productive, they write a ton." *TheNotebook* pursued this line of attack by firing three of its most famous staff journalists, who had been there from the start, and replacing them with young bloggers who were less expensive and published more frequently. Noah, a former editor, analyzed the rationale behind this decision:

> The layoffs took place during the fall of 2011.... They fired the people who were most expensive and least efficient. I mean, "least efficient"—the people who were the most expensive and the least productive. When you have to cut back and you don't have as many programmers as you want, and

there are people on the staff who are making six-figure salaries and writing once a week.... You could hire two or three people who are young and can produce 5 to 10 pieces of content a week.

Among these "productive young writers," as Sam called them, was Martin, a blogger hired in 2011 who specialized in economic topics. His productivity scared many of the other writers, who felt unproductive by comparison. As another journalist jokingly commented, "Martin writes thirty stories a day! That's barely an exaggeration! I could never do that, I don't have that in me.... I wake up and he's already written three blog posts, written seven tweets.... I'm just drinking my coffee! He's like a robot (*laughs*)!" Robot jokes apart, many writers and editors at *TheNotebook* complained about an acceleration in the rhythm of publication, which they argued went hand-in-hand with more superficial editing, as well as a decline in the length and depth of the articles.

The Invisible Work of Visibility: Recipes for Traffic Maximization

In addition to publishing more and faster, the chase for clicks took another central form at *TheNotebook*: it involved significant efforts in terms of traffic maximization to ensure that the website's articles would be visible online. The word "visibility" has become a catchall term in the digital economy: organizations and individuals alike are increasingly expected to build their online brand by promoting content that is likely to go "viral," to "trend," or to get some "buzz"—that is, to get the attention of internet users across the web.[4] This competition for attention is often analyzed as a natural force: in the digital world, analysts speak of "organic" traffic when an article or a meme becomes viral on Facebook or Twitter. The organic metaphor implies that visibility is something that grows on its own, independently of human intervention.[5]

But achieving online visibility is far from a spontaneous process. In fact, ensuring even minimum visibility takes a lot of work. As media scholar Brooke Erin Duffy shows in her study of fashion bloggers, becoming famous on social media entails constant effort and relentless discipline.[6] Similarly, in web journalism, writers and publishers devote significant time and work to achieve visibility. Articles need to be posted on the right platform, at the right time, and with the right headline in order to have a chance to "go viral." In the jargon of internet publishing, writers need to carefully "promote" their articles and "cultivate" their online "community" of dedicated fans and "followers."[7] Such efforts are then often minimized and promptly forgotten: the activities devoted to making online content "visible" are usually delegitimized in web newsrooms, resembling what Susan Leigh Star and Anselm Strauss call "invisible work"—the backstage, mundane, infrastructural, and often gendered activities allowing organizations and systems to function. In the words of Sarah T. Roberts, they take place "behind the screen": after all, not everyone wants to be seen tweaking the market for attention.[8]

At *TheNotebook*, the road to online visibility took two main directions. A first strategy was search engine optimization (SEO), the broad set of techniques employed to have one's articles appear at the top of search engine results for a given query. Google now functions as a "master switch" for many publishers: appearing at the top of Google's search results can mean life or death for a publication. Thus, *TheNotebook* hired a SEO specialist, Moira, along with another technology specialist, with the task of increasing the site's visibility on Google and other search engines. Though Moira had no formal training in computer programming or data science, she had learned the tricks of the trade during her early days as a writer and editor at the *Huffington Post*, one of the first newsrooms to invest heavily in SEO. With *TheNotebook*'s developers, Moira improved the website's ranking on Google. She also proceeded to train the staffers by organizing regular sessions where she taught them the best recipes to improve articles' rankings on search engines. These techniques became routinely used by editors in *TheNotebook*'s newsroom, who referred to Moira as their "data guru," as described in the following observation note.[9]

Observation
TheNotebook
October 17, 2012

Mary has been a copy editor at *TheNotebook* for two years. I am sitting at her desk while she edits an article on Afghanistan. On the right side of her computer, a sheet of paper is scotch-taped that says:

The 7 secrets of a SEO:
1. Think like a googler
2. Go after terms you can win
3. Word order matters
4. Get it fast, get it first, get it right

5. The ":" and the "?" are your friends
6. Use CAPSLOCKS on media
7. Hyperlink keywords

The 6 SEO No-No's
1. Putting *TheNotebook* in the SEO line
2. Author's name in SEO line
3. Wordiness before key words
4. Don't be clever, be obvious
5. Only having one paragraph
6. Not considering SEO when you write the SEO line

Mary explains that this comes from her latest training session in SEO with Moira, whom she called their "data guru," a couple of weeks before. She finishes editing the op-ed on Afghanistan and says: "Now I'm adding some key words, 'Obama,' 'Romney,' 'debate,' to capitalize on traffic, since they talked about it yesterday." [*The observation took place the day after a presidential debate.*]

In the meantime, the short note scotch-taped to Mary's computer shows how deeply engraved in the daily practices of the newsroom the search for traffic had become. Traffic maximization was a matter of constant attention for most copy editors and staff writers: in Moira's words, "not considering SEO when you write the SEO line" was a "no-no." As in other cases of invisible work, young female employees like Mary were often in charge of these meticulous activities—women remain overrepresented in copy editing, where they work as the "little hands" or "housekeepers" of online publishing. They were the ones implementing traffic maximization strategies, which were then perceived as a low-prestige task. As historian Mar Hicks documents, this is far from a unique case: after all, women made up most of the workforce in the early days of computing, before being replaced by men as programming became more prestigious.[10]

This note also reveals how the skill of writing headlines evolved over time. Moira's scotch-taped guidelines read: "Don't be clever, be obvious." For many traditional print editors, this would have been anathema. In the words of Esther, *TheNotebook*'s first culture editor, who had spent most of her career working for print publications: "We were *not* [*her emphasis*] maximizing for search engines. I'm realizing that I'm a dinosaur here. The article itself would have one title and that's where my artistry would come in. I love clever titles! It wasn't designed to maximize the search engines."

Contrary to what Esther implied, however, the "artistry" involved in writing good headlines did not disappear with SEO. Instead, online articles began to have multiple headlines. A straightforward SEO headline appeared in the article's URL (the web address as indexed by the search engines), but there were two other levels of headlines explicitly designed to attract readers' attention: the headline that appeared on the website's homepage, as well as the (different) headlines written for Twitter and Facebook, which were devised to be engaging and pun-driven.

In addition to SEO, *TheNotebook* developed another strategy to increase the website's visibility. Over time, the editors started paying more attention to social media expertise, also called "community management"— a specialty that encompasses the skills and efforts needed to attract readers and develop loyalty for a given brand on social media platforms. In order to tap into social media traffic, *TheNotebook* created the position of "social media editor" (SME), which was filled by Josh, a former editorial assistant. Josh became responsible for optimizing the website's content on Facebook, Twitter, and (to a lesser extent) Instagram and the now-defunct Google Plus social network. As he told me when I sat with him, his job was to "curate" the website's pages on social media platforms by tweaking the headlines, updating the pictures, and repeatedly posting selected articles on Facebook or Twitter in the hope that they would reach a larger audience.

Observation
TheNotebook
October 18, 2012

I am sitting with Josh, the social media editor of *TheNotebook*, in his cubicle. Josh explains that he "did a bit of everything" before being put in charge of social media when it became, in his words, a "big thing." Josh is currently posting a tongue-in-cheek article about a cooking recipe in *TheNotebook*'s Twitter feed. I am surprised, because I noticed that this specific article had already been posted on *TheNotebook*'s Twitter account the night before.

> AC: So you posted it last night on Twitter and now you're reposting it?
>
> JOSH: Yes, with a slightly different wording.
>
> AC: Do you often do that?

JOSH: Yes, two times, three times for each article. Depending on the time of the day, you get different categories of readers ... and it helps if the headline is not exactly the same. It's the same thing on Facebook.

AC: What's most important, Facebook or Twitter?

JOSH: In terms of traffic, Facebook is twice as important ... but we have way more control on Twitter. On Facebook, traffic comes from organic sharing, not from our page. Also, on Facebook you can only post once per hour, even less, so you have to wait.... It's because of their algorithm; it doesn't work as well when you post things too often. Whereas Twitter, you can post it as often as you want. I always change the headlines for Facebook and Twitter.

Josh then starts working on another article about a funny advertising campaign. The article was published the day before on *TheNotebook*'s website with the following headline: "The Cleverest Ad You'll See Online." Josh changes it for Facebook and puts instead: "No hyperbole, this is the best campaign ad you'll see." He laughs: "Yeah, the word "hyperbole" always works well on Facebook!"

This was another aspect of the invisible work of visibility: the repeated and constant promotion of articles on social media platforms, at different times of the day, with different headlines or stock images, all in order to tap into sources of traffic that the story may have missed. Such routines soon became part of the daily life of most web newsrooms, including *TheNotebook*. Yet these were met with more resistance at *TheNotebook* than at other places. Many of the editors and staff writers, especially the ones who had been there from the early days, were reluctant to use social media. Noah, the former editor mentioned above, recalled his feelings of frustration with his colleagues at the time:

When I started, *TheNotebook* was still a new media company.... Even though it had been around since the mid-90s, most people thought of *The-Notebook* as a new kid on the block. But by 2007–2008, people started to have the sense that *TheNotebook* was an old media.... I could see the older people at *TheNotebook* saying, "I think Twitter is ridiculous." I could see myself aging into that category. I remember, the guy who ran the magazine, when Twitter was coming out, he called his assistant and asked her to show him how to use Twitter. That really bugged me! Here is that guy who made his career convincing investors that he knows the latest technology and yet he has his 24-year old assistant teach him how to use the simplest tool. It makes you wonder whether *TheNotebook*'s efforts to "leverage Twitter" were based on any valid intuition about the internet … or on a pathetic grabbiness.

Noah's dispirited comments highlighted an interesting aspect of *TheNotebook*'s evolution: the fact that its age—and the age of its managers and employees—became a liability over time. At the turn of the 2010s, *TheNotebook* already looked like part of the "old media." Analysts started to describe the website as old-fashioned, not "agile" enough to survive in the rapidly changing tech environment.

"Agile," "disruptive," "nimble," "pivoting": one cannot overestimate how central these terms have become in the current media landscape. For many companies—especially those that had been around for a while—keeping the appearance of technological "nimbleness" gradually became as important as producing quality content. *TheNotebook* was no exception to the rule. It took immense efforts on the part of its editors and managers to "get" social media, efforts that Noah criticized as "pathetic grabbiness." This grabbiness, however, can also be described as the institutional evolution that enabled *TheNotebook* to survive for more than twenty years.

LaPlace in the Storm

On the other side of the Atlantic, we left *LaPlace* in a period of experimental bliss. Over time, however, this collective enthusiasm was replaced by fatigue and doubts. As Marina, the managing editor, philosophically commented, euphoria could not last forever:

> After the first years of euphoria when they were working all the time, partying together all the time, thinking that they were the pioneers of the news, well, there was a normalizing process. A normalization of life, first, because people had gotten older, they had girlfriends, they wanted to buy an apartment, these kinds of things. But the working conditions weren't changing. There was a lot, a lot, a lot of work! And the editorial project was fuzzy. At the beginning, they were inventing and having fun, but the other media started doing the same. So they were having doubts.

To some extent, what Marina called a "normalizing process" is what sociologists would call a classic case of routinization of charisma. As the organization got older, the workers started questioning the authority of the founders and realized that the working conditions at *LaPlace* were less than ideal.[11] Yet there was another set of causes for this transformation of the working atmosphere: the company was already running short of money. A year after the publication was launched, the founders had to raise capital from new investors, bringing in an additional one million euros in order to develop and expand the website. The four founders kept the majority of the shares, but the new investors made stern recommendations: if the company was not able to make a profit soon, they would have to fire several employees, something that the founders—unlike *The-Notebook*'s managers, who had no problem firing people—vehemently refused to do.

As in the United States, the French market for online news was also becoming increasingly competitive. Other successful news websites had emerged. *Mediapart*, created in 2008, became well known for its scoops incriminating Nicolas Sarkozy. *OWNI*, launched in 2009, published cutting-edge data journalism and technology coverage. *Atlantico*, which started in 2011, was directly inspired by the U.S.-based website *Politico*. The French version of the *Huffington Post*, which was created in early 2012, was also attracting a growing number of visitors. In the meantime, however, advertising revenues remained low. As André told me: "We operated under the illusion that if we proved our journalistic value the business side would follow.... We were told, 'if you get one million unique visitors you'll get one million euros of revenues.' It didn't work that way. To use a term in vogue these days, we underestimated how 'disruptive' online media would turn out to be." The journalists had completed their part of the deal, but advertising revenues fell far short of a million euros and *LaPlace* was still in the red.

The founders tried several different strategies to increase revenues, all of which took a toll on the staff's time and energy. Like *TheNotebook*, and largely inspired by their example, *LaPlace* developed sub-sites, including one on economic topics, in hopes of attracting more lucrative advertising contracts. These were never profitable, however, and closed after a year and a half. *LaPlace* also created a monthly print magazine, which required extra work from staffers and was quickly abandoned. The most long-lasting initiative was to sell training programs to companies who wanted to train their employees in web journalism: *LaPlace*'s journalists and editors took turns teaching online search techniques, fact-checking, and digital writing skills. By 2011, everybody in the newsroom was exhausted and pessimistic about the future. The early days of editorial pioneering and playfulness seemed far away. When recalling these years, Philippe, the editor-in-chief, explained: "We were very anxious about money. We were really worried that six months later we wouldn't be there anymore. In 2007 the economy was good in France, the ads were working well. Then there was a crisis in 2008, the downturn in 2011. It was hard.... We started the training seminars because the shareholders were worried and were asking us to fire our staff. We said no. We said that we were going to find something else." The atmosphere in the newsroom was tense. In Marina's words: "The founders were having a lot of trouble—they were worried, they were looking for money everywhere, the shareholders were causing trouble, the training programs had just started.... People were tired and doubtful."

The Sale to LeGroupeMag and the End of the Collaborative Ideal

In 2011, the founders decided to sell the website to a media company, LeGroupeMag, which already owned 3 percent of *LaPlace*'s shares. Created in the 1960s by a left-leaning investor who had made his fortune in another business, by then LeGroupeMag was a mid-sized media group that owned a popular political magazine and several specialized magazines. LeGroupeMag's chairman respected *LaPlace*'s editorial project, as *LaPlace*'s founders repeatedly emphasized, and paid about 7 million euros for *LaPlace*, which the founders considered to be a generous offer. The sale meant higher wages for the journalists, who would be given a 10 percent pay raise. LeGroupeMag also promised new hires and increased technology budgets while reassuring the journalists about the editorial independence of the publication.

The staff had mixed feelings about the transaction. The journalists profoundly disagreed with the ways that the negotiations with LeGroupe-Mag had been conducted. The founders had kept the negotiations secret until the last possible moment (they argued that they had been sworn to secrecy about the sale): the journalists only learned about it a couple of days before the public announcement. More profoundly, many of them felt betrayed by the founders' decision to sell, as well as by the profit that the founders realized in the financial operation. The founders, they felt, disrespected the sacrifices that the staff had endured during the website's early years in the effort to secure its survival as an independent publication.

The journalists also resented the amount of the raise, which they viewed as inadequate in light of their investment in the editorial project and the long years of underpayment that they had accepted.

A couple of weeks after the announcement of the sale, I had coffee with Sarah, a long-time staffer, on the rooftop of *LaPlace*'s building, looking out at the panoramic view of the city. Sarah was agitated. She explained that the staff writers were in the process of creating a representative body (*société de journalistes*)—similar to a union but more specifically concerned with journalistic independence and ethical guidelines.[12] After a while, she told me: "The bosses don't really care about money, which is kind of paradoxical given that they just cashed in a big bag of money. André is not going to buy ten expensive suits and drive a fancy convertible.... It's not his style. But still, I don't forget that he got a million euros and that I participated ... a lot ... in the valorization of this business and that I didn't get a bonus or anything." Fancy convertible or not, Sarah realized that she had contributed through her constant and underpaid efforts to the "big bag of money" that André, Philippe, and the other founders got from the sale. Former managing editor Gabriella, who had left the website before the sale, had a more analytic take on the situation:

> From the start there was an ambiguity at *LaPlace* ... in part because of the personalities of the founders, they don't like conflict, but it was also because of the lack of financial means.... The discourse was, "We're a participatory website, we're collaborative, this website is your website." When in fact, no, it's a private business, with founders who own shares! A business that became more valuable as the capital increased.... There was this emotional blackmail about the survival of the company: "We could never have made it without you." Well, when at the end you sell the company ... In fact, we, the staff, the unpaid bloggers, we all created additional value for the founders' shares!

Most of the staffers, freelancers, and bloggers felt that they had been somewhat cheated by the founders. Until then, they had understood their work for *LaPlace* as participation in an experimental, collaborative adventure. They did not mind being underpaid (or in the case of many bloggers, unpaid) because they thought that they were participating in an important editorial and political project. Yet the sale underscored that *LaPlace* had been a for-profit business from the start. The staffers and bloggers realized that their nonstop work and emotional involvement had increased the value of a company that had always been a commercial asset. *LaPlace*'s "ambiguity"—as Gabriella put it—had been unveiled by the sale.[13]

Traffic, Traffic, Traffic

As Newspapers Inc. had for *TheNotebook*, LeGroupeMag had high expectations for *LaPlace*. LeGroupeMag's decision to acquire *LaPlace* came with a clear mandate: traffic growth. By adding *LaPlace*'s number of monthly visitors to the ones that LeGroupeMag's publications already had, the company hoped to join the top echelon of Médiamétrie//NetRatings' media rankings, enabling them to charge higher advertising rates. Hence, after a few months, the chase for clicks was back, but this time under direct pressure from LeGroupeMag: *LaPlace* had to find ways to increase traffic without spending more money.

How would they do it? The editors came up with several strategies that were very similar to the ones at *TheNotebook*. Like the New York publication, the French website developed editorial partnerships, which included foreign magazines with francophone content, artistic magazines, and collaborations with blogging platforms around the world. Unsurprisingly, these partnerships took a lot of work: the journalists spent many hours selecting and editing the content provided by the website's partners in order to make it fit with their editorial line. A second strategy was to pressure the staffers to cover breaking news in real time with short, witty articles usually based on aggregation or news wires. Similar to what we saw at *TheNotebook*, *LaPlace*'s staff resented this evolution and complained that the multiplication of short articles did not leave them enough time to focus on the long-form investigative articles that had made the website successful in earlier years.

Another solution, specific to the French website, was to have more blogs. As we saw in chapter 2, participatory content had always been part of *LaPlace*'s project, but during and after the sale the number of bloggers increased exponentially—up to 76 blogs in 2012. From the start, *LaPlace*'s founders had decided that they would not pay their bloggers. This nonpayment policy became problematic after the sale to LeGroupeMag: many bloggers who cared about *LaPlace*'s collaborative and participatory ideal felt betrayed by the sale, and they repeatedly told the staffers and founders they wanted compensation. Editors tried to manage these tensions while still increasing the number of blog posts published on the website, which took a toll on their time and morale.

In addition to publishing more and faster, the French editors also started paying close attention to traffic-related technologies. As at *The-Notebook*, they turned to search engine optimization and social media expertise. Gael, one of the website's senior editors, became the SEO specialist and community manager and directed the efforts of the newsroom in making its editorial content more visible online. In 2012, *LaPlace*'s two copy editors, who were also in charge of posting articles on the content management system (CMS) of the website, had the same routines as at *TheNotebook*: they wrote different headlines for the homepage, the SEO line, the Facebook page, and the Twitter feed; they carefully inserted key words in order to increase the ranking of the articles on Google; they tweaked the articles' headlines for Facebook and Twitter; and they started tracking how many readers came from these different platforms. As Gael explained to me, the editors were getting a much clearer sense than before of the different types of readers that the website was attracting:

> Our readers ... Their profiles are becoming more and more diverse. We have internet users who read our articles on Facebook—they read our paper through their friends' links, or they "like" our page on Facebook, but they never go to the website directly. They're younger, 25 or 30 years old, whereas our average reader is more like 30–35 years old. But our returning readers, who are usually the ones who post comments all the time, every day or almost every day, they hate Facebook because of its use of private data, because of its ideology.... These readers are very important for our identity, they've been there from the start, but it's only 300–400 people whereas we're getting 80,000 readers through Facebook. The numbers are just different.

Paradoxically, as *LaPlace* better understood its sources of traffic and the preferences of its audience, editors and journalists started paying less attention to the loyal readers—the so-called "neighbors"—that had been there from the start. As Gael pointed out, although these long-time readers had been essential for the identity of the site, they did not "count" much in quantitative terms—or, as we will see, according to the click-based evaluation gaining ground in the Parisian newsroom—compared to the masses of readers coming from Facebook and Twitter. The interactive relationship that *LaPlace*'s staffers had put in place with their online public during the early years of the website was replaced over time by a more quantitative, data-driven understanding of algorithmic publics, as we will develop in the next chapters.

Isomorphic Convergence

Did these parallel traffic-driven strategies result in any actual convergence between *TheNotebook* and *LaPlace*? To go beyond the discourses of journalists, I collected quantitative data about the two websites. With the help of computer scientists, I conducted a web crawl of all the articles published by the two websites between 2009 and 2014. We gathered 90,270 articles for *TheNotebook* and 60,816 articles for *LaPlace*. The quantitative findings confirm the journalists' declarations and reveals striking processes of convergence between the New York and Parisian websites.

First, the journalists had a point about publishing more and publishing faster. Figure 3.1 shows the evolution of the number of articles per month published on the two websites. In 2009, *TheNotebook* published an average of 603 articles each month. By 2013, the New York website had more than doubled its production, with an average of 1,342 articles published per month. Similarly, *LaPlace*'s publication rhythm picked up in the second half of 2011. Whereas the French website published an average of 620 articles per month in 2010, by 2013 this number had reached 877 articles per month—a 41 percent increase. Both websites also started publishing an increasing number of short aggregation-based blog posts after 2011.[14]

Not only was there more content published overall; the analysis also indicates that the mean number of articles published per author per month also increased significantly over the period. Figure 3.2 shows that the monthly articles-per-author figure grew from 4.5 articles in 2009 to 5.2 in 2013 at *TheNotebook*—a nonnegligible increase from 54 to 62 articles per author per year. At *LaPlace*, the mean number of articles published per author per month grew from 3.9 articles to 5.2 articles—from 47 to 62 articles annually—over the period. In other words, both *TheNotebook*'s and *LaPlace*'s staffers ended up writing more than before, independently of the number of new writers hired to help with content production.[15]

These convergent evolutions between *TheNotebook* and *LaPlace* in turn resemble what sociologists Paul DiMaggio and Walter Powell call "institutional isomorphism" in organizational fields. According to DiMaggio and Powell, when fields become structured—that is, when the interactions, awareness, and information flows between actors of a given sector reach critical levels—the organizations of that field tend to converge and become more alike. DiMaggio and Powell further identify a specific type of convergence, "mimetic isomorphism," which tends to occur in situations

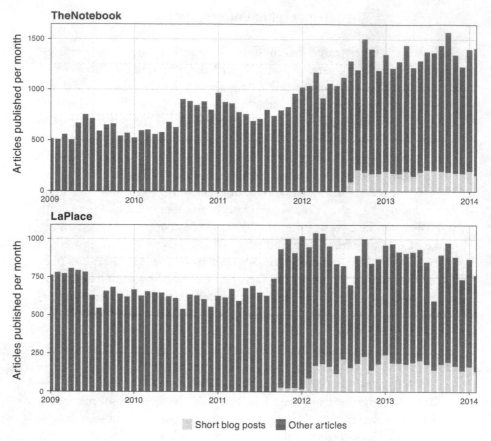

Figure 3.1. Number of articles published per month, *TheNotebook* and *LaPlace* (2009–2014).

of uncertainty: when organizations are not sure about the best course of action to improve their standing or revenues in a given sector, they often imitate their most legitimate competitors, hoping to send signals of modernity and prestige to their funders, peers, and customers.[16]

The fact that *TheNotebook* and *LaPlace* adopted the same strategies to maximize traffic, even though they were on different sides of the Atlantic and had little direct contact at that point, makes them a striking case of isomorphism. Faced with marked pressures to increase traffic, but not knowing exactly how to achieve that goal, they imitated the strategies of news websites they perceived to be more successful than themselves—in this case, the *Huffington Post*, *BuzzFeed*, and *Gawker*. In so doing, they not only hoped to improve traffic numbers but were also sending signals

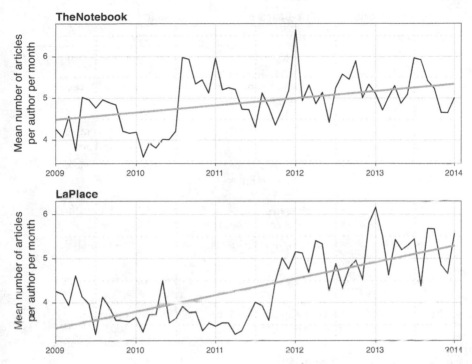

Figure 3.2. Mean number of articles published per author per month, *TheNotebook* and *LaPlace* (2009–2014).

of legitimacy and modernity to investors and advertisers. As a consequence, the length of the articles and rhythm of publication of the two websites converged.[17]

Editorial and Click-Based Evaluation

Taking a step back, the chase for clicks led to the emergence of a similar tension at *TheNotebook* and *LaPlace* between competing definitions of their journalistic mission—more specifically, between what I call an *editorial* and a *click-based* mode of evaluation. By mode of evaluation, I mean all the cognitive, discursive, and practical operations by which people categorize and hierarchize ideas, objects, and practices.[18] Table 3.1 provides ideal-typical descriptions of the editorial and click-based modes of evaluation, comparing their definitions of journalistic excellence, measurements of success, temporal frames, and relevant units of analysis.[19]

Table 3.1. Editorial and Click-Based Modes of Evaluation

Evaluation	Editorial	Click-based
Definition of journalism	- Original reporting - Background information - Blog posts are not valued - The news dictates the format of the article	- Communicating with readers - Being "webby," "reactive" - Long articles are deemed "boring" - The audience dictates the format of the article
Signal of success	- Being followed by other media outlets and news agencies - Compliments by colleagues and competitors	- Number of page views, likes, and tweets - "Going viral," "trending," "buzz," "organic traffic"
Time frame	- Slow; long-term editorial strategy	- Fast; real-time analytics
Unit	- Collective (site, section)	- Individualized (writer, article)
Related concepts	- Autonomous pole (Bourdieu 2006) - Professional logic (Thornton et al. 2012) - News as information (Schudson 1978)	- Heteronomous pole (Bourdieu 2006) - Market logic (Thornton et al. 2012) - News as stories (Schudson 1978)

First, editorial and click-based evaluations come with different views on what constitutes good journalism. According to the editorial definition, journalism is about providing quality information to the public through original reporting and background research. Depending on how complex the news is, the length of the articles will vary. This definition builds on the "news as information" paradigm described in chapter 1, which emerged in the late nineteenth century as journalism became professionalized. In contrast, according to the click-based mode of evaluation, journalism is first and foremost an act of communication with online readers: no efforts should be spared to make stories enticing, witty, and funny. According to this view, which bears similarities with the "news as story" paradigm, readers tend to get bored when articles are long and arduous. Therefore, brevity and light blog posts are preferred, regardless of the complexity of the information provided.[20]

The two modes of evaluation come with different signals of success. According to the editorial mode of evaluation, recognition by one's peers is essential: a good article is one that gets compliments by editors, colleagues, and competitors. As we saw in chapter 2, for *TheNotebook* and *LaPlace*, this is what created the high emotional energy and feelings of pride that dominated the early years of the two newsrooms. Instead, in the click-based mode of evaluation, success is primarily quantitative and comes from the audience: having high traffic numbers and mentions on social media platforms is of utmost importance. This data comes mediated through specific metrics, visualizations, and technological artifacts, the reception of which I will examine in the next chapter.

The two definitions also rely on distinct time frames and units of analysis. Editorial evaluation understands journalism as a long-term and collective enterprise based on the quality of the output of a publication over several years, usually under the tenure of a given editorial team. For *TheNotebook* and *LaPlace*, this meant experimenting with formats and creating their own original editorial line. In contrast, the click-based definition focuses on instantaneous success, usually at the level of the individual writer, measured through real-time audience metrics: what matters most is to "go viral," rather than any assessment of the long-term impact of the article.

Last but not least, each mode of evaluation participates in—but cannot be reduced to—wider ways of organizing the world. Thus, editorial evaluation shares characteristics with professional and autonomous logics, in the sense that the actors involved draw on norms and values that are specific to the field under consideration to resist what they perceive as an encroachment of commercial concerns. In contrast, click-based evaluation bears similarities with market-based and heteronomous logics, in the sense that actors tend to mobilize external indicators of popularity as a way to legitimate types of content that are perceived as "light" or less serious.[21] As we will see in the next chapters, however, this does not exhaust the meanings of traffic numbers, which represent more than just market pressures.

The relative balance between editorial and click-based evaluation changed over time at *TheNotebook* and *LaPlace*. During the publications' early years, when the two teams had high editorial ambitions and few expectations of being "normal businesses," editorial evaluation prevailed and click-based evaluation was low. As we saw in chapter 2, audience metrics were then notably absent from the daily routines of the newsrooms. When the two websites experienced increased pressure to enter the chase for clicks, and following isomorphic pressures towards convergence, the click-based mode of evaluation became more prominent and came into acute conflict with the editorial definition that had prevailed until then. Through web analytics, click-based evaluation became more visible, individualized, and instantaneous, making increasingly pressing demands on the editors and journalists as they tried to navigate the tumultuous waters of online news production.

Conclusion

This chapter followed *TheNotebook* and *LaPlace* as they abandoned their utopian ideals to enter the chase for clicks, opening the door of their newsrooms to web metrics. The two websites faced similar economic pressures to make a profit and came up with identical solutions—ranging from editorial partnerships to SEO techniques—in order to publish more, faster, and to attract traffic without increasing their costs. This backstage and invisible work took a lot of time and energy from staffers and copy editors. Over time, journalists at *TheNotebook* and *LaPlace* experienced a similar conflict between editorial and click-based definitions of their work, identity, and organizational goals.

Interestingly, this gradual—and unintentional—process of convergence had more long-lasting consequences on the two publications than the conscious process of imitation that we saw in the previous chapter, when we examined how *LaPlace* explicitly replicated some of the *TheNotebook*'s innovations. In spite of the system of public protection and subsidies put in place to help shield French news organizations from market pressures, *LaPlace* ended up adopting the same traffic-driven techniques as its American counterpart, leading to similar complaints among staffers about the decrease in quality and standardization of its editorial line.[22]

If we stopped here, it would seem that *TheNotebook* and *LaPlace* were stuck in an inexorable process of convergence, spiraling down towards the lowest common denominator induced by the chase for clicks. Yet the differences between *TheNotebook* and *LaPlace* did not, in fact, disappear. As we will see, the two organizations developed distinct uses of web analytics and different relationships with their algorithmic publics. This in turn came with important consequences for their news production process, compensation systems, and contributors' careers. The second half of the book explores these differences.

CHAPTER 4

The Multiple Meanings of Clicks

Journalists and Their Algorithmic Publics

When web journalists talk about the kind of articles that attract a lot of clicks, they often use the word "trash," in English and in French. In fact, some of them go further, deploying the metaphor of prostitution. For instance, Philippe, *LaPlace*'s editor-in-chief, told me how the editorial team had come up with the term "the whore's spot" (*la place de la pute*) to describe a specific location on the website's homepage where they often posted popular articles:

> We're always trying to find a balance between serious and light articles, short and long papers.... The second article on the homepage, we call it PDLP for reasons that, shall we say, should remain confidential [*laughs*].... I don't even remember where it came from, I think that one day one of us said, "put it in the whore's spot" [*place de la pute* (PDLP)], we laughed, and it stayed. "Whore" is for whorish [*putassiers*] articles, it doesn't have anything whorish really but it should be a racy article, either a polemical piece, or something light, or something about sex. It's not the headline, so we can't be accused of having trashy headlines, but still it's on top of the homepage. We don't post anything degrading ... but we try to put fun things there.

To Philippe, popular articles were "racy" or even "whorish." He emphasized that *LaPlace* would not post "degrading" pieces at the top of their homepage because they did not want to be accused of being "trashy." He was not the only one: many web journalists in New York and Paris distinguished clickbait from quality content using what sociologist Viviana Zelizer would call a "hostile worlds" repertoire. They relied on strongly normative words to contrast the instrumental rationality of traffic-driven articles and the purity of "serious" editorial news content.[1]

Most of the journalists developing the metaphors of trash, indecency, and prostitution were men, whereas many of the writers who covered popular but low-status beats (sex, gender, lifestyle, celebrities, and so on) were women. By granting a new visibility to these low-prestige topics, web analytics transformed the internal status dynamics of news organizations—a process that incumbents (usually highly educated white men) typically criticized as an encroachment of "whorish" commercial criteria into the editorial sanctuary of newsrooms. Female writers covering low-prestige but popular beats countered with click-based arguments. They typically emphasized not only the economic value of their production, but also their connection with online readers and their skill in seizing on topics that people found relevant.[2]

I argue in this chapter that audience metrics caused more than a mere intrusion of market concerns in editorial processes, or even a reorganization of status and gender hierarchies in web newsrooms. By putting clicks at the center of newsrooms, analytics software programs made a new category of actors *present* in the daily life of editors and journalists: they materialized the complex and distributed collectives of online readers, what I call "algorithmic publics," in the lifeworld of web journalists. From the perspective of journalists, online readers are now algorithmically sorted twice: first when they see and click on news articles on the algorithmically mediated feeds of social media platforms and search engines, and second when their clicks are aggregated and displayed through dashboards in web newsrooms.[3]

Here I use the concept of "publics" broadly to include multiple kinds of communicative exchanges—online and offline, deliberative and agonistic, specialized and generalized. What matters for my argument is that publics always have a civic potential, at least for the journalists who rhetorically mobilize publicity in defining their professional identity. Compared to the related concept of "audiences," publics have two characteristics: they refer to communities with some form of collective agency, instead of haphazardly assembled spectators; and they are firmly anchored in the democratic polity, both as consumers of information and as citizens endowed with political legitimacy. Both aspects are important when analyzing how journalists make sense of their publics and how these representations affect the production of news in the United States and France.[4]

Given the amount and granularity of digital data gathered about online users, one could expect journalists and editors to be able to assess with a great deal of certainty the identity and preferences of their algorithmic publics. Instead, I find that algorithmic publics remained a deeply elusive and contested object in web newsrooms—not unlike the "imagined communities" analyzed by Benedict Anderson. Journalists in New York and Paris projected complex and ambiguous meanings onto their algorithmic publics; they mobilized distinct imaginaries to make sense of them; and they oscillated between widely different definitions of their readers in the process. As we will see, journalists in New York primarily relied on a commercial understanding of traffic numbers. They relied on the data at their disposal to reinforce their conceptions of algorithmic publics as fragmented entities and as commodities whose comments did not say much about the quality of their writing. In contrast, in Paris journalists entertained a more ambivalent relationship with their publics, evoking both their commercial side and their civic potential. This chapter documents how digital metrics take strikingly distinct meanings depending on their institutional context and how the history of the U.S. and French journalistic fields help to make sense of these differences.

Counting Clicks at *TheNotebook* and *LaPlace*

As we saw in the previous chapter, beginning in 2008 and 2009, both *TheNotebook* and *LaPlace* faced strong pressure to attract more traffic. They started publishing more material at a faster pace, with a new focus on search engines and social media optimization. They also began paying closer attention to their online audiences. In their quest to increase their traffic, and at about the same time, *TheNotebook* and *LaPlace* eventually turned to the same innovation to track the behaviors and preferences of their readers: web analytics software programs.

In New York, *TheNotebook*'s marketing department had been using analytics since the late 1990s, relying on Omniture and Comscore. From its early days, *TheNotebook*'s sales representatives had a clear idea of who their audience was. For instance, in 2002, *TheNotebook*'s marketing team wrote to potential advertisers: "*TheNotebook*'s audience is educated, affluent, and influential. 61 percent of *TheNotebook* readers have a college degree or higher. 69 percent of the audience is between the ages of 25–54. The mean income is $90,108 and the median income is $73,728." They described their readers as "seasoned online users" and "savvy online shoppers." Their marketing department used a more detailed version of this audience profile to attract advertisers and set the rate of their online inventory.[5]

The New York organization began using Google Analytics as early as 2005, but it was only after Sam's promotion to editor-in-chief in 2008 that top editors started to rely heavily on real-time data. In 2009, *TheNotebook* licensed Chartbeat, which was gradually installed on most computers in the newsroom. Sam also hired a new director of technology, who developed an in-house program in parallel. During my years of fieldwork, the website relied on no fewer than five different analytics programs. Sam described this careful attention to web metrics as one of his main accomplishments: "Anyone in my position would have done it, but now we have a new person who runs technology for us.... So we're being much more conscious about data and using data. The first ten years that *TheNotebook* existed, we didn't really think very much about traffic in an explicit way, people were always very scared of it. So we really pushed on that."

The situation was more artisanal at *LaPlace*, which relied on (only) two software programs to track traffic: Google Analytics, which they began using in the mid-2000s, and Chartbeat, licensed in 2010. Chartbeat was also installed on most computers in the newsroom. Gael, *LaPlace*'s social media editor and community manager, recalled how they acquired Chartbeat: "Our web developer is the one who found out about Chartbeat. Beforehand, we were making do. But we're not as sophisticated as most American newsrooms.... Here it's less precise."

In spite of their different locations, the two websites thus started using the same analytics tools at about the same time. During my fieldwork, they both used Google Analytics and Chartbeat, two programs produced by U.S.-based companies and used around the world. At *TheNotebook*, the decision to license Chartbeat was a top-down process initiated by the editor-in-chief, whereas at *LaPlace* the advent of metrics was a bottom-up initiative started by a web developer. These differences were not merely anecdotal, as we will see, because editors and journalists in fact made sense of web analytics—and, through metrics, of their algorithmic publics—in nearly opposite ways at the two websites.

Trust in Numbers at *TheNotebook*

In the New York newsroom, most editors considered web metrics to be reliable indicators that were helpful for guiding editorial and managerial decisions. This was made evident in the course of an interview I had with Sam. The editor-in-chief had just explained to me how, under his direction, *TheNotebook* had more than doubled the amount of content they published every month. When I asked why, Sam replied:

> The fact is ... that what we see in our data is that the more we publish, the more readers we get.... Here, I'll show you [*he opens the in-house software program that shows traffic trends over time*]. If you look here in particular— this is how much we publish. There is almost a direct link with traffic. There

are some exceptions, I could explain why.... The green line is the number of articles we publish. The red line is the number of blog posts. So we're trying to publish more. Because ... more gets us more. All the evidence that we have from our own data suggests that the more we publish the more readers we get.

When asked about one of his decisions as editor-in-chief, Sam immediately turned to the question of data, which had not been mentioned until that point in the interview. He understood this data as a "fact," or even a piece of "evidence." But it was not enough to tell me about the data: Sam also felt compelled to open their in-house analytics program to show me the correlation between numbers of articles published and traffic patterns. Sam used analytics as a justificatory tool when asked about an important editorial decision he made. In the face of radical uncertainty about the determinants of online popularity, he protected himself from external criticism by justifying his editorial decisions as based on "objective" criteria. In so doing, he projected strong beliefs certainty, impartiality, and rationality—onto the data itself.

Sam was not the only one at *TheNotebook* to understand analytics as an unproblematic piece of evidence. Section editors also routinely relied on web metrics when making editorial decisions. As Emma, one of the editors, told me. "I do not diminish the importance of numbers. That's not all that matters ... or we would only be doing cat videos [*laughs*]. But journalism is a marketplace. If no one reads your articles it's that there is something wrong, the packaging is wrong or the article is not good." For Emma, traffic numbers had a clear meaning that needed to be taken into account, either to better understand what was "wrong" with an article or to boost the popularity of a piece that was already doing well. Like Emma, most web editors at *TheNotebook* welcomed the information they received about their readers and interpreted this data as an indication of the success of a piece in the "marketplace" of attention. They used it for multiple editorial decisions, as illustrated in the following observation with Tom, the homepage editor at *TheNotebook*.

Observation with Tom
TheNotebook
October 17, 2012

Tom works in a separate office alongside the open space where most staffers are located. He is looking at two large computer screens in front of him and constantly checks a program that is an overlay of Chartbeat and the in-house program. For each article on the homepage, the overlay shows a red or a green sign, which changes in real time depending on how many people are clicking on each article compared to predictions based on earlier traffic.

One of the headlines has a red sign. Tom says "ok, maybe it's time to change this one." He scrolls down the website.

> TOM: So … what's going well? Yes, the post-debate thing about sexual dominance…. [*laughs*] Well, this explains that, people click because of a base instinct…. I don't think that I need to promote it.
>
> AC: Are there things that you never put on TAP 1 [*the top location for a headline on the homepage*]?
>
> TOM: Yes…. There are things that are enormously popular but that won't do for TAP 1. Like our advice column [*a column that gives facetious advice about sex, relationships, and family life*], it's very smart and fun, but it's not something that people need to read in order to become informed citizens of the world…. In this case, editorial value trumps popularity. Same thing with a blog post, we won't put it on TAP 1, it's not our work, it shouldn't be there.

Tom relied on real-time analytics when deciding which articles to "promote," that is, to move to a higher position on the homepage. He compared the observed click-through rate and the predicted one. When a headline was not doing as well as predicted, Tom's reaction was quick: he moved the article further down on the homepage. Yet there were also limits to this data-driven approach, because high popularity did not systematically translate into editorial promotion. For instance, Tom pointed out that he never posted a "sex and gender" advice article on top of the homepage: these articles were popular but "wouldn't do" for the most prestigious spot on the homepage. In such cases, Tom's editorial judgment overrode the click-based mode of evaluation.

Traffic numbers also provided sufficient justifications at *TheNotebook* for cutting or dropping entire sections. For instance, in 2011, the website cut its international coverage when one of the senior writers in charge of international news was fired. Tom, the homepage editor, commented on this decision: "It's true that we scaled back our international coverage…. We didn't have the resources, and there wasn't enough interest among our readers." In this case, the preferences of the readers were cited as a sufficient criterion to cut the international section—or at least to justify it *post hoc*.[6]

Similarly, *TheNotebook* stopped covering large parts of the arts scene, including classical music, opera, and dance performances. Esther, the former culture editor, recalled the pressure to do more "lowbrow" culture coverage in the early 2000s: "I was aware that the culture section was the least read. I didn't take that personally. I think that in all magazines the culture section is the least read. There was a constant tension between highbrow and lowbrow culture.... I was definitely under pressure to do more lowbrow. And I just pushed back, I viewed it as part of my job to push back!" Eight years later, after Esther's departure, the magazine had stopped covering highbrow culture altogether. It specialized instead in articles about television series, a "niche" for series addicts who regularly visited the website to get updates, according to Noah, a former editor and staff writer: "The staff keeps paying attention to what is successful on the site. They realized that *The Sopranos* and *The Wire* blog posts were very successful." Editors used web analytics to identify what online readers were clicking on and tweak *TheNotebook*'s coverage to cater to these specific audience niches. This perception of online readers as having discrete preferences that could be catered to was part of a broader understanding of their algorithmic publics as fragmented and commodified—I will return to this point later.

In addition to making editorial decisions based on audience data, *TheNotebook*'s editors also relied on analytics in their management of the staff. They strongly and openly encouraged staffers to think about traffic and pay attention to web analytics. Sam explained his strategy as editor-in-chief: "We made a decision here to be very frank with our writers about what our business challenges were, about what we would do on the business side. We just say, 'Here are the needs that we have, we need to prove to the advertisers that we are a sufficiently large site, we need to get traffic, how do we do that, what can you do to help us?' And my sense is that people have been incredibly eager to do that."

TheNotebook's editors developed an array of techniques over time to make internet metrics omnipresent in the daily routines of the newsroom. Moira, former editor at the *Huffington Post* and "traffic guru" of *TheNotebook*, was influential in the process. As she told me,

> At *TheNotebook*, they have a strong editorial voice, they do excellent journalism, and they have high standards. I didn't want to alter that core, but my mandate was to get more traffic—they didn't have a clear strategy about how to do it. One of my first moves was to make people more familiar with traffic and traffic numbers. Now everybody has access to Chartbeat.

When I arrived, people talked very differently about traffic. People saw it as threatening, debasing. That's not the case anymore.... I wished people used the programs more. But there was a lot of catching up to do.

Reports were regularly emailed to all editors, staffers, and contributors, with a ranking of the "top ten articles" for the day, week, or month, the "most-emailed" articles, the "most-shared" articles on Facebook and Twitter, etc. For a while, the entire staff also attended weekly meetings to gather ideas about the best ways to use different technologies at *TheNotebook*. This was not an editorial meeting: it was solely oriented towards improving the website and attracting more readers. Last but not least, the management briefly tried to implement a performance-based compensation system, in which bonuses would be distributed to section editors depending on their traffic numbers. Noah, a former editor, recalled these developments with mock terror:

> You know this David Mamet movie in which a corporate guy is coming to a company and says: "Next week you're going to have to make as many sales as possible, the guy who makes the most sales is going to have a new car, and the next one is going to have steak knives and everyone else is fired." ... At *TheNotebook*, they said that there were going to break out traffic number by section, and they had meetings with everyone, and they said: "Here is what your numbers are all like, your goal is 50% by next year." And I really got the sense that, well, if you don't make your numbers, you're in trouble.[7]

For a while, *TheNotebook* tried to imitate the performance-based compensation system of *Gawker*, one of their New York rivals. At that time, every *Gawker* writer and editor was assigned traffic targets for the upcoming year and received a bonus whenever they reached it. A landmark of the *Gawker* newsroom was a giant screen called the "Big Board," which featured Chartbeat's real-time ranking of the most popular articles of the day, along with the name of the author and the number of unique visitors for each piece.[8] *TheNotebook* never went as far as *Gawker*, although its top editors were tempted to follow the same direction. They briefly created a performance-based bonus for section editors, but this measure was soon abandoned, probably because it required a degree of monitoring that was beyond the capabilities and interest of *TheNotebook*'s management.

Overall, the picture that emerged at *TheNotebook* was one of what historian Theodore Porter called "trust in numbers." Not only did *The-*

Notebook's editors understand web analytics as reliable and unproblematic indicators; they also projected strong values and beliefs about rationality and objectivity unto these quantitative tools. In this, their attitudes were analogous to that of the U.S. Army engineers studied by Porter. According to Porter, engineers promoted quantitative calculations of cost-benefit ratios for expensive public works as a way to protect themselves from external criticism. In his words: "A decision made by numbers ... has at least the appearance of being fair and impersonal."[9] Similarly, faced with growing pressure from their parent company to attract traffic without clear guidelines about how to achieve this goal, *TheNotebook*'s editors mobilized web analytics as a discursive and practical strategy—one that could shield them from the intrinsic uncertainty they experienced when making editorial decisions that could damage or ensure the survival of their publication.

Ambivalence at *LaPlace*

At the Parisian website, editors had a more conflicted and ambivalent relationship with analytics. Whereas *TheNotebook*'s editor-in-chief insisted on the "facts" provided by audience metrics, *LaPlace*'s editors were more reluctant to use Chartbeat, for reasons that Philippe, the website's editor-in-chief, explained:

> I don't follow Chartbeat much.... I try not to look at it. When you look at Chartbeat all the time, you make choices that might not be the best ones for the identity of the media. If we only cared about the number of clicks, about Chartbeat, it would be simple, you know, we would only write about celebrities. Celebrities ... it always works. But the issue then is that we would become a celebrity website and that's not the kind of credibility we're looking for.... In the long run, when it gets too trashy, people move somewhere else. So we don't write about celebrities. I mean, we do, but only when it's related to politics, to a scandal, but we don't write about celebrities just to write about them. We don't do that.

Philippe openly criticized Chartbeat, which he believed created incentives—like covering celebrities and tabloid news—that went against the best interest of the publication. Yet this opinion was not shared by everybody in the French newsroom. For instance, Marina, *LaPlace*'s managing editor, had a somewhat different position. Marina came to *LaPlace* in 2010 after a career at women's magazines, where she was an editor, and at print newspapers, where she worked as a freelancer. She explained how much she loved Chartbeat:

> I'm a Chartbeat addict! I look at Chartbeat all the time. When I arrive in the morning, I start my computer, and the three screens that I open are *LaPlace*; Chartbeat; and Gmail. I then see immediately how things are going.... I need to feel what the internet users are reading, what is going on in France and in the world and with our readers. Chartbeat is a tool that gives you the possibility to feel that.... You see what's going well on Twitter, Chartbeat, Facebook, and you start moving your ass [*tu te bouges les fesses*] if nothing works.

Marina did not seem to share Philippe's distrust of web analytics, but her understanding of Chartbeat was nonetheless very different from the one developed by *TheNotebook*'s editors. She did not describe Chartbeat as a "signal" providing "evidence." Her fondness for Chartbeat was more impressionistic: it allowed her to get the pulse of her online readers. In the process, Marina described *LaPlace*'s algorithmic public as a unitary and vibrant entity—one that existed "out there" and needed to be understood on its own terms. Yet even Marina had doubts about the relevance of clicks as an indicator of journalistic value. For instance, she expressed how her confusion grew once the excitement caused by the frantic rhythm of online traffic wore down: "When you start, you get super excited, you get a lot of comments and a lot of clicks on an article and you think, wow, it worked really well! But later you start thinking, 'Maybe it wasn't that good, maybe it wasn't that important ...' It's hard."

Traffic numbers did matter in making editorial decisions in the Parisian newsroom, but only to a limited extent. Similar to *TheNotebook*, editors at *LaPlace* relied on Chartbeat when deciding which articles to promote: articles that were doing well were put on top of the homepage, whereas articles that attracted fewer readers than expected were downgraded to a lower position. As at *TheNotebook*, there was a subtle equilibrium to reach regarding headlines. As Philippe explained, they tried to strike a fine-grained "balance" between "serious" and "light" articles on the homepage: "We never put any article from the 'sex and gender' section as a headline or a super-headline, I'm very careful about that." Tellingly, editors at *LaPlace* had exactly the same—somewhat disingenuous—rule as at *TheNotebook*: articles about sex were never posted on top of the homepage, but were put instead in the second most visible location on the homepage (the "whore's spot" mentioned earlier), where they would gather attention and clicks without contaminating the editorial integrity of the homepage.

Beyond these apparent similarities, however, important differences emerged between the two organizations. For instance, editors at *LaPlace* steadfastly refused to cut sections that were not successful in terms of traffic. On the contrary, they understood it as their duty to provide important news about technical or demanding topics, even though the articles were typically not popular with online readers. As Marina, the managing editor, told me: "The headline ... If it's something about Syria, well, our readers don't care about Syria, there will be only 4,000, 5,000 clicks, which is not a lot for the headline, but we'll still do it.... Some pieces are not read a lot online but they're super important on the website."

Philippe confirmed this view by explicitly relying on the editorial mode of evaluation: "There is a credibility criterion to take into account. I'm going to give the readers what they want to see on their favorite website.... They might not click on the page, but it gives some credibility to the website." In contrast to *TheNotebook*, where the international section was cut down, editors at *LaPlace* continued to post articles about international news, even though they knew that such articles would attract little traffic. For the French editors, and in line with the traditional goal of guiding public opinion, part of the editorial mission of a good publication entailed publishing articles that their public *should* care about—even if they did not end up reading these pieces. According to Philippe and Marina, having serious articles about demanding topics was a way of maintaining *LaPlace*'s prestige, and therefore its audience, in the long run.

Another essential distinction between *TheNotebook* and *LaPlace* regarded the use of internet metrics as a management tool. *LaPlace*'s editors and managers did not send daily reports to their staff with rankings of the most popular articles or moot the possibility of performance-based bonuses. On the contrary, they tried to cheer up staffers disappointed by their articles' lack of popularity. For example, one day, as we were talking about an article written by a staffer in the culture section, Marina told me: "The articles that she writes about culture, graphic novels, it's always around 5,000 clicks but we're really supporting her. Sometimes she's a bit discouraged, she works for four days on something and she only gets 4,000 clicks.... But I tell her, 'No, listen, you're building a community, it's something that we value a lot.'"

Overall, when it came to analytics, the picture that emerged among the French editors was one of ambivalence. On the one hand, the Parisian editors were well aware of the limitations of Chartbeat. They believed that focusing on Chartbeat would lead to poor editorial decisions. They frequently pushed back against traffic imperatives and instead prioritized alternative editorial projects, such as public interest stories and articles that helped build a community of dedicated readers. At the same time, they saw in Chartbeat a valuable—if impressionistic—tool for understanding what resonated with their algorithmic public. Unlike *TheNotebook*'s editors, who saw Chartbeat as an unproblematic source of traffic data, editors at *LaPlace* constantly second-guessed their uses of the analytics software program, worrying that it did not accurately represent what readers truly cared about (even if they did not click on the articles), or that it would lead them to prioritize "degrading" articles instead of important ones.

Given these differences in how editors used and interpreted analytics at *TheNotebook* and *LaPlace*, how did staffers make sense of traffic numbers in each organization? One could have expected each staff's interpretation to be in line with the position of the editors: trust in numbers at *TheNotebook*, ambivalence at *LaPlace*. Yet paradoxically the staffers at the two websites had almost opposite reactions.

TheNotebook's Staff: Distancing as Passive Resistance

In the New York newsroom, staff writers adopted a distanced attitude towards audience metrics: journalists frequently asserted that they did not pay much attention to the number of page views that their articles attracted. Take Martin, the staff writer mentioned in the previous chapter who specialized in economic topics. When I asked him whether he checked his metrics, he answered: "Hmm ... I try not to look at traffic too much because at the end of the day it doesn't depend on me but on the editors, it depends on where my posts are put on the website." Sean, another writer, confirmed:

> I have access to traffic numbers.... They keep sending me links where I can log on and see all that stuff. In great detail [*laughs*]! Might be Omniture ... I can't even remember which proprietary thing they use. So, I have access to something that shows all those stats ... and I do not look at them. I just don't bother. It's not worth it to me. On the homepage, they have a box with the "top ten most read," "top ten on Twitter," I'll look at those when my stories are up, like "Oh, is it catching on?" But that's it. I don't go to

Omniture or Chartbeat or whatever it is that they use and obsessively look at the stats. I find it kind of stressful and I try not to get too wrapped up in that.... I would certainly prefer not to have to pay attention to that stuff at all and do good work and stuff I'm proud of.

Such reactions were widespread among *TheNotebook*'s staffers, who said that they did not systematically check their traffic numbers despite being repeatedly sent links and passwords by the editors and management. Like Sean, many writers noticed when their articles appeared in the "top ten most read" list, but they also explained that it was more important for them to do "good work" and write articles they were "proud of," in Sean's words. As Jack, a staff writer who specialized in short blog posts about breaking news, told me: "My breaking news posts are doing great in terms of traffic, it's been a success, and the content is very good, so the editors are happy. I'm aware that the management is happy with it. But the staff, it's different—they don't care. When a video goes viral and gets many more page views than a long-form article, well, no one at *TheNotebook* will think that it is of better value. I've never seen that." Similarly, take the following exchange with Alec, a staff writer to whom I asked whether other staffers talked about traffic in the office:

AC: Do they often talk about traffic at the office?

ALEC: During the day, chatting around the office and stuff, I don't think so. Much more often you'll hear people say, "Oh I really liked that piece" or "I thought that was a really smart take." And once in a while you will hear someone say, "do you know how well that piece is doing?" Once or twice when they mentioned the traffic it was kind of a surprise, it was an outlier, they may talk about it, like "Oh my god, look at the traffic, this piece is blowing up." Once in a while you'll hear that. But much more often they talk about the journalism itself.

Interestingly, the metaphor that emerges from the staff writers' description of online popularity is that of a fluke—a surprising and positive development, but one that is not particularly meaningful.[10] During my days of observation in the newsroom, this discursive indifference of staff writers towards metrics was confirmed by their work practices. I often witnessed traffic-oriented conversations at *TheNotebook*, but only behind closed doors, when top editors met to talk about data and traffic—for instance when they discussed headlines, which they often tweaked whenever they thought that articles were underperforming in terms of traffic. In contrast, no staffer checked traffic numbers in the open-space section of the office while I was there. Staff writers spent a lot of time on *TheNotebook*'s home-page, email, the content management system, search engines, instant messaging, and social media, but I did not see any of them looking at Chartbeat or Google Analytics, though they had access to all of these programs.[11]

This relative absence of traffic talk in the newsroom, however, did not mean that *TheNotebook*'s writers were not aware of traffic numbers. As we saw, they received numerous emails every week about traffic; they also usually knew whether they were in the "top ten" most visited articles or not. Yet they did not seem to take traffic numbers to heart. Instead, staff writers at *TheNotebook* appeared to understand internet metrics as a technical game—one that editors had to master but one that was not particularly meaningful. As Martin suggested above, he interpreted his traffic numbers as a reflection of how his articles had been promoted on the website—for instance, whether they had posted on top of the homepage at a propitious time—but such decisions were made by editors, not him.

This led staff writers to be openly critical of their editors' traffic-oriented strategies, which they often found problematic for the quality of the website. Thus, many writers vehemently criticized two of the tactics developed by *TheNotebook*'s editors to maximize traffic: pagination (a trick by which articles are divided into two or three pages, automatically doubling or tripling the number of page views and impressions counted compared to single-page articles) and slideshows (each image counts as a page, so a slideshow with ten images would receive ten page views or impressions if the reader viewed all the slides). As Jane, a former copy editor already introduced, explained: "When *TheNotebook* started publishing slideshows they were doing this fairly unique thing, they were essays with images that were supposed to advance some kind of argument. And then we moved to the same model that other websites have, where it's just about traffic. There is no real text, only captions. It's just that.... You get more clicks. I mean, it's cheating!" Similarly, Noah, already mentioned above, reminisced:

> I remember when *TheNotebook* started paginating, in '05 or '06. That was something I was opposed to because it was so clearly.... There is no way you could argue that readers would actually enjoy that. You'll antagonize your readers but you're doubling your traffic. Oh yeah! That's why everybody started paginating. And even when you click "single page" when you start reading the article, it counts as a click. When it's a three-page article, you triple your page views. But people don't really make it to page three.

That said, in spite of the strong judgments they passed on these "cheating" strategies, staffers also emphasized that they understood the pressures faced by the editors. As Jane told me, editors were under strong pressure from the parent company to attract more traffic; she thought that they were only "doing their best to make the publication survive." In this view, checking metrics and traffic considerations were part of the bundle of tasks assigned to editors. In Sean's words: "Editors ... It's part of their job to know that stuff, to really understand SEO and make good SEO lines, to understand what kinds of stories are going to do well and what kind probably aren't.... My editor, all day she's on Omniture, Chartbeat, whatever this is, she's looking at that. But it's not my job to look at that stuff. My job is just to hand them my copy and hope that it's good."

Writers thus drew strong distinctions between the respective roles of editors and writers in the New York newsroom. According to them, one of the responsibilities of editors was to take care of traffic-related consid erations. Writers saw *TheNotebook*'s editors as doing what they had to do—pagination, slideshows, and so on—in order to squeeze out more clicks from their online publics. This allowed staff writers to focus on their own role, which they defined as writing "good copy." By drawing such a sharp line between the professional roles of editors and writers, and by refusing to take responsibility for metrics-related optimization, the staffers were not complying with their management's goal: after all, as we saw earlier, editors wanted them to "help" with traffic in addition to writing quality content. For *TheNotebook*'s staff writers, distancing themselves from traffic concerns was an act of passive resistance.

LaPlace's Staff and the Emotional Power of Clicks

At first glance, the Parisian staffers seemed more cynical about traffic than their New York counterparts. They often relied on a moralizing repertoire when analyzing the types of topics that got high numbers of page views. For example, during a cigarette break in front of the office with two staff journalists in February 2012, I asked them what kinds of articles were usually chosen as headlines for the website. They immediately replied: "A headline piece ... Well, when you have some sex, or Sarkozy, or a touch of racism, it works! [*they both laugh*]." Other staffers confirmed these views: "We know the recipes to get more traffic: kittens and sex, obviously!"

In spite of these sarcastic comments, web metrics and the subject of traffic were ubiquitous subjects of conversation during my days of field-work in the French newsroom, to a much greater extent than at *TheNotebook*. This stemmed in part from the design of the website itself: one of the most striking characteristics of *LaPlace*'s homepage during this period was that it prominently featured the number of visits, likes, tweets, and comments for each article. Consequently, online readers and *a fortiori* journalists had access to audience metrics. In fact, staff writers told me that they found this information difficult to ignore. One of them, Louise, explained: "It's hard not to look at the number of clicks, because it's very visible on the website's homepage, you see. I can't avoid the number of clicks. It's already a lot to deal with." Staffers felt that it was impossible for them to ignore the number of page views their articles received, because it was the first thing they saw on the website's homepage.[12]

In addition to the basic metrics featured on *LaPlace*'s homepage, the Parisian staffers also obsessively followed Chartbeat. During my days of fieldwork, each time an article was posted online, the writer and editors in charge usually opened the Chartbeat window and followed how popular the article was during the first minutes after its publication. For instance, one day in January 2012, Lise and Vicente—two journalists in the sports section—had just finished editing an article about a French athlete prosecuted for assaulting a woman at his sports club. Vicente announced: "We're going to post it!" Lise then told me: "I'm a bit scared ... of everybody. The sports fans, the feminists, everybody! [*Laughs*] I'm really stressed out!" Right after the article was published, Vicente opened Chartbeat and turned to me: "You know this program? It's the hell of *LaPlace* ["*c'est l'enfer de LaPlace*"]. You can see how many people are visiting the website, around 1,500 right now, which articles they are reading, what country they live in, and also what they typed on Google that led them to the article. For example, Lise's piece, it's doing well! Here, a guy typed 'video sexual assault.' [*Laughs*] It's 11 a.m., and the guy is looking for a video of sexual assault! Weirdo."

Vicente used Chartbeat to check how the article was doing, and also to get a sense of what kinds of readers were clicking on it (including the personal tracking information about what had brought some "weirdo" to the article). He described Chartbeat as "hell," a term that has a double meaning—one with a spiritual component, as the nether realm in which people suffer everlasting punishment, the other more secular, describing a state of misery and torment. Such eschatological language echoes a comment made by Bourdieu about the journalistic field (specifically television) where, he argued, "ratings have become the journalist's last judgment."[13] Certainly, *LaPlace*'s staffers and editors kept referring to traffic numbers as an essential arbiter of individual and collective worth. In addition to checking Chartbeat constantly, they also frequently switched back and forth between editorial and traffic-oriented repertoires when discussing news articles. The interactions that surrounded the following piece reveal the intermingling of click-based and editorial evaluation in the Parisian newsroom:

Observation
LaPlace
February 2, 2012

10 a.m.
Marc, one of the interns, just finished writing an article listing different solutions for erasing one's traces on the web. The article takes on a witty tone while providing a critical overview of online surveillance and giving advice about how to avoid it. The first sentence gives a sense of the rest of the article: "Surfing on the web is like jumping in wet cement: it leaves indelible traces (almost) everywhere."

11:30 a.m.
MARINA (managing editor) to Lucie (copy editor): "What about the title ... "A little guide to the web"? No, it sounds too condescending. "The guide to ..." And what about the image? [*The image shows footprints on melting snow.*]

LUCIE: I like it. It's beautiful, melting snow.

MARINA: Yes, but it's only melting snow. [*To Marc*]: This image ... it's cute but it doesn't connect to the topic. The rest is great. I found your article really clear.

3 p.m.
LUCIE to Marina: Marc's piece is doing great.... I'm looking at Chartbeat and it gets a lot of visitors. Should we turn it into a super-headline [*"super-manchette": a banner that fills the entire top third of the homepage*]?

[*Several staff writers who overhear the exchange stand up and come to Lucie's table to check Chartbeat with her. Marina comes close as well.*]

MARINA: I like the new headline, "Surfing incognito on the web."

LUCIE: Should we do it? Come on, let's do it!

MARINA: But then we need a PDLP [*"place de la pute," the second space on the homepage, where Marc's article was originally located*]. Do we have an extra one? No? What about you guys in the sports section? Nothing? Never mind. Okay, let's do the super-headline.

5:30 p.m.

ANDRÉ (chairman, just coming back from a meeting): That's a great headline! And it's doing well too, the number of visitors is huge, even without Google. Maybe we only get readers who feel guilty about something they did online. But we don't have anything to feel guilty about [*"on n'a rien à se reprocher"*]. [*They all laugh.*] Already 20,000 visitors!

MARINA: But it's not only a guide to erase your dirty secrets ... I mean, it's also about privacy. What if the CIA forces Google to give up all of its data?

MARC: Yeah ... there is some political relevance to the piece.

6 p.m.

VICENTE (staff writer, coming back from an interview): Hey, great piece! It's a hit! I feel super incognito right now! [*He laughs and several staffers make jokes about what he might have to hide.*]

These exchanges give a sense of the multiple registers used by *La-Place*'s editors and staffers to talk about their work. Marina and Lucie started by discussing the best headline for Marc's article. Later in the day, Lucie noted that the article was doing well in terms of traffic and asked Marina whether they could promote the article as a "super-headline." Several staffers heard that something was going on; they collectively decided to promote the piece. Later in the afternoon, *LaPlace*'s chairman entered the room and immediately commented on the super-headline, without sitting down, which meant that he must have checked the article's traffic numbers on his smartphone. He congratulated Marc, drawing both on editorial criteria ("A great headline!") and click-based arguments ("And it's doing well, too!"). In the early evening, another staff writer, Vicente, congratulated Marc, saying that his article was not only "great" but also a "hit" (*ça cartonne*)—one of the Parisian staffers' favorite expressions when talking about traffic.

Contrary to *TheNotebook*, where editors were the only ones discussing metrics and did so behind closed doors, traffic numbers were a public affair at *LaPlace*. Editors, managers, copy editors, and staff writers constantly commented on web analytics in the open space. During these discussions, everyone switched back and forth between editorial and click-based evaluation: "good" articles (editorially speaking) were also articles that "did well" (quantitatively speaking). Conversely, articles that were flops (quantitatively speaking) invited the editors' suspicions (editorially speaking). This back-and-forth between the two modes of evaluation was made clear during one of *LaPlace*'s editorial meetings.

Observation

LaPlace

January 12, 2012, 9:30 a.m.

> CLÉMENT (intern): I'm thinking of writing a piece about the fines you get when you travel to Italy.... In fact, when you're French you don't have to pay them because you can ask for a fair trial in French and they don't have the means to organize that.... I find it interesting.
>
> PHILIPPE (editor-in-chief): Great.... That could be a banner on top of the homepage. What an internship, Clément! You've already written two top pieces, three soon, with thousands and thousands of clicks! We're going to hire you, you know that!
>
> ALEXANDRE (staff writer): Yeah, you know how much we care about page views! [*Everybody laughs.*]
>
> EDITH (copy editor): There's also this fun topic ... Giscard [*the former French president*] wants to be buried in his private garden, but it's not allowed in France, except in Corsica.
>
> SARAH (staff writer): I can feel that this is a 100,000-click topic [*everybody laughs*]!
>
> MARINA (managing editor): Well, funeral laws are really interesting.
>
> EDITH (copy editor): The last idea is about the monthly private budget of Sarkozy.
>
> PHILIPPE (editor-in-chief): This would be a 3-million-click article!

Editorial meetings are important rituals of newsroom life. During these weekly meetings, the Parisian staffers and interns pitched their ideas for the upcoming week in front of the editors and the rest of the team. The group then reacted to the different ideas, praising or critiquing them. At *LaPlace*, many editorial meetings involved traffic discussions. Editors and journalists reacted immediately to article proposals by commenting on the number of page views that they were likely to attract. These traffic-oriented comments in turn often led to newsroom banter and cynical jokes about the publication's priorities. Philippe welcomed Clément's proposed article on the best way to evade fines when traveling to Italy, complimenting him—somewhat ironically—on finding a subject that would attract "thousands and thousands of clicks." On the other hand, the idea of writing an article about funeral laws in France was dismissed because it would have been a flop in terms of traffic ("I can feel that this is a 100,000-click topic," Sarah interjected sarcastically).

Perhaps unsurprisingly, given how central traffic talk was in the Parisian newsroom, *LaPlace*'s journalists explained that they experienced strong emotions depending on the popularity of their articles. In the words of Louise, a staff writer: "Yes, I look at traffic numbers. I don't think that I choose my topics based on it but I look at it and it makes me happy. It's a stupid reward.... When you see that a piece is working well you're happy. It's like a reflex." Good numbers made writers "happy," even when they thought that it was illegitimate (or "stupid") to feel that way. In contrast, bad numbers tended to produce feelings of anxiety, as exemplified by Agnès, who wrote in the culture section:

> When you have an important topic, a topic that matters ... and you get 2,000 clicks ... then you're really mortified. So okay, you know your way around, you know that's the way it works ... but you have a ghost whispering in your ear, "not cool." On the contrary, it always makes me feel much better when I post a paper online and it gets 40,000 clicks. Then it's cool. So then you realize that it's important because you're very happy when your paper has a large audience. Anyway, it's almost like a natural law, at least for me: after 10, 12 pieces that didn't work, you give yourself a break and you write a short piece that is going to be a hit! You don't sell your soul to the devil, no, no, but you just reset the scale.

Agnès knew that "bad" numbers made her unhappy, so she developed a strategy to "reset the scale" when things were not going well: if several of her articles were flops, she wrote pieces that she knew would be popular.

Not unlike Vincente, who described Chartbeat as "hell," Agnès drew on otherworldly metaphors ("ghost," "devil") when talking about the pressure to get high traffic numbers. As we will see, this ambiguous, internalized, and emotional relationship to metrics resembles disciplinary power—a diffuse and pervasive type of control analyzed by Michel Foucault. In contrast, *TheNotebook* relied on a well-defined authority structure based on clear incentives, strong internal boundaries, and centralized hierarchies—a kind of managerial power that can be described as bureaucratic. We will return to this distinction between disciplinary and bureaucratic power in the next chapter.

Between the "Wall of Separation" and Civic Imperatives

Overall, at *TheNotebook*, a strong division of labor emerged between editors and staff writers. Editors were expected to handle traffic-related concerns: they paid close attention to click-based imperatives, repeatedly asking staffers to help them achieve traffic goals. This in turn provoked a counterreaction among the staffers, who quietly engaged in passive resistance, drawing on their professional ethos and on the editorial mode of evaluation to shield themselves from the editors' demands. Hence, despite the editors' pressure to attract more traffic, staffers in the newsroom remained relatively buffered from web analytics.

LaPlace did not have such a division of labor. Instead, the professional roles of editors and staff writers largely overlapped. As we discussed in the previous chapter, the founders of the Parisian website could not help but realize that traffic was essential for the survival of the publication. Unlike *TheNotebook*'s editors, however, they did not change their editorial line or fire employees. Over time, the relative absence of specialization between editors and staffers in turn left both groups ill-prepared to handle the strain of having to maximize traffic numbers.

Where do these distinct newsroom dynamics come from? We saw in chapter 2 that *TheNotebook* and *LaPlace*'s editors had spent the first half of their careers working for print publications. When trying to solve the challenges of creating a new type of publication in a rapidly changing environment, Sam, Emma, Philippe, Marina, and their colleagues relied on what they knew best: they drew on the specific set of cognitive categories, justifications, and organizational forms that developed over time in the print newsrooms of their respective countries. In the process, they reproduced the strategies and institutional recipes that emerged as part of the different histories of U.S. and French journalistic fields.

In New York, that meant drawing on the "wall of separation" and strict division of labor between editors and journalists of the "high modern" era described in chapter 1. Web journalists at *TheNotebook* were able to adopt a distanced attitude towards metrics, but only because editors bore the responsibility of maximizing traffic numbers. In contrast, the paradigm of self-regulation that emerged in France after the Second World War was not based on walls of separation or on a strict division of labor but instead on a civic ethos, for editors and staff writers alike, to guide and shape public opinion. Hence, editors at *LaPlace* saw it as their primary role to publish "important" pieces, even though such pieces were not popular with their readers, in line with the ambition prevalent among French intellectuals to provide political and cultural guidance to a broad public. As commercial pressures became more prominent in the newsroom, however, editors were not able to buffer their staffers from the click-based imperative. Over time, metrics became integrated into a broader form of anxiety about journalistic performance in the competitive market for online news.

These organizational dynamics, inherited from previous phases of their national journalistic fields, shed light on the distinct uses of traffic metrics at *TheNotebook* and *LaPlace*. Yet there is more to the difference between the two websites than simple variation in the division of labor and reception of market pressures between editors and staff writers. More profoundly, journalists did not *see* the same things when they looked at metrics. In New York, journalists interpreted clicks as the manifestation of an algorithmic public they saw as fragmented, commodified, and largely uninteresting except for commercial purposes. In Paris, editors and journalists scrutinized metrics to interact with an algorithmic public understood as unitary, active, and endowed with civic and political will. The rest of this chapter turns to these differences and examines their effects in the two newsrooms.

TheNotebook: Segmenting the Algorithmic Public

On the American side, editors and journalists primarily interpreted traffic numbers as commercial indicators. As such, they were either acted upon (by the editors) or kept at bay (by staff writers), but there was little mystery regarding the object that web analytics purported to represent:

for *TheNotebook*'s editors and writers, analytics were primarily about the "marketplace"—in Emma's words—of online attention. In this digital marketplace lived the algorithmic public of the New York website. Yet there was nothing particularly meaningful about the online readers of *TheNotebook*. Take what Noah told me about the coverage of television series at *TheNotebook*: "There are people who are obsessed about pop culture, about what you might think is trashy. And they want to find a magazine where there are smart people, so to speak, talking about their favorite TV show. That's a sweet spot for *TheNotebook*.... You get readers who are obsessed with the show, and then they become obsessed with having *TheNotebook* people writing about the show and they come back multiple times and are desperate for more."

"Trashy," "desperate," "obsessed," "sweet spot": the words Noah used to describe *TheNotebook*'s readers leave little to the imagination. For the New York–based journalists, audience metrics offered useful feedback for finding audience niches, catering to them, and maximizing revenues. But the tastes of these algorithmically mediated publics were not particularly valued by the journalists, who often deprecated their reading habits and short attention span. As one staff writer wrote in a humorous article, addressing his piece to online readers: "I'm going to keep this brief, because you're not going to stick around for long."[14] Many writers further complained about the lack of attention of online readers, especially when they realized that the average time spent on their articles was under a minute. As one journalist complained, "people don't really make it to page three.... When you look at the stats, 40% look at the second page, and then on page three it's 10%, it's kind of dismaying. So when you ask me 'do you look at your stats,' well, if you get 70,000 unique users, you know that realistically only a third of these people have read through the end of your article."

In addition to criticizing the reading habits of their readers, the New York journalists clearly categorized their algorithmic public into disparate segments. *TheNotebook*'s editors and staff often praised their loyal readers—the online readers who frequently returned to the website, who were typically urban and highly educated, who "got" *TheNotebook*'s style and contrarian jokes, and whom they described as "prepared for the complexities of a typical article from *TheNotebook*." In contrast, they disparaged occasional readers who came through social media platforms and search engines, who didn't necessarily know *TheNotebook*'s brand, and whom they perceived to have less desirable socio-economic characteristics than the "loyal" ones. *TheNotebook*'s editors criticized these "strangers," as they called them, who "may not be familiar with *TheNotebook*—they may not even know of its existence—and they have been lured to the article by a short, snappy headline."[15]

Overall, the New York-based journalists and editors described their algorithmic public as a segmented entity—one whose prevailing preferences did not strike them as particularly meaningful or interesting, except for commercial purposes. For all of these reasons, journalists explained that the preferences of online readers did not provide valuable feedback about the editorial quality of their articles. Instead, they saw audience metrics as the latest iteration of the multiple commercial encroachments that characterized U.S. newsrooms since the development of a mass market for information.

LaPlace: Engaging the Algorithmic Public

Things were different in Paris. At *LaPlace*, journalists and editors cared about their algorithmic public as it was represented through the Chartbeat dashboard. This public was in turn imbued with elusive and contradictory meanings. Unlike what we saw at *TheNotebook*, *LaPlace*'s editors and staffers did not have clear-cut categories to hierarchize their online readers into distinct segments. Instead, their online public remained a unitary whole—one with mysterious preferences, in spite of the Chartbeat data everyone at *LaPlace* followed so avidly. As Louise, a staff writer, once told me:

> What I find annoying is that our audience is not well defined. It's never been defined. We don't have any studies about our readers. I think it's important to know who we're writing for, but the bosses told me: "No, we write for everybody." Well, I don't think so! But here no one wants to know. I think we miss a lot of opportunities. We get the number of clicks, but we don't understand *why* [*her emphasis*].

This lack of precision did not stem from a lack of data: as we saw, *LaPlace* relied on several analytics tools, including Chartbeat, to track the preferences of their readers. But the French editors did not analyze the data in the same way as their New York counterparts. Louise thought that this was a conscious decision: the editors hoped to "write for everybody," she said. This universalist conception of the public as including all potential—in addition to actual—readers was confirmed by the editors when I interviewed them. For instance, Eric, founder and top editor, explained in a somewhat tendentious way: "We're not writing with our nose right on the audience's preferences. We're building our website based on an editorial project that is designed to attract and interest people."

For Eric and the other editors, success was a matter of appealing to the taste of "the people" (*les gens*). But how could *LaPlace*'s team know what people wanted? It was, at the end of day, a somewhat magical process. For instance, Marina, mentioned above, repeatedly emphasized how she trusted her intuition to interpret Chartbeat and get a sense of what the public needed. In her words, it was essential "to stay in touch with what's going on for our readers" (*il faut garder le contact avec ce qui se passe pour nos lecteurs*).

Intuition, attraction, touch, feeling … Far from the number-driven mindset in place at *TheNotebook*, many of the Parisian journalists saw it as their role to "charm" their readers. At *LaPlace*, web analytics functioned as an intuitive gauge of public opinion and public relevance: good traffic numbers meant that a writer had reached their public (actual and potential); bad traffic numbers indicated that the communication process with the public had failed.

At the same time, *LaPlace*'s editors and journalists could not help but realize that their online audience was also a commercial target to monetize. Thus, the Parisian journalists faced an intrinsically problematic tension between contradictory definitions of their algorithmic public: it was a civic entity that should be guided towards quality information *and* a commodity that needed to be coaxed into clicking at any cost. This tension was made particularly clear during an episode of acute conflict that took place after the sale to LeGroupeMag. Responding to the repeated requests from the new parent company to attract more traffic, *LaPlace*'s top editors sent an email to the staff, entitled "the battle for the audience." In it, they asked staff writers to do their part in bringing more traffic to the website:

> What is at stake today is the role of *LaPlace* as an independent site, in the context of a brutal acceleration of the commercial crisis that touches all the media…. We need to realize that growing our audience is vital in this context of crisis. Reaching this goal depends on the behavior and mobilization of each and every one of us…. Many recent examples show that we have much to gain from being more reactive and covering hot news right when it occurs. This is important for the editorial line of the website and in order to win the battle for the audience.

A follow-up email further specified that writers would be evaluated based on traffic from then on:

> You will all be scheduled for individual meetings. We will talk about our goals and see where we stand.... The programmers are working on a program that we will use to track these objectives. Every month, the machine [*sic*] will send you a summary of your publications, as well as the total number of articles on the website. The email will also include figures about the evolution of the number of visitors.

Unsurprisingly, *LaPlace*'s staff reacted negatively to these expectations. During several meetings of the *société de journalistes* that they had created earlier that year, the staffers drafted a collective email to the management, in which they criticized the top editors' "obsession" with "quantitative goals"—an obsession that they described as "demoralizing" and "counterproductive." They countered with a radically different picture of *LaPlace*'s role and relationship to its public. As they wrote in their response, "*LaPlace* [is] an independent website which invents, innovates, creates, entices, amuses, instructs, inspires, refuses to comply, and bears responsibility for its choices. We need a young, innovative, independent, and different media, now more than ever." Half seducing, half guiding, the Parisian journalists put the emphasis not on the commodified side of their algorithmic public but instead on the authentic and civic nature of their relationship with "the people."[16]

Thus, *LaPlace*'s editors and journalists interpreted traffic numbers in deeply ambiguous and contradictory ways. Clicks were criticized and cynically disparaged as indicators of market pressures, but in between their jokes, journalists and editors understood web metrics as a fuzzy signal of their relevance to the mood and opinions of a broad, civic, and unitary algorithmic public. Over time, this somewhat magical communion with the public increasingly clashed with the pressure from the editors and the parent company to consider algorithmic publics as a commercial target.

Conclusion

In this chapter, I examined how web journalists made sense of audience metrics in New York and Paris. At *TheNotebook*, a relatively consistent understanding of metrics emerged: editors and journalists described web analytics as reliable measurements used to target a commodified, fragmented, and superficial public. Consequently, they either doubled down on metrics or kept them at a distance, depending on their role in the newsroom. At *LaPlace*, journalists projected ambiguous and contradictory meanings onto web analytics and, through them, onto their algorithmic publics. They oscillated between a commercial transaction with their readership—which they criticized as a form of prostitution—and a more engaged communication process with a unitary public endowed with civic and political agency. This ambiguity resulted in a widespread fixation on traffic numbers.

These differences were in turn shaped by specific organizational forms and relationships with the public as they developed over time in the U.S. and French journalistic field. At *TheNotebook*, the marked division of labor between editors and staff writers enabled journalists to preserve some amount of professional autonomy. In contrast, the emotional weight placed on metrics at *LaPlace* came with a stronger emotional involvement of journalists themselves in the chase for clicks as a manifestation of their relevance in the public sphere. These interpretations of traffic numbers in turn came with clear ramifications for the balance between editorial and click-based evaluation. As we shall see, this profoundly influenced the production of news at the two websites.

Digital metrics, then, function as complex symbolic entities: they always stand for more than just themselves. In newsrooms, analytics represent the public (or, using the term invoked earlier, they "appresent" it on screens), a crucial but contested entity in journalism. By comparing the strikingly different uses and meanings projected onto digital metrics—and, through metrics, onto algorithmic publics—by editors and staff writers in New York and Paris, I wish to show the interpretive flexibility of algorithms and analytics. Beyond the specific case of journalism, this reveals the essential role of institutional contexts in shaping the meanings of metrics.

CHAPTER 5

The Fast and the Slow

Producing Online News in Real Time

News organizations are characterized by an intrinsic tension, as sociologist Gaye Tuchman first pointed out: news is by definition unpredictable because it depends on each day's events, but media companies need to put together a highly standardized product regardless—be it a newspaper or a television show—at the same time, day after day. Thus, news organizations need to find ways to "routinize the unexpected" and streamline the production of information.[1]

Traditionally, print newsrooms achieved this by relying on hierarchical and compartmentalized structures. As Herbert Gans argued in the 1970s, the journalistic distinction between "hard" and "soft" news, together with the somewhat "military" division of labor he found between editors and staff writers, enabled magazines and television networks to standardize the daily processing of unpredictable events. Editors-in-chief played the role of general managers in this production process. Every day, they made sure that that no important topic was overlooked, that articles were ready on time, and that editorial quality remained high. All of this took place under strict time and economic constraints—in the words of economist Jay Hamilton, "a world of multiple scarcities."[2]

At first glance, things could not be more different in online news. After all, there are no time or space limitations on the web: editors can theoretically publish as much as they want, whenever they want; the cost of maintaining the servers remains more or less the same. Yet online production comes with new constraints, the most important of which is the pressure to publish constantly—what journalism scholar Nikki Usher calls the "immediacy imperative." Web editors need to keep their homepage up to date by publishing fresh content 24/7, year-round. In a way, this belief in immediacy is the logical development of traditional journalistic values. After all, immediacy has been baked into the very concept of "news" since the advent of periodicals in Renaissance Europe. If digital technologies make it possible to cover breaking news in real time, why shouldn't news websites take advantage of this?[3]

Yet the ideology of immediacy comes at a cost. In the words of Alexis Madrigal, former editor of the *Atlantic Online*: "Let me give you this hypothetical. You are a digital editor at a fine publication. You are in charge of writing some stuff, commissioning some stuff, editing some stuff. Maybe you have an official traffic goal, or (more likely), you want to be awesome, qualitatively and quantitatively.... You need to do great stuff. But hell, you're posting all the time! How do you do great stuff? You find ways to optimize between speed and quality. Everyone has their own coping strategies. And it's always gonna be a tradeoff. "[4]

Madrigal merely mentions the existence of a "tradeoff" between speed and quality, but others are more pessimistic. For instance, journalist Dean Starkman criticized web newsrooms for being on what he called a "Hamster Wheel" of immediacy: "the Hamster Wheel isn't speed; it's motion for motion's sake. The Hamster Wheel is volume without thought. It is a news panic, a lack of discipline, an inability to say no." Others have argued that web newsrooms suffer from "Attention Deficit Disorder," with "little clear strategy about how, when, and why stories should be posted." Overall, scholars find that publishing news in real time comes with problematic side effects in terms of quality.[5]

In this chapter, I revisit how the immediacy imperative affects the editorial strategies of editors and journalists. The comparison between *TheNotebook* and *LaPlace* reveals that the two newsrooms experienced an acute conflict between click-based and editorial definitions of journalistic quality. They faced a similar dilemma between the pressure to publish frequently and their desire to write "important" pieces. Yet the two organizations handled this tension in almost opposite ways. In one case, specialization prevailed. In the other, flexibility and versatility were the order of the day. I will analyze these differences in terms of *bureaucratic* and *disciplinary* power. I find that *TheNotebook* relied on a bureaucratic framework based on centralization, strong hierarchies, and marked internal boundaries between click-based and editorial concerns. In contrast, *LaPlace* drew on a disciplinary form of managerial power based on decentralization, fuzzy boundaries, and a constant overlap between editorial and click-based considerations. The chapter shows how these distinct organizational dynamics shaped the work practices, office spaces, and even the homepages of the two websites.

TheNotebook and the Distinction between the Fast and the Slow

As we saw earlier, starting in 2008–9, *TheNotebook* faced strong pressure from its parent company to publish more content and attract more traffic. For a while, the chase for clicks was overwhelming. Many staffers worried that quick posts were taking over and that the publication was becoming too similar to *TheNotebook*'s nemesis, the *Huffington Post*. Benjamin, managing editor, recalled how he felt at the time:

> If *TheNotebook* had been only going in the direction of publishing more, publishing shorter, publishing more quickly ... that would have troubled me a little bit, because I don't want *TheNotebook* to become the *Huffington Post*, I don't want to just be reacting to the news. Traditionally *TheNotebook* has thought of itself as a magazine, not as a news site exactly. We like to bring perspective and point of view and hopefully surprising arguments to the news. Obviously, it's harder to do that when you're publishing more and publishing more quickly ... with the same number of people [*laughs*]!

Though Benjamin acknowledged the difficulties associated with publishing at a faster pace without additional resources, he also believed that *TheNotebook* had managed to maintain its editorial identity over the years. When asked why, he—like many others—told me about the distinction between the "fast *Notebook*" and the "slow *Notebook*." In the New York newsroom, the expression "fast *Notebook*" referred to all the short articles published on the website. These pieces were also called "blogs"—a term that comes with multiple meanings in the digital world but one that at *TheNotebook* simply referred to short articles (about 500 words long instead of the regular length of 1,000 words).[6]

Blog posts were supposed to be "reactive," in the sense that journalists were expected to publish them as quickly as possible after the event that motivated the post. For that reason, blog posts did not necessarily go through the full copy-editing circuit: many writers were allowed to publish the posts themselves in order to accelerate the publication process. These short formats also overwhelmingly drew on news aggregation. Aggregation—the repackaging of information published elsewhere—was first popularized by blogging venues and websites like the *Huffington Post*. After denouncing it as outright theft, traditional journalistic outlets gradually adopted the practice, which became part of standard newsroom routines. This was the case at *TheNotebook*, which relied heavily on news aggregation for its fast articles.[7]

What did that leave for the "slow *Notebook*"? When staffers talked about the "slow" part of the website, they referred to all the long-form and carefully researched articles published on *TheNotebook*. These pieces were intended to mark the reputation of the publication as a smart, original website with a distinctive voice on subjects ranging from politics to culture and technology. Some of these articles featured original research and investigations. Others were more literary, developing complex arguments or new angles on a given topic. No effort was spared to ensure the quality of these longer articles. Writers could take up to several days—and sometimes much more—to do research and get feedback on their pieces. Such articles always went through the full copy-editing circuit. They also often received careful attention from the media department in terms of illustrations and images.

At *TheNotebook*, all the writers knew where they stood in the distinction between the "fast" and the "slow." Many of them strongly identified with one side or the other. For instance, Jack, a writer for the breaking news section, clearly identified with the fast part of the website when he described his daily work routines:

> I wake up at 7 a.m. and I start reading the news. If there's some kind of breaking news I'll sit down at my desk right away. If not, I'll start working one hour later. The idea is to be the first responder when something important happens. At *TheNotebook*, when something happens, the writers think about it, they write a piece, and they react six hours later with a thoughtful, great piece. My role is to put something out there *immediately* [*his emphasis*], not six hours later! It's important for the readers to know that they can come to *TheNotebook* for this kind of breaking news.... On an average day, I write six or seven posts. We use the same software as the rest of the staff, but we're on our own, we have to be faster. It's not like them, they're slower, they take more time editing.

Jack carefully distinguished between what he did as a "fast" writer—being a "first responder," writing "immediately," "having to be faster"—from what the slow writers did. Other writers, like Noah, claimed to be able to engage both in the fast and slow parts of the website:

> There was this idea that *TheNotebook* would have a "fast" and "slow" component and that we needed to figure out the right mix. But some people on staff are just "slow *Notebook*," they don't want to do the fast stuff. And there are some people who are only fast. I was more of a "slow *Notebook*" ... but I have kind of a trashy mindset. In a way, I'm a bit of a hybrid. I don't like content for the sake of content, it really annoys me when people just throw things up without working hard; I could never dash off a piece in an afternoon instead of researching and reporting for a day and a half.... But on the other hand, I wasn't super slow. The stories that would interest me get a lot of clicks. I am interested in weird news, I'm not interested in

serious things. I think my aesthetics were sellable but in terms of tempera-
ment I was "slow *Notebook*."

Interestingly, Noah equated the fast *Notebook* with covering "trashy"
topics that got a lot of clicks, whereas Jack focused instead on the rhythm
of publication to characterize the distinction between fast and slow. On
paper at least, the fast *Notebook* did not restrict itself to any topic in particular: it featured short blog posts about a variety of topics ranging from
politics to culture, gender, and economics. Yet Noah's comment revealed
a slippage between faster tempo and traffic-driven content. Indeed, there
was a strong alignment between the fast/slow distinction at *TheNotebook* and what I have analyzed as "click-based" and "editorial" evaluation. As we saw in the previous chapters, click-based evaluation values
quantitative success in terms of page views, likes, and tweets, whereas
editorial evaluation pays closer attention to the internal qualities of articles and feedback from one's peers and superiors. The fast *Notebook*
participated in the click-based logic, in the sense that writers had to publish frequently in order to attract traffic, whereas the slow *Notebook* bore
closer affinities to the editorial definition of journalism, in the sense that
articles were primarily assessed based on their internal quality.

TheNotebook's editors claimed to play the role of arbiter between
click-based and editorial priorities: they saw it as their responsibility to
fine-tune the relative balance between fast and slow articles. They pointed
out that both strategies were essential for the success of the website. For
instance, Sam, the website's editor-in-chief, explained:

> We do a lot of long-form journalism. It's something obviously I'm very
> proud of, we made an explicit investment. It's our belief that for *TheNote-
> book* to make a difference, we can't serve little nuggets all the time, we need
> to show them longer stories.... If you do only blogs, I think that we would
> start to diminish our brand, so we have to go in depth in issues. And some-
> times these longer series do have economic value ... sometimes they don't
> but they have a huge morale value for the staff. People like it, it's an oppor-
> tunity that they really wouldn't get at a lot of other places.

After contrasting the "little nuggets" of the fast, click-driven articles with
the "longer stories" of the slow, editorial part of the website, Sam relied
on several justifications when talking about long-form articles. He explained how proud he was of the slow *Notebook*, which came with a
"huge morale value" for the journalists. Yet he simultaneously drew on
economic arguments, describing slow stories as an "investment" for the

"brand" of the magazine, which often—but not always—had immediate economic value (by which he meant that these articles brought in high traffic numbers). Benjamin, the managing editor, relied on similarly bifurcated justifications when he described one of the main initiatives on the slow side: the long-form "fellowship program," which enabled full-time journalists on staff to take up to six paid weeks in order to do research and write longer articles that they could subsequently turn into books. As Benjamin told me:

> Hopefully everything we do is thoughtful. But long-form pieces can go places that a shorter piece can't. The most successful long-form piece we did was Emma's, she started covering that beat almost like a newspaper reporter would have, eventually she wrote a 10,000-word essay that then became a central element of her book. It was great for *TheNotebook*: the readers were really interested in it, it was wildly successful in terms of traffic. That's the best-case scenario. Emma also became the go-to expert on the topic. She was on television multiple times; when she goes on a show it says "Emma, senior editor at *TheNotebook*," so there is growing brand awareness.

For Benjamin, not only did long-form pieces have intrinsic editorial quality; they also came with a clear economic value for *TheNotebook* because they increased the prestige and "brand awareness" of the publication while sometimes being "wildly" successful in terms of traffic. The editors thus often switched back and forth between editorial and click-based justifications when explaining how and why slow articles mattered for the publication.

These justificatory switches confirm another important point about *TheNotebook*'s internal organization: the strong division of labor in place between editors and staff writers, introduced in chapter 4. Whereas *TheNotebook*'s staff writers primarily understood their role as providing quality content for the website, editors had a more instrumental orientation: they saw themselves as being in charge of deciding which topics should be covered while making sure that traffic numbers remained stable. Editors almost never published articles of their own on the website: this was perceived as a waste of their time and a potential encroachment on the turf of their staff writers. Instead, they specialized in writing headlines. There was a dedicated meeting every day during which top editors brainstormed ideas and came up with attractive headlines for the articles to be published the next day.

Interestingly, *TheNotebook*'s web editors created a hierarchical space that resembled the traditional organization of American print and television newsrooms. Herbert Gans observed that U.S. editorial departments he studied in the 1970s featured a strong division of labor, which he compared to an "assembly line." He also noted that, unlike staff writers, top editors were very much aware of how their product was faring in commercial terms, meeting with corporate executives at least once a week and integrating economic constraints discussed in these meetings into their decisions about what to publish.[8]

As we saw in chapter 2, most of *TheNotebook*'s editors spent the first half of their careers working at print publications. When trying to figure out how to publish quality content in a real-time, click-driven digital landscape, they relied on the organizational forms that emerged over time in the U.S. journalistic field and that they had witnessed in the newsrooms where they had worked before starting *TheNotebook*'s adventure. The New York editors thus defined their role as arbiters of the relative balance between click-based and editorial goals in a highly specialized newsroom. In the process, they established strong boundaries between the two modes of evaluations, all of which were mirrored in the infrastructure of the newsroom.

Symbolic Boundaries in the New York Newsroom

During my fieldwork, I realized that *TheNotebook* was crisscrossed by symbolic boundaries that established multiple distinctions in the daily life of the organization. All employees were engaged in what sociologist Thomas Gieryn calls "boundary-work": an array of rhetorical and material strategies designed to purposely "construct ... social boundaries that distinguish between intellectual activities."[9] A first order, horizontal, was based on the distinction between fast and slow news. A second order, vertical, stemmed from the hierarchy separating journalists and editors. These symbolic boundaries shaped many of *TheNotebook*'s activities and physical environment. Here I examine three of them: the organization of its office, its employment statuses, and the structure of its homepage.

We begin with a description of the newsroom's office itself. Spaces, buildings, and offices can provide telling symbolic representations of the power structure and occupational dynamics of an organization, particularly where space is scarce and rents expensive.[10] *TheNotebook*'s office, located in Lower Manhattan, was no exception (see figure 5.1). Top editors had the best position on the floor: they occupied individual offices, which had a window and a pleasant view of the street. Managers and

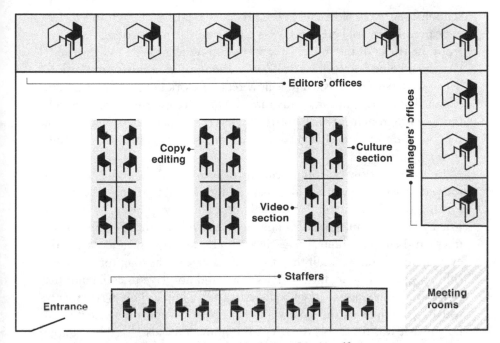

Figure 5.1. Sketch of *TheNotebook*'s office.

technology specialists ran a close second: they had individual offices, but no windows. The rest of the editorial team was dispersed in the open space through several cubicles. These cubicles were in turn organized either by section (culture, politics, etc.) or by function (copy editing, social media editing, etc.). Several cubicles were reserved for the exclusive use of fast writers. This was the case for the video section, where staffers put together short video-based blog posts about breaking news events. As I realized when I started spending time in *TheNotebook*'s office space, the layout of the New York office thus mirrored not only the hierarchy between top editors and staff writers but also the distinction between the fast and slow parts of the website—and, through them, between click-based and editorial evaluation: they were literally not sitting in the same place.

Strong symbolic boundaries also regulated the employment structure in place at *TheNotebook*. There the distinction between fast and slow jobs was even more obvious. Fast positions were usually low-prestige, entry-level, and precarious: almost all the dozen or so fast writers who worked for the website during my fieldwork were contractors without benefits. These writers were typically just starting a career in journalism: many of them were young, in their mid-twenties, just out of college or journalism school; a few were older and in the process of transitioning from a different career. Many told me that they were there to acquire writing skills and learn the tricks of the trade. They were hoping to become full-time staff writers at some point, either at *TheNotebook* or at another publication. These writers were expected to follow regular work hours, from 9 a.m. to 5 p.m. They could not take advantage of the long-term journalism fellowship program mentioned above, however: as independent contractors, they were *de facto* excluded, since that program was reserved for full-time employees.

In contrast, slow positions tended to be reserved for more seasoned journalists who had worked for other prestigious publications—the *Washington Post*, the *Atlantic*, *Newsweek*, etc. The slow journalists on staff usually had full-time jobs with benefits. They had a more flexible schedule than their fast counterparts: they could take up to several days (and even up to several weeks, if they took advantage of the long-form fellowship program) to write their articles. They did not have to come into the office every day; instead, they could work from home. Slow writers were usually conscious of the luxury of their position and often mentioned how nice it was to be able to write from home; they also liked being able to focus on long-form articles. After all, it is these deeply researched articles that allow journalists to build their reputations, negotiate higher salaries, and get more lucrative book contracts. Being a slow staff writer was a good route to becoming an editor: several top editors at *TheNotebook* had been long-form writers before being promoted.

Unsurprisingly, slow writers were often critical of fast articles and looked down on content aggregation—and more broadly on click-based content—which they argued often went hand-in-hand with a decline in editorial quality. As Margaret, a former newspaper editor who had recently started freelancing for the slow *Notebook*, told me:

> The blog posts are just less ... I mean, you can make a single point in a blog post and that's fine. So it's not just a question of length. There is more of a high bar for the articles than the blog posts.... Sometimes you slave over a piece for five days and it gets no attention and then you toss up a blog entry in an hour and a half and it gets tons, tons of attention and comments—and you don't even think it's that good!

According to many slow writers, fast articles were simply not very good in editorial terms, by which they meant that blog posts did not feature original reporting, did not advance new arguments, and were more likely to contain typos and grammatical infelicities because they were not closely edited. In the words of Jane, a former assistant editor: "We started having more blog posts, in contrast to essays … faster editing.… What we considered to be an article or an essay was a little bit more in-depth, longer, maybe had some reporting, and had to advance some kind of argument, or some kind of take. And a blog post was just like: 'This happened. Here is a video.' You could really tell the difference."

Like Jane, many slow writers criticized the multiplication of fast blog posts on *TheNotebook*'s website, which they associated with mission drift. As Esther, the former culture editor, told me, "*TheNotebook* risks tipping over to the chase for clicks over quality. At the time, we were obsessed with generating original content. Now I feel that there are many more partnerships, appropriations, and theft of material." Aaron, a long-time contract writer, also described what he saw as a decline in originality: "The idea of being a magazine where you had your regular political columnists, your foreign affairs columnist.… It's much less visible. Now it's more like a big bazaar where you just click on it and if you don't like it you move on. They have to feed the machine."

Yet Aaron's perception of *TheNotebook*'s homepage as a "big bazaar" where blog posts and long-form articles appear without any distinction is not quite adequate. Even though it could seem disorderly, *TheNotebook*'s homepage in fact mirrored the consensus of the editors and staff writers over the relative quality of fast and slow articles, while also reinforcing existing distinctions between fast and slow news. This can be seen in figure 5.2, a schematic diagram of *TheNotebook*'s homepage on the morning of April 18, 2014—an unexceptional date towards the end of my fieldwork.[11]

At first sight, Aaron seems to be right: out of the eighteen pieces featured on the homepage of *TheNotebook* that morning, only eight are full-sized articles; the remaining ten pieces are blog posts or quizzes. Yet a closer look reveals subtle hierarchies. For instance, the most visible spot on the homepage, on the top left, is a long-form piece written by one of the slow staffers. This is not an anomaly: the website had an explicit policy of always featuring slow articles on the top left of the homepage (the rationale behind that rule being that blog posts and fast articles were not representative of *TheNotebook*'s editorial line). Blog posts were posted instead in the more cramped parts of the homepage, such as the columns on the right and bottom left of the screen. Fast articles thus remained less visible and were placed in a less prestigious spot than slow articles on the

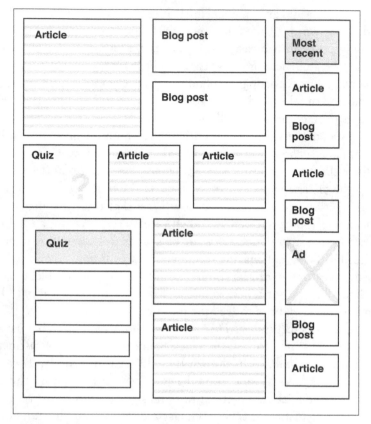

Figure 5.2. Homepage of *TheNotebook*, April 18, 2014, 11:30 a.m.

website's homepage. As we saw in the previous chapter, this organization of the homepage did not emerge in a social vacuum, nor was it accidental. In fact, *TheNotebook*'s editors spent a lot of time and effort to strike the right balance between click-based and editorial goals when deciding where to post articles on the website's homepage.

The design of the homepage, along with the spatial organization of *TheNotebook*'s office and the employment status of its workforce, all helped to reinforce the symbolic boundaries in place in the New York newsroom, compartmentalizing the fast, slow, high, and low segments of the organization. These complementary forms of boundary-work kept editorial and click-based evaluation apart, structuring in profound ways the daily functioning of the New York website.

LaPlace and the Multiplication of Editorial Formats

LaPlace faced a similar tension between click-based and editorial evaluation, but the French team developed different strategies for handling it. The Parisian editors and journalists did not use the clear-cut categories of fast and slow to describe the kinds of pieces published on their website. Instead, they relied on a variety of terms: "papers" (*papiers* in French, a more informal word than *article*), "HuffPos," "blog posts," and "testimonies" (*témoignages*).

"Papers" meant original articles, usually around 1,000 words long.[12] As in the New York newsroom, these articles went through the full copy-editing circuit at *LaPlace*. They had to be approved by senior and copy editors before being published on the website. These long articles usually featured original material (interviews or original documents) and innovative angles. They belonged to the editorial mode of evaluation.

"HuffPos" in turn referred to short articles—500 words maximum—that linked to news published elsewhere. This was the equivalent of what *TheNotebook*'s journalists called "fast" articles. As at *TheNotebook*, these were short, quickly written, and reactive articles; they clearly participated in the click-based logic. Most people at *LaPlace* held these pieces in low esteem. As Philippe told me: "We have a format of paper that's called a 'HuffPo,' in our slang. A HuffPo is when we steal ... when we write a paper based on someone else's information, with a link."[13] The name was a denigrating reference to the content published by the *Huffington Post*. As Alexandre, one of the staff writers, explained:

> It's called "HuffPo" because the *Huffington Post* invented this model. It works like this: you see some important news in another newspaper, *Le Parisien* or whatever.... You use this information, you don't say *"Le Parisien* said that" but you write "this news revealed by *Le Parisien* is interesting because" and you give a new angle, it's quick and easy to do.

Blog posts on the French website were no shorter or more lightly edited than regular articles. Instead, the distinctive mark of blogs stemmed from their authors' nonjournalistic status. *LaPlace*'s staff writers repeatedly emphasized that bloggers were not professional journalists, but instead were academics, activists, experts, or politicians who wanted to share their opinion or knowledge of a topic. (However, as we will see in the next chapter, bloggers' actual ambitions were in fact more varied.)

LaPlace's last editorial format consisted of "testimonies" (*témoignages*). These were articles written by internet users about their experiences or opinions on a specific subject. Unlike blog posts, testimonies were not part of a series: they were one-time opportunities for readers who felt strongly about a topic to share their views on the website. These pieces, often heavily revised by editors, were highly popular and attracted a lot of page views. They were also ubiquitous. In quantitative terms, 3,088 blogs and testimonies were published on *LaPlace* between 2007 and 2012. In other words, 23 percent of all the content published on the Parisian website was written by nonjournalists.[14]

Compared to *TheNotebook*'s classification system in terms of fast and slow, *LaPlace*'s staffers relied on a third, participatory category. Formats like blogs and testimonies existed outside of the editorial versus click-based distinction: they were explicitly designed to solicit user-generated content, which was not the case at *TheNotebook*. Whereas *TheNotebook* had never put in place an editorial structure for publishing participatory content, *LaPlace*'s team believed from the start that their readers should contribute to their editorial agenda. When the time came, they heavily relied on their online readers to help feed the website and attract more traffic.[15]

Informality in Action

Overall, the Parisian newsroom did not rely on the division of labor so central in the organization of the New York newsroom. Instead, flexibility was paramount, in several ways. First, no one exclusively wrote long-form articles: editors *and* journalists, staffers *and* freelancers, short-term *and* long-term employees alternated between writing long articles and putting together quick HuffPos. Everybody was expected to help with the most pressing task at hand, be it writing a HuffPo, helping out with an investigation, or editing the text of a blogger. As I witnessed during my days of fieldwork, many journalists would start their work day by writing a HuffPo in the morning, then go out to conduct an interview or attend an event for a longer article, then come back to the newsroom in the late afternoon to write a second HuffPo, before starting to compose a longer article that would be published the next day.

This constant back-and-forth was mirrored in the employment structure of the organization. *LaPlace* did not have the same hierarchical system as *TheNotebook*. The stratification between staff writers and editors played a less prominent role in the Parisian newsroom. There was little division of labor between them. Take the case of articles: although staff journalists and freelancers wrote the majority of the articles, top editors also frequently contributed. In fact, as of 2012, the writer who had published the highest number of articles on the website was André—founder, chairman, and editor-at-large—with 2,408 articles. Philippe, the editor-in-chief, came in fifth with 1,851 articles.[16]

This absence of division of labor between editors and staff writers was made clear during my fieldwork. Over the course of informal discussions, editors would often get excited about a subject and offer an amusing or controversial take on the topic. The staffers would then tease them to write it up, appealing to their editorial skills: "André, you *have* to write this HuffPo! Only you can do this, it's going to be *so* good," etc. As a result, editors frequently chimed in with short pieces and op-eds— after all, they had been prominent journalists before starting *LaPlace* and sometimes missed their writing days, something staffers were aware of. Regardless of age, employment history, and professional status, everybody at *LaPlace* was expected to participate in the collective effort to feed the site—and contribute to click-based evaluation—by churning out quick HuffPos every couple of hours to keep the homepage "fresh."

Similarly, the production of headlines was not as compartmentalized at the Parisian website as it was at *TheNotebook*. Whereas *TheNotebook*'s editors met behind closed doors every day to discuss headlines, headlines at *LaPlace* were usually negotiated throughout the day. Once an article had been reviewed by a copy editor and a managing editor, the staff writer, the copy editor, and the managing editor would often meet at the copy editor's desk to brainstorm the best possible headline for the article. I discussed an instance of this process in chapter 4, when Marina, Lucie, and Marc discussed the headline for Marc's piece on incognito browsing. While the managing editor always had the last word, copy editors and staff writers could also defend their opinions. This constant back and forth and relative absence of specialization between editors and staffers was facilitated by the spatial organization of the French offices, represented in figure 5.3.

Except for the zone of grey in the diagram (where the training programs mentioned in chapter 3 took place and where I often conducted my interviews), there were no cubicle dividers and no separate offices in *LaPlace*'s open space. Everybody—staff writers, editors, managers, developers, and even administrative and marketing staff—worked in the same open space. The "bosses' table" (*la table des chefs*), as the editors' table

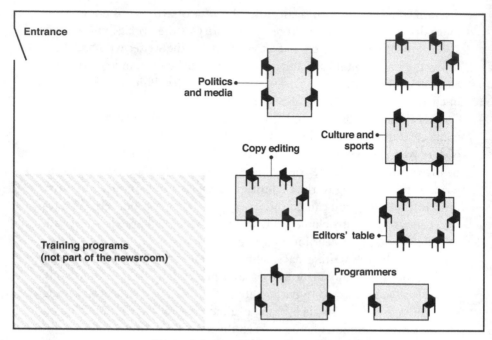

Figure 5.3. Sketch of *LaPlace*'s office.

was colloquially named, was located in the middle of the room, surrounded by the staffers' tables, the computer programmers' table, and the copy editors' table. Whereas in *TheNotebook*'s newsroom, staff writers did not face each other (their individual desks faced the cubicle dividers instead), *LaPlace*'s section editors, staffers, and interns all sat around the same tables. Most journalists at *LaPlace* mentioned this open-space organization of the office on their own during the interviews, usually as a signal of the "start-up" spirit and informality of the news organization; they compared it to the other—usually print—newsrooms where they had worked, which they said always had separate offices for the technical and marketing staff.

This absence of a separation in *LaPlace*'s office between editors and journalists or between slow and fast writers came with clear effects on the atmosphere of the newsroom. Since there were no dividers, editors and staffers overheard everything that was spoken at a normal conversational volume. As a result, *LaPlace* was a noisier newsroom than *TheNotebook*. Journalists were often chatting and making jokes; they stood up and moved to other tables to talk with their colleagues about their

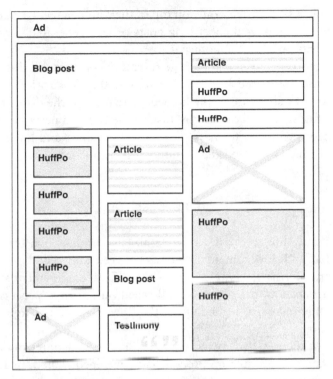

Figure 5.4. Homepage of *LaPlace*. April 18, 2014, 1:15 p.m.

HuffPos and headlines. When a discussion took too long or when other staffers started complaining about the noise, people would often go out for a cigarette and coffee break on the rooftop of the building, which was used as a meeting place. Most of the interactions between editors and staff writers took place informally, either in the office or on the rooftop.

Such an informal organization was also manifest in the structure of *LaPlace*'s homepage. Figure 5.4 sketches the homepage of the Parisian website on April 18, 2014—the same date as the diagram of *TheNotebook*'s homepage earlier in this chapter. There were fewer full-fledged, original articles on *LaPlace*'s homepage that day than on *TheNotebook*'s: only 21 percent (three out of fourteen) of the articles published on *La-Place*'s homepage that day were full-size articles (more than 1,000 words), compared to 44 percent (eight out of eighteen) on *TheNotebook*'s homepage. On that day, the piece published on the most visible spot of *LaPlace*'s homepage—the top left—was not a full-fledged news article but instead a blog post written by an outside contributor. Contrary to *TheNotebook*'s rule to publish slow articles only on top of their homepage, *LaPlace*'s top editors frequently posted short blog posts or user-generated content on the most visible part of the homepage.

This organization of the homepage reveals the distinct priorities of *La-Place*'s editors compared to *TheNotebook*'s. In the New York newsroom, we saw how the structure of the homepage reinforced the distinction between the fast and the slow. In contrast, in the Parisian newsroom, more heterogeneous editorial formats—fast and slow, short and long, professional and amateur—coexisted without clear distinctions.

"It's a Mess"

LaPlace's daily life revealed a relative absence of symbolic boundaries between fast and slow content, as well as between editors and journalists. The editorial formats, organization of the offices, employment statuses, and the structure of the homepage all relied on informal processes and priorities that changed depending on the time, person, and topic under consideration.

During *LaPlace*'s first years, this informality had not troubled the staffers: the news production process had developed somewhat haphazardly during the meetings in André's kitchen, before the website was even launched. Coordinating half a dozen journalists at a time when there was little division of labor between the founders, editors, and staff writers seemed easy. Yet as the size of the newsroom staff kept growing—up to twenty or so employees in 2013—these informal interactions became more problematic. Often, staff writers would receive different directions from multiple editors, which resulted in missed deadlines. They frequently complained that the newsroom was a "mess" (in French, *le bordel*, or bordello, a word that takes us back to the prostitution metaphor analyzed in chapter 4). The managing editors—usually women—would try to fix this messy situation by creating new structures organizing the news production process, but these initiatives typically failed, usually because the staffers and founders did not make significant efforts to implement the new guidelines. Gabriella, a former managing editor, recalled her feelings of frustration:

> I tried to get things more organized, but people were nostalgic about the good old times of the early years, when it was a mess.... I wanted to have an editorial meeting every morning, where writers would have to come with

ideas. But people were stressed out about having a morning meeting. Well, in every newspaper, there is a morning meeting where you present your ideas, that's the way it works! But everybody was awkward. So instead it became, "OK, now only people who have ideas will present them." Same thing, I wanted to have a board on the wall with every ongoing project. I thought that we needed a bit of planning ... and they were against it! Philippe said, "OK, let's stop using boards, we'll go back to the way it was." I tried to organize the newsroom, I really tried! But it didn't work.

After the sale to LeGroupMag, the confusion grew. The founders worried that the homepage was not "fresh"—i.e., that its content was not updated frequently enough. They complained that staff writers did not take the mission to write HuffPos seriously, which resulted in a static homepage that would not attract potential readers. Staffers argued that it was hard to switch back and forth between short HuffPos and longer editorial projects. As Alexandre, a staff writer in the politics section, told me: "Nowadays I end up having to write a lot of short articles on a daily basis and it cuts into my longer investigations and my investigative articles.... I keep saying that we should spend more time on things, explore things that are not obvious, but we're becoming more and more dependent on the rhythm of other media." Staff writers criticized what they saw as editorial drift and a decline in the quality of the website. In the words of Gabriella, a former managing editor, the pressure to publish constantly "creates burnouts. It never ends. There is this ambivalence: you say that you don't want to cover everything ... but you end up giving in to the temptation to do everything. That's what happened to us."[17]

Whereas the New York newsroom resolved the tension between editorial and click-based evaluation by creating a clear distinction and division of labor between fast and slow articles, *LaPlace* did not develop similar strategies. Instead, the Parisian newsroom retained the informality of its early days, which left most editors and staffers dissatisfied with the relative balance between editorial and click-based content on the website.

Bureaucratic and Disciplinary Power

Taking a step back, what do these organizational dynamics tell us about the kind of managerial power in place at *TheNotebook* and *LaPlace*? Studies of work and workplaces have long contrasted different ways of organizing production processes. On the one hand, scholars have traced the diffusion of "bureaucratic" templates across organizations. These involve clear hierarchies, centralized power structures, strict rules, and predetermined sanctions in cases of infringement of the rules.[18] On the other hand, researchers have analyzed a different kind of power, which they describe as diffuse, normative, pervasive, with fewer written rules and sanctions. Power then works through "capillarity," in the sense that it is often inscribed in minute detail and relies on internalization rather than upfront imposition: workers learn through trial and error the "right" way of doing things. This is what Foucault and others have described as "disciplinary" forms of power.[19]

Here I use ideal-typical versions of these two paradigms to clarify some of the differences between *TheNotebook* and *LaPlace*. Note that these simplified models are not usually found in totally pure forms in the social world, first because most organizations exhibit intermediary features and second because bureaucratic and disciplinary power can operate together.[20] While the rest of this chapter contrasts *TheNotebook* and *LaPlace* in terms of their bureaucratic and disciplinary dynamics, other aspects of the daily lives of the two organizations did not match the starkly simplified ideal-types depicted here.

Table 5.1 relates the concepts of bureaucratic and disciplinary processes to the tension that *TheNotebook* and *LaPlace* experienced between editorial and click-based concerns when they entered the chase for clicks. Overall, *TheNotebook*'s internal dynamics resembled those of the bureaucratic type of power, in the sense that the New York newsroom was highly centralized and hierarchical, with clear internal boundaries separating click-based and editorial evaluation. In contrast, *LaPlace* bore similarities with the disciplinary ideal-type: it had a flatter hierarchy, weak internal specialization, and was characterized by constant overlap between editorial and click-based priorities.

These distinct forms of organizational power structured many aspects of the newsrooms' daily operations, including their use of audience metrics, their definition of algorithmic publics, and the kind of information they produced. First, the production of information at the two websites was profoundly shaped by these distinct regimes of power. As we saw, at *TheNotebook*, strong hierarchical and horizontal boundaries organized content production through the distinction between the fast and the slow and the division of labor between top editors and staff writers. As we will analyze in the next chapter, this compartmentalized management of editorial and click-based priorities was mirrored in a compensation system

Table 5.1. Bureaucratic and Disciplinary Power

	Bureaucratic power	*Disciplinary power*
Managerial authority	- Centralized, hierarchical	- Unclear, diffuse, "flat" hierarchy
Rules	- Clear	- None (or vague)
Sanctions and rewards	- Material (fines, layoffs) - Administered by the centralized authority	- Mostly symbolic - Internalized and self-administered
Balance between modes of evaluation	- Strong boundaries, compartmentalization, separation between click-based and editorial evaluation	- Weak boundaries, informality, constant overlap between click-based and editorial evaluation
Role of metrics	- Measures of performance, initiated and controlled by centralized authority	- Unclear (measure of value), no central control, individualized relationship to metrics
Algorithmic publics	- Commodified, passive, segmented	- Ambiguous, engaged, commodified *and* civic
Related concepts	- Bureaucratic control (Gouldner 1954, Edwards 1979) - Utilitarian power (Etzioni 1961), - Sovereign power (Foucault 1995)	- Hegemonic (Burawoy 1979) & normative control (Etzioni 1961, Kunda 2006) - Disciplinary power (Foucault 1995)
Example	- *TheNotebook*	- *LaPlace*

based on hierarchies and secrecy. In contrast, *LaPlace* was characterized by a relative absence of specialization, which informed the news production process: in the open space, everyone did a bit of everything and wrote editorial as well as traffic-driven pieces.

These kinds of managerial power also shaped how editors and staff writers used audience metrics. As we saw in the previous chapter, at *TheNotebook*, editors relied extensively on web metrics to make editorial decisions and manage their staff, but these direct pressures were met with indifference and disdain on the part of the staffers, who did not feel threatened by metrics and engaged instead in buffering strategies. Here again, *TheNotebook* relied on strong internal boundaries, a marked division of labor, and clear rules regarding performance. On the contrary, at *La-Place*, both editors and staff writers manifested ambivalent attitudes towards traffic numbers, asserting that traffic was a poor criterion for making decisions but also paying constant attention to web analytics and expressing feelings of shame and dejection whenever their articles attracted low numbers of page views. Hence, at the French website, the use of audience metrics resembled disciplinary processes, individualized and internalized.

Last but not least, these distinct organizational dynamics shaped how journalists defined their algorithmic publics. In the New York newsroom, the website's online public was conceptualized as commodified, segmented, and largely irrelevant for staff writers—in line with the hierarchical and compartmentalized culture of the organization. In the Parisian newsroom, the relationship between journalists and their algorithmic publics was much more ambiguous. Everybody at *LaPlace* was both critical of traffic *and* obsessed with clicks. Journalists developed a contradictory understanding of their publics as both commodified and civic—one that mirrored the absence of boundaries and overlap between click-based and editorial evaluation. The Parisian journalists translated disciplinary pressures to get high traffic numbers into an emotional quest to seduce their algorithmic publics.

Conclusion

Confronted with a similar pressure to publish all the time, *TheNotebook* and *LaPlace* needed to find a balance between the click-based imperative and their editorial ambitions. They relied on similar distinctions—though they gave them different names—between short, fast-paced, aggregation-based content on the one hand and long-form, investigative articles on the other.

Yet the two publications organized their news production process in different ways. In New York, multiple symbolic boundaries structured the bureaucratic organization of *TheNotebook*: the categories of fast and slow, along with the hierarchies separating editors from staff writers, affected many areas of the website's life, from editorial formats to the structure of office spaces, employment status of writers, and organization of the homepage. In contrast, everyone did a bit of everything in *LaPlace*'s disciplinary system. This informality and lack of specialization were mirrored in the layout of their open-space office, the organization of their workforce, and the fuzzy rules guiding the publication of articles on the homepage. Even the relationships between journalists and their algorithmic publics reinforced these distinct forms of control. In one case, publics were segmented and valued differently based on one's position in the newsroom. In the other, editors and journalists nurtured an almost mystical communion with "the public" at large, while also making cynical comments about its commodification.

By showing how digital metrics become integrated in broader organizational dynamics, this chapter reveals the dialectical relationship between algorithms and their contexts. The previous chapter showed how institutional contexts, linked to national fields, shaped the meanings of web analytics at *TheNotebook* and *LaPlace*. Here I take the analysis a step further by demonstrating that journalists' and editors' daily use of metrics contributed to reinforcing organizational and cultural differences between the two publications. At *TheNotebook*, metrics were used to strengthen existing boundaries; at *LaPlace*, metrics functioned as a kind of organizational vortex, preventing other forms of structuring from taking place.[21] By connecting the organizations' uses of metrics to these broader types of managerial power, this chapter seeks to change how we think about the effects of metrics on organizational life. Contrary to the widespread belief that metrics necessarily encourage convergence, it shows how data can be mobilized to reinforce preexisting differences, within and between organizations.

As an ethnographer, I should note that the absence of structure at the French organization made fieldwork hard to organize. For one thing, the internal functioning of the newsroom kept changing. Over the course of my fieldwork, the frequency and length of editorial meetings at *LaPlace* underwent multiple transformations, as did the procedures for pitching articles, the guidelines for managing bloggers, and the editorial priorities of the website. Roles, schedules, and responsibilities also fluctuated in unpredictable ways. Multiple times, I came to the newsroom to attend a particular meeting, learning only when I arrived that it had already taken place, been cancelled, or rescheduled to another date and time. Conflicts kept erupting—from the sale to LeGroupeMag to the "battle for the audience" episode—to the extent that it was sometimes hard to keep track of what was going on between staffers and editors. In comparison, *TheNotebook* was a haven of stability. Meetings took place on predictable days and times. The editorial organization of the newsroom kept revolving around the distinction between the fast and the slow. People moved in and out, but the structure of the newsroom was largely impervious to these changes. Overall, *TheNotebook* was a more stable and less contentious place than *LaPlace*—and nowhere were these differences more striking than when it came to the thorny question of compensation.

CHAPTER 6
•••••••••••

Between Exposure and Unpaid Work

Compensation and Freelance Careers

On March 4, 2013, the veteran journalist Nate Thayer, well known for his coverage of military zones in Cambodia and North Korea, published a post on his blog entitled "A Day in the Life of a Freelance Journalist, 2013."[1] Thayer simply copied and pasted an email exchange he had with a web editor of the *Atlantic Monthly*. The editor was interested in publishing a version of an article that Thayer had posted that day on NKNews.org. When Thayer expressed his interest and asked for more information about the format and fees, the *Atlantic* editor wrote:

> Thanks for responding. Maybe by the end of the week? 1,200 words? We unfortunately can't pay you for it, but we do reach 13 million readers a month. I understand if that's not a workable arrangement for you, I just wanted to see if you were interested. Thanks so much again for your time. A great piece!

To which Thayer responded:

> I am a professional journalist who has made my living by writing for 25 years and am not in the habit of giving my services for free to for profit media outlets so they can make money by using my work and efforts by removing my ability to pay my bills and feed my children.... I appreciate your interest, but, while I respect the Atlantic, and have several friends who write for it, I have bills to pay and cannot expect to do so by giving my work away for free.... Frankly, I will refrain from being insulted and am perplexed how one can expect to try to retain quality professional services without compensating for them.

Thayer's blog post launched a fierce debate that resounded on Twitter and in the journalistic world for weeks. A couple of days later, Ta-Nehisi Coates, a high-profile writer at the *Atlantic*, added his contribution to the debate:

> I've been watching all of this with some curiosity, mostly because I got my start at the online *Atlantic* working for free.... I wanted exposure. I was

not a "young journalist." This was not my chance to break into the profession.... [But] I could not convince editors that what I was curious about was worth writing about. Every day I would watch ideas die in my head.... What the internet offered was the chance to let all of those ideas compete in the arena, and live and die on the merits.... I was ecstatic any time anyone took my ideas seriously enough to offer them a platform.[2]

Coates reminds us that passion—the inextinguishable desire to write and share one's ideas with a public—played a major role in his decision to pursue a journalistic career. At that time, the prospect of reaching readers and working with writers he admired was enough to make Coates "ecstatic," regardless of monetary compensation. This strategy eventually paid off. Coates became a national correspondent for the *Atlantic*, a celebrated author, and the recipient of a "Genius Grant" from the MacArthur Foundation.

The last word on the matter might nonetheless go to Nate Thayer. After giving dozens of interviews about the incident and participating in more conferences than he could remember, Thayer sarcastically summarized his take on the whole affair: "This particular post has gotten more attention than anything I've spent my entire adult life researching. I've gotten more than 20,000 hits in the past hour. The irony is that I haven't made a penny off of any of this."[3]

Compensation, Careers, and Identities in Online News

This controversy about unpaid freelance work, and more generally about how to make a living as a web journalist, takes place at a time when compensation has become an increasingly thorny question in the media landscape. For most of the twentieth century, journalism as an industry relied predominantly on salaried employment: most journalists would start their careers with short-term contracts before getting a full-time position in a newsroom, perhaps moving once or twice when opportunities arose. Journalists were mostly "company men"—or, in the words of sociologist William H. Whyte, "organization men"—who were committed to the newspaper they worked for. On the reception side, readers frequently ignored bylines and paid more attention to the newspaper they were buying than to the names of individual journalists.[4]

Things have changed. The number of journalists who have temporary, part-time, or freelance positions has been increasing steadily over the past decades, in the United States and in Europe.[5] Even when journalists get full-time positions, they often move to a different newsroom after a couple of years—hoping to take their readers with them. Many are now conscious of being a "brand name," whose prestige and reputation need to be carefully curated on social media platforms, independently of the publications they work for.[6]

Journalism has joined the growing ranks of the so-called "gig" economy, an encompassing term that describes an employment paradigm in which short-term and project-based work are replacing full-time and long-term salaried positions as the dominant form of employment. In 2017, the Bureau of Labor Statistics reported 15.5 million people as self-employed in the United States. From low-skill jobs to highly skilled occupations like computer programming, graphic design, and academia, short-term and independent forms of employment permeate an increasing number of sectors. The emergence of digital platforms promoting independent contracting at scale—from Uber to Amazon Mechanical Turk, UpWork, Care.com, and TaskRabbit—further accentuates these trends.[7]

To date, most studies of the gig economy have focused on what workers have to gain, or lose, from these flexible patterns of employment. Less is known about the institutional side of the story. How do managers decide to hire and compensate independent contractors? How do these institutional choices in turn shape the careers and identities of individual freelancers?[8] Here I examine these questions in the case of web journalism. As we saw in the previous chapters, web editors gradually realized that they needed to publish more content than ever before to stay afloat financially. To do so, they relied on a growing number of flexible workers. Yet they did not necessarily have enough resources to pay everybody a living wage. So whom did editors prioritize when they allocated their budgets?

When deciding on compensation and contracts, employers need to reach an agreement about "what counts" and why: salaries always mirror the interplay between different—and often conflicting—criteria of evaluation.[9] *TheNotebook* and *LaPlace* were no exception: the compensation practices developed by the editors to handle contract workers reflected the tension between click-based and editorial modes of evaluation.[10] Yet the distinct internal dynamics and kinds of managerial power in place at the New York and Parisian websites also shaped their compensation practices. In New York, a stratified compensation system was developed. In Paris, formal equality prevailed, but with multiple exceptions.

For the freelancers involved, this meant paying close attention to their digital metrics, and in particular to their number of followers on social media platforms, which they analyzed both as a symbol of professional recognition and as an indicator of market success. Even though freelance journalists in the United States and France relied on the same metrics-driven tactics to manage their compensations and careers, they used distinct discursive repertoires to make sense of their precarious situations. Overall, this chapter shows how digital metrics can become proxies for reputational value and professional success in a competitive employment market.

Secret and Hierarchies:
How *TheNotebook* Handled Its Freelancers

A typical relationship between a news organization and its freelancers looks something like the following. A freelance writer reads the target publication regularly and knows some journalists or editors working there; she comes up with an idea for an article that could be a good fit for the website in terms of topic and style. The freelancer then contacts one of the editors, sometimes out of the blue but more often through a friend or colleague's recommendation. She pitches her article, explaining the angle of the piece in what she hopes is a concise and enticing manner. The editor replies with an answer that ranges from "sounds great" to "not a good fit for us," with many nuances of "perhaps" in between. In the best-case scenario, a back-and-forth ensues in which the editor gives feedback to the freelancer about her article project.

The discussion between the editor and the freelancer then transitions from the content to a contract. The editor indicates the rate for a freelance piece of this type, the number of words, and the deadline. Sometimes news websites are not inclined to pay for the piece in question. Sometimes they offer to pay, but not much. Sometimes they are willing to pay but refuse to provide an advance, which means that the freelancer will have to write "on spec"—on a speculative basis, not knowing whether their piece will be eventually accepted and paid for.[11] Freelance writers can try to negotiate each of these points, but they often do not have much room to maneuver, especially when they are not regular contributors. They frequently hear that the offered rates are "the website's policy": if freelancers are not happy with it, they can sell their piece somewhere else. The younger the writer, the less likely she is to be able—or even willing—to negotiate. This was what Mara, a twenty-six-year-old writer straight out of journalism school, experienced when she wrote a piece for *TheNotebook*. In her words:

> The editor was very straightforward. When he said he would take the pitch, he told me it was $300. Then the second piece I wrote I didn't ask. You know, I was happy with the $300. It's the most an online outlet has paid me for anything, even though it's a bit hard to judge because it's a long piece and everything. And then when I wrote about the cheerleaders for them, I didn't ask about the rates because I was happy with what I had gotten before but he then offered me an extra $100 to help with the slideshow.

Mara did not negotiate: she was "happy" with the rate and thought that the whole thing was straightforward. Other writers, however, did not find the process so transparent. Paul, a twenty-nine-year-old freelancer, expressed puzzlement about his freelance work for *TheNotebook*. His rate changed over time, but he did not know why: "The small posts are all $75 apiece. The larger ones ... the first one was $200 and the second one was $300. I don't know why it's different.... When I realized this, it was like three months later, so I didn't ask about it. I'm trying to pitch another article, we'll see how it goes."

A closer analysis of the determinants of freelance rates at *TheNotebook* reveals a complicated picture, and one that evolved significantly over time. From its beginning, *TheNotebook* relied on freelancers to publish articles on the website. In the words of Esther, the culture editor of the publication in the 1990s: "I was expected to have at least one or two articles up every day. I was given the budget to commission things. We paid a great deal more in those days. It went as high as $1,200 an article.... We were trying to prove that we could be as good as a printed magazine. We had more money, a little more money, than places like the *New Republic*."

After the sale to Newspapers Inc. in 2004 and the pressure from the new parent company to publish more, the number of contract workers dramatically increased at *TheNotebook*, and the rates fell. As Sam, *TheNotebook*'s editor-in-chief, told me: "A story that we paid $1,200 for in 1996 ... we might pay $200 today." For many freelancers, this decrease in rates was hard. Aaron, who had been freelancing for *TheNotebook* since the 1990s, recalled: "When I began writing my column, I was paid $1,200. And then around 2003 they cut my pay, and also cut the pay of all contributors who were making a lot. A few years later I convinced them to go up to $1,000 on the basis of inflation alone. They kind of relented ... and then this fall they cut it again, down to $500."

Interestingly, the rates freelancers mention receiving are different: $200, $300, $500 ... Why are writers compensated differently? Seniority and experience certainly play a role: older, more experienced, and well-known writers are paid more than young and unknown writers. Yet there were also cases that did not quite fit this pattern. When I asked *TheNotebook*'s editors about these discrepancies, they remained rather vague. As Sam, *TheNotebook*'s editor-in-chief, put it: "The actual rates now, I mean it varies, there are certain people who are under contract with us who make more and others who make less. It depends on the ... the particulars of it." Over time, I realized that the most striking aspect of *TheNotebook*'s compensation system was that there was actually no single rule for deciding on compensation. Top editors had a great deal of autonomy in deciding which rate to apply. Thus, there was a lot of variation between how one editor and another thought about compensation.

One can compare the justifications of Karen and Emma, two section editors at *TheNotebook*. As Karen, a science editor, told me, "[Rates] are a complicated thing.... It depends on what they were paid before. I ask the previous editor or the other editors and I pay them the same amount. For people who are not professional writers, like tenured professors, they're used to writing all the time, we don't pay them. Also we don't pay people who have a book coming up, it's like promotional material, an excerpt from the book. And the others are paid a couple of hundred dollars." Emma, a legal and political editor, later offered her perspective:

> EMMA: The contributors who contribute episodically are not paid a lot ... $100 or $200 for legal pieces, and up to $400 for gender pieces. It depends on the time they spend on the article, and also whether they are journalists who are supporting themselves with their writing. The legal pieces are paid less because it's lawyers and judges and they don't care about the money. On the other hand, Alma, who writes on sciences and technology, she's paid more, $400, because her articles are great, she's been with us for a long time, and it's exactly the line of *TheNotebook* ... also, she does well on traffic.
>
> AC: So you also take traffic into account?
>
> EMMA: Yes, it's important ... in that order: time spent, how interesting it is, and traffic.

Karen and Emma's freelance rates depended on a long list of criteria: the amount of time it took to write the piece, the quality and overall interest of the article, the writer's fit with the editorial line of the website, whether they were supporting themselves with their writing, how long they had been writing for *TheNotebook*, how much they were paid before ... and of course whether their articles were popular online. Perhaps unsurprisingly, *TheNotebook*'s editors were more likely to pay a higher rate when the freelancers' traffic numbers were high, as Emma mentioned.

But there were also differences between Emma and Karen's compensation systems. For instance, Emma tried to compensate everybody—even a small sum—whereas Karen had explicit rules about when *not* to compensate people. A variety of arguments were used to justify unpaid work. If the writer had just published a book, editors considered the piece to be "promotional material" and refused to pay. Similarly, tenured professors, whom Karen described as "writing all the time"—an interesting characterization coming from journalists who also write all the time—were often asked to write for free. None of these criteria, however, was absolute. As another section editor told me, "There have been occasions where we're working with someone who has a new book and they are willing to essentially trade work for the exposure.... So we don't pay them. But there are also cases like that where we pay people.... It's on a case-by-case basis."

Thus, the decision not to compensate someone remained highly idiosyncratic, as was the decision to pay a writer a higher rate than someone else. The cases of Sean and Margaret, two freelancers who wrote regularly for *TheNotebook*, provide striking differences:

> SEAN: Each year I produce about thirty stories, plus four multi-part features or longer articles. That's about fifty articles. I'm on contract.... My high point was in maybe 2006–2007, I was making $72,000 from *TheNotebook*. It's $65,000 now, something like that.
>
> MARGARET: It gets all lumped in one sum, which is $1,600 a month. I get that for blogging two times a week and writing two articles. So it has never been clear to me what is for what but I would estimate that it's $600 for each piece. So that's 1,200 [*for the articles*] and 400 bucks for the blogs.

Sean and Margaret both freelanced occasionally for *TheNotebook* before being offered annual contracts—they still work as individual contractors but on an annual basis. Sean, 38 years old, was formerly a staff writer at a large and prestigious national magazine. He was paid $65,000 for about 50 articles per year, which amounted to approximately $1,300 per article. Margaret, 36, had formerly been an editor and staff writer at a prominent daily newspaper. At *TheNotebook*, she was paid $19,200 per year for a total of about 120 pieces, including 24 long pieces, which amounted to $160 per article (mixing together short and long pieces)—an extremely low rate compared to Sean.

Yet there was no obvious reason to pay Margaret less than Sean. They were both mid-career journalists who had been on staff at prestigious publications. They both supported themselves with their writing. They both had been writing for *TheNotebook* for some time, which meant that editors could trust them. So why pay Sean three times more than Margaret? The short answer to this question is: probably no one knew, not even the editors themselves.[12] Sean and Margaret wrote for different sections of *TheNotebook*. The most likely scenario is that their editors never discussed their respective rates. Knowledge about compensation was indeed strictly hierarchized and compartmentalized at *TheNotebook*, as I realized during a day of observation in the New York newsroom.

Observation
TheNotebook
March 20, 2013, 9 a.m.

I'm sitting with Mary, an editor at *TheNotebook*, in her cubicle in the open space. We talk about her work as an editor for the poetry section. Mary describes the different types of poems that she commissions. I am curious about the freelance rates for poems—how does one decide how much a poem is worth? After a while, I ask:

> AC: And ... how much do you pay for poems?
>
> MARY: Hmm ... I don't know if I'm allowed to tell you that.... Let me check with Ben [*the managing editor*].

Mary stands up in the open-space and calls Ben, who is sitting in another cubicle:

> MARY: Ben, can I tell her how much we pay for poems?

A long silence ensues.

> BEN: Hmm ... I would prefer if that remained confidential.

Mary mumbles "sorry" before getting back to work. I curse silently and write down: "Why did she have to yell it? Now no one will be willing to tell me about money!"

As embarrassing as this rebuff was in the moment, it gives a sense of the cloud of secrecy surrounding compensation at *TheNotebook*—and of the prohibition against discussing salary in white-collar professions in the United States more broadly. Editors were reluctant to answer when I asked them how much they paid their contributors. Like Sam above, their replies usually involved a version of "it depends"; they would not get into the details.

This reluctance certainly made sense when interacting with outside observers like myself. Yet it was also emblematic of a more systematic containment of information flows at the New York website. Indeed, very few people had a panoptical view of the compensation system in the newsroom. Sam, the editor-in-chief, gave a lot of autonomy to his section editors, who managed their budgets as they saw fit. Section editors in turn rarely compared or harmonized their rates, relying instead on their predecessor's practices to decide how much to compensate writers. This path dependency led to major gaps in the rates for freelance pieces. Most freelancers did not know about the gamut of rates in place at *TheNotebook*. During my days of fieldwork, freelancers often asked me whether I knew how much other writers were paid, a question I answered with the same sheepish response as *TheNotebook*'s editors, usually muttering something along the lines of "it depends." Unwittingly, I had become part of the secrecy and compartmentalization process in place at the New York website regarding freelance rates.

Compensation at *LaPlace*: Flat Rates and Their Exceptions

On the other side of the Atlantic, *LaPlace* also needed as many writers as possible in order to publish more and faster. In a similar manner to what we saw in New York, the Parisian editors increased the number of external contributors they worked with. Yet instead of having a sliding compensation scale based on the seniority and skill of the freelancer, *LaPlace* put in place a flat rate for *all* freelance pieces: 120 euros per article, regardless of author, length, quality, or popularity. Such a flat rate was highly unusual in the French media landscape, where most news organizations paid their freelancers by the page, or *feuillet*.[13] Freelancers criticized this system. For example, Gabriella, who returned to freelance for *LaPlace* after leaving her post as managing editor, and Anne, a regular freelance contributor, both complained about their compensation:

> GABRIELLA: I know that a freelance piece will be paid way under the
> market rate at *LaPlace*. They don't use the regular freelance rates,

which are rates by the page. Instead, they have flat rates, 120 euros for the article, whatever the length. Well, it's not enough.

ANNE: The rate used to be 100 euros. Now it's 120 euros. It's not well paid, because it's 120 euros for the whole package…. When you work with a photographer, you have to share, so that's 60 euros each, it's really not much. But I knew that when I started to work as a freelancer for them. They don't have any money.

The two writers had starkly different profiles. Gabriella, 42, had been *LaPlace*'s managing editor between 2007 and 2010, after which she worked as a staff writer at a prestigious national magazine before turning to freelance writing. Anne, 29, had only recently graduated from journalism school and began her career as a freelance writer in Senegal. In spite of Gabriella and Anne's distinct levels of seniority and experience, they were paid exactly the same meager amount, a situation both of them lamented.

Why did *LaPlace* start relying on flat freelance rates in the first place? It is here essential to remember the climate of the Parisian website during its first years of existence—the "fan club" period analyzed in chapter 2. As we saw, there was little money to spend then: most of the initial capital had been eaten up by programming and office-related costs. The founding team also had a strong egalitarian ideology, inspired in part by their left-leaning and countercultural beliefs. Given these early beginnings, it is not surprising that the Parisian editors came up with a system of flat rates for all freelance pieces: instead of having to define different wages and rates, they decided to have as flat a hierarchy as possible.

In parallel, the editors put in place a highly compressed salary scale within the newsroom. According to several journalists, the wages of the highest-paid employee in the Parisian newsroom (André, founder and chairman) were only 2.5 times higher than those of the lowest-paid employee (Colette, administrative assistant). The variance between the wages of the staff writers themselves was smaller still. Journalists mentioned that the least well-paid journalist earned 1,800 euros per month (after tax), while the highest-paid earned 2,500 euros per month. This scale did not account for the differences in ownership shares between founders and employees. Yet, at least on paper, *LaPlace*'s wages and rates mirrored its egalitarian values, while also minimizing the organization's payroll expenses.[14]

Another striking aspect of the system was the amount of unpaid work taking place at *LaPlace*. From its early years, the website had incorporated what the top editors called their "participatory DNA," or the belief that internet users should participate in the daily life of the website. They welcomed user-generated content, creating specific editorial formats to help organize and structure it. It was clear from the outset that this participatory content would not be compensated. The editors saw these formats as an opportunity for online readers to express their views. They argued that bloggers received ample nonmonetary compensation for their contributions: a platform for their ideas, increased visibility and exposure, quality feedback on their articles, and so on. As Gael, one of *LaPlace*'s editors, explained:

> I disagree with the idea that bloggers should be paid. Bloggers contribute for lots of different reasons, you know: because they want to participate in an ongoing debate, because they want exposure, they want to share their expertise.... A couple of bloggers make a living out of it, they're invited everywhere and they are paid for what they do, but it's rare and it doesn't make much sense to me. You also have students who want to see their articles online, who want to improve their writing skills—they have different priorities.

Over time, however, *LaPlace*'s relationship with its bloggers changed. As the editors came to realize that they needed to publish more content in order to attract traffic, they consciously reached out to increase their number of external contributors. Because the number of contributors kept increasing while in-house editorial oversight did not, bloggers began to feel that they were not receiving enough feedback on their work and complained about the low visibility of their articles on the website, which they interpreted as a lack of attention and promotion on the part of the editors. They also felt betrayed by the sale to LeGroupeMag. Not unlike the unpaid bloggers in the United States who brought a class action lawsuit against the *Huffington Post* after its sale to AOL in 2011, *LaPlace*'s bloggers contributed, through their unpaid work, to the creation of a valuable company that had then been sold for millions of euros. They did not sue the founders, but they argued that they should at the very least be compensated for their work now that *LaPlace* belonged to a larger media company.[15]

The relationship between journalists and bloggers became contentious and strained, which came with position-takings on both sides. The Parisian editors and journalists established strong distinctions between "professionals" on the one hand and "amateurs," on the other. Professional journalists, in their view, naturally deserved to be paid: it would have been unfair and exploitative not to compensate them. Yet their standards were strikingly different for "amateurs"—by which they meant bloggers. Indeed, most editors and staff writers did not believe that bloggers needed to be compensated. As the editor-in-chief, Philippe, told me:

> So the official position here is to say that when an article features journalistic work … reportage, interviews, investigations … we pay. And when the bloggers are people who have another job and a salary—academics, for example—then it's like people who write op-eds in newspapers, so we don't pay them. In exchange, they don't have a lot of constraints, in terms of deadlines, formats, length, etc. They're free … as they would be on any blog.

Not unlike what we saw at *TheNotebook*, *LaPlace*'s editors believed that people who had another position and a source of income—academics, politicians, experts, and so on—did not need to be paid for their articles. They equated their blog posts with "op-eds," most of which are unpaid, and relied, somewhat sheepishly, on the argument that bloggers were "free" to write the way they wanted.

What emerged from the staffers' discourses was a specific view of "professional journalism"—a label they equated with easily recognizable values, including original reporting, innovative angles, conciseness, and strong copy-editing skills—in line with the editorial mode of evaluation analyzed in the previous chapters. Staffers relied on editorial evaluation to describe their own professional skills; they criticized bloggers for not having these skills and merely providing what they perceived as unsubstantiated opinions. They also emphasized bloggers' lack of professional ethics. This was made clear by Alexandre, a journalist in the politics section:

> Bloggers and journalists, it's just not the same job. Journalists have a responsibility.… One of the most important things with journalism is ethics. For example, in 2010, there was a rumor saying that Carla Bruni-Sarkozy was cheating on her husband [*Nicolas Sarkozy, then President*]. Journalists had known about it for a long time but we didn't say a thing. One day, a blog hosted by the *Journal du Dimanche* posted: "Gossip: Carla is sleeping with X." The day after, many newspapers wrote "the prestigious *Journal du Dimanche* says …" But the man who posted this was a young guy from the marketing division. His job was to create some buzz and get clicks. So he posted this and then went home, thinking "I had a good day." These people are not journalists. A regular journalist would never do that. We would never publish gossip. It's libel.

Unsurprisingly, most of the bloggers disagreed with these blanket characterizations of their lack of ethics and poor writing skills. As Hugo, a long-time blogger for the Parisian website, told me: "The better the blogger, the more professional they become, either because they have a large audience or because newspapers contact them to write articles because of their blog.... At some point they become more like a journalist. It's easy to become a journalist, there's no specific training to become a journalist."

Like Hugo, many bloggers protested against the staffers' binary classification of "professionals" versus "amateurs." They argued instead that their work was very close to journalistic standards. As Chloe, a graduate student who blogged for *LaPlace*, hoping to transition to a career as a writer, explained: "they're incredibly demanding at *LaPlace*.... It's not like the other blog platforms. It's almost like a newspaper article, and incidentally they use my articles on the homepage.... I knew from the beginning that I wouldn't be paid, but when I spend a month writing a piece [*laughs*] ... I can't do that every other day, right, because I'm not paid!" Hence, the relationship between *LaPlace*'s editors and bloggers was rife with conflict surrounding the connection between professionalism and compensation.

Over time, I also realized that there were exceptions to the website's official line about not compensating bloggers. Some bloggers *did* in fact get paid. Unsurprisingly perhaps, most of these exceptions related to the online popularity of a blogger's production. Take the example of Lou, a blogger who wrote about LGBTQ topics for the website:

> I already had a blog that was extremely successful, so when we started talking about my blog, I asked for three things. First I didn't want any salary or work contract, because I already have a day job. Second, I told them that I didn't want to cost more than what I would bring. I wanted to support them and bring extra revenue to the website. Third, I told them that I wanted a percentage of what my pieces would bring in terms of advertising revenue.... We calculated together how much the advertising revenue was for every hit. I was paid two or three times a year, with a maximum of 600 euros per month.... I wasn't the only one to be paid this way, but my blog was making 10% of the overall traffic of *LaPlace* at that time.

Lou was not a journalist and did not want to become one. Originally trained and employed as an engineer, Lou had a highly successful blog, attracting hundreds of thousands of visitors every month. A transparent negotiation took place, in which the editors agreed to give Lou a percentage of the advertising revenues produced by the blog. In this case, the deal was clearly anchored on traffic numbers from the start, independent of any consideration about ethics or professionalism. In other cases, such as that of Celia, another blogger, things were more ambiguous.

Click-based compensation at *LaPlace*: Comparing the accounts of Sarah, section editor, and Celia, blogger

Celia's main job is as an editor at a women's magazine. She used to be an unpaid blogger for *LaPlace*, but her status changed in late 2011, when she started to receive a freelance rate for her articles. I conducted two interviews about her situation: one with Sarah, the section editor in charge of Celia's pieces, and the second with Celia herself. Their accounts differed.

> SARAH: Celia will now be paid as a freelancer. Whenever the bosses think that a piece is worth it, that there is some journalistic content, she will be paid. So she changed status, from blogger to freelancer.... For a long time, the bosses relied on the same argument, "she writes for fun." But they realized that she brought them so much that they had to pay her. She writes pieces that are hits.... The best example is the XXX [*product name redacted*]. The bosses realized that this piece had brought 7,500 euros with Google ads because whenever people search for XXX online our piece comes second.... So it was 7,500 euros of benefits. I didn't tell her, but when Philippe told me that, I thought: "It would be nice to find a hundred euros for her from time to time, wouldn't it?" [*Laughs*]. I mean, she brought a lot of traffic and a lot of money to the website, her pieces are long-tail pieces, they are well referenced on search engines, and she writes about topics that get searched a lot online. But she doesn't know the mechanism.

> CELIA: Now I'm paid. It has been a month. If I understand correctly, we're now four bloggers who are paid, four professional journalists.... It was complicated for *LaPlace* not to pay bloggers who do exactly the same job as professional journalists, bloggers who are in fact professional journalists.

When Sarah mentioned Celia's recent shift to being compensated for her writing, she first emphasized the high journalistic value of Celia's articles, before moving to a quite different justification in order to explain why she started getting paid, namely, that her articles attracted a lot of traffic and therefore brought in high advertising revenues. As Sarah explained, somewhat ambiguously, the top editors "realized that she brought them so much that they had to pay her." Yet Celia was not aware that this was the main cause for this change in her status: she believed that it was because she was a "professional journalist." Celia did not know that they attracted a lot of traffic. Using Sarah's words, she was not aware of the "mechanism" that made *LaPlace*'s editors decide to compensate her.

Compensation between Bureaucratic and Disciplinary Dynamics

The differences between *TheNotebook* and *LaPlace* should begin to sound familiar at this point. Here again, we see the ramifications of click-based considerations and audience metrics. To keep their homepages fresh, the two websites relied on an increasing number of external contributors. Yet neither *TheNotebook* nor *LaPlace*'s editors were able—or willing—to pay everybody the relatively high wages that had been common in previous decades. At *TheNotebook*, the editors decided to allocate their budget through a hierarchical pay scale. contributors were paid a wide range of rates, editors had autonomy in deciding how much to pay people, and click-based evaluation played an important role in the decision-making process. In contrast, *LaPlace*'s editors decided to enforce a flat rate for all freelance pieces, regardless of length, quality, or the writer's seniority. In parallel, they relied on a system of unpaid work by not compensating nonprofessional writers, whom they called "bloggers," even though this rule came with exceptions for highly popular writers.

Hence, both at *TheNotebook* and *LaPlace*, compensation mirrored the tension between editorial and click-based definitions of journalistic quality introduced in the previous chapters. According to the editorial criterion, only professional journalists should be paid, and experienced journalists should be paid more than "rookies." In contrast, according to the click-based criterion, writers should be compensated proportionally to the traffic and advertising revenues they brought to the website, regardless of the editorial quality of their pieces. These two compensation scales often clashed. The most experienced journalists did not necessarily attract the highest number of page views. Conversely, the most popular articles did not always conform to editorial standards of journalistic excellence.

In order to deal with these contradictions, editors at *TheNotebook* and *LaPlace* put in place an asymmetrical management of information flows. This meant remaining silent about whom was paid, how much, and why. At *TheNotebook*, editors did not disclose information about wages and rates to anyone. At *LaPlace*, editors kept silent about the multiple exceptions to the "official" rates. Editors also switched between different repertoires of justifications whenever they had to talk about compensation. When addressing professional journalists, editors typically relied on editorial arguments, emphasizing the writing skills, editorial fit, and seniority of a writer to justify how much they were being paid. When engaging with bloggers or popular writers, editors turned to click-based arguments in order to justify their decisions, acknowledging that compensation was indexed on the number of page views and "virality" of a writer's production. *TheNotebook* and *LaPlace*'s editors routinely alternated between these arguments when accounting for the complex sets of determinants that guided compensation decisions.[16]

In spite of these similarities, however, important differences emerged between the two websites. Somewhat predictably, *TheNotebook*'s editors did not shy away from hierarchies when deciding how much to pay their contributors. *TheNotebook*'s compensation system further amplified the already stratified and bureaucratic system in place in the newsroom by attaching different dollar amounts to writers. In contrast, *LaPlace*'s editors rejected the idea that some of their individual employees were more valuable to the organization than others: the compressed salary scale and flat freelance rates reflected such beliefs. This was accompanied by the creation of an outside category of unpaid contributors, as well as by multiple exceptions, all of which reflected and reinforced the disciplinary system in place at the French website.

Metrics and Exposure

How did these compensation systems affect the career strategies of freelance writers working for *TheNotebook* and *LaPlace*? More broadly, how did freelancers make sense of their independent status? From historical representations of "grub street hacks" to depictions of precarious bloggers ready to sell their soul for a penny, there is often some stigma associated with independent editorial work.[17] Yet the freelance journalists I met with strongly disagreed with these gloomy depictions. Throughout the interviews, they explained that they would not exchange their position for a salaried one: their independent status, they said, was the only option enabling them to be autonomous. As Sean, who wrote for *TheNotebook*, told me:

I used to work as a staff writer for [a large national magazine], but I couldn't write with the voice I wanted to write with. Anything that was fun had been taken out of it. I quit in 2000 to drive around the country with my then-girlfriend and figure out what I wanted to do. I started freelancing that fall. At the time I thought that I would try it and probably go back on staff ... but I ended up staying freelance all this time because I really like the flexibility, I love the freedom of it.

No schedule, no hierarchical superior, absolute autonomy—Sean's situation sounds idyllic. Yet this autonomy often comes at a cost given the competitive economic landscape freelance journalists operate in. Specifically, freelancers explained that they had to make constant trade-offs about when and where to work. Should they write for Publication A, which paid well but was not prestigious? Or for Publication B, which did not pay well but was a well-known name? Or should they say yes to Publications A *and* B, sacrificing sleep and leisure?

When managing their work schedules and professional careers, freelancers found it emotionally exhausting to engage in such relentless arbitrage. They knew all too well that they were forced to make hard choices.[18] As Nikos, a freelance illustrator for *LaPlace*, put it: "As a freelancer, you realize that time is money: when you don't work you lose money. I only take two weeks of vacation per year ... and that's when [*with an ironic tone*] my 'best friend' at the communication agency takes his vacations. I have to be alert at all times. And of course I work on weekends." For him, being a freelancer meant constant efforts, because his employment schedule entirely depended on the desires and timelines of his clients.[19]

This double-sided aspect of freelancing—absolute autonomy and relentless constraints—resonates with Foucault's analysis of neoliberalism in *The Birth of Biopolitics*. According to Foucault, workers in the contemporary economy are increasingly asked to behave as "entrepreneurs of themselves," understanding their own bodies and skills as a form of capital that can be invested to maximize returns. Such an entrepreneurial ideology may be empowering and provide a sense of independence, but it also comes with an instrumental orientation towards the self. Freelance workers have to engage in the same kind of decision-making as managers or executives. Yet they are managing their own selves instead of acting upon the external world.[20] The freelancers I met with did not discuss their work in these terms, but they certainly emphasized the counterintuitive sides of their independent status. For instance, they said it was hard to say no to work: they often felt that they had little choice about which jobs to take. In the words of Marie, a 30-year-old freelancer in Paris, unpleasant gigs were often the only way to remain afloat financially:

> Now there is a system of "shifts" in large web newsrooms: they need three teams of freelancers to cover the news all day long. It's a way to pay the bills: you work for seven hours in a row and then you go home and you're done. People tell you what to do, they boss you around, and you work like a dog.... But then I can do fun things on the side.... I create slideshows with sound recordings. It's my hobby. Sometimes I make money out of it but usually I don't and when I do it's almost nothing.

Marie did shifts in big newsrooms, a job she found uninteresting and tiring, in order to subsidize her "hobby," which was to make slideshows with soundbites. Those were rarely compensated, but she did not care. In organizing her career, Marie established strong distinctions between her money-making activities, which she was not emotionally invested in, and her passion, for which she did not expect to be compensated. Many freelancers developed similar distinctions to justify their professional choices. For example, John, 29 years old, had a day job in an advertising company and wrote on the side for *TheNotebook*. For him, success was all a matter of time and persistence:

> I have different degrees of happiness. I've reached one of them, which is that someone is paying me to write about something that I love. So I've already gone that far and that's great. But I also have an advertising day job and honestly it takes a lot of my time. Ten years from now I really hope to just be writing non-fiction and not subsisting on advertising or another side job.

John congratulated himself on getting paid to do what he loved and compared it to earlier times in his career when he wrote without getting compensated for it. Many freelancers agreed that unpaid work was at times an absolute necessity. In order for writers to get started in journalism, they need to build their reputation: their ability to make a living in the long run depends on having other people know about their work. Prestigious and well-known publications are well aware of that. As a result, they often pay very little or nothing at all—a state of affairs that freelancers usually accept when the publication provides good visibility or *exposure*, as journalists label this reputational work.[21]

Freelancers faced explicit trade-offs between compensation and exposure. Take Anne, the freelancer for *LaPlace* mentioned above: "*LaPlace* pays very poorly. It's bad.... But it's offset by their visibility. Now that I regularly write for them, a lot of people, journalists but also other people, have contacted me because they've seen my papers on the website. That's why I transferred my blog from [another website] to *LaPlace*: it's more visible and it's more prestigious too." In New York, Margaret, the former newspaper editor who freelanced for *TheNotebook*, made similar points:

> Other places pay much better, but I got many work opportunities because of what I do for *TheNotebook*. Oh yeah ... For example, the *New York Review of Books*, which pays really well, I got an email from an editor, whom I didn't know at all, who said, "I saw that you wrote this piece for *TheNotebook*, would you like to write a piece for us on a similar topic?" At some point I talked to a *New York Times* editor about an idea and he said, "I'm familiar with your work from *TheNotebook*." It's interesting to me because when I was writing for [a national newspaper], well it's older and more prestigious, but the way the website is designed, people didn't see my stuff, I would work on these pieces and they would just disappear! It was like it didn't exist. But *TheNotebook* really knows how to exploit the stories and show them to the readers.

Anne and Margaret agreed to write for *LaPlace* and *TheNotebook* because the websites provided good exposure, even though they paid relatively little. Margaret further distinguished between prestige and exposure. The national newspaper she used to work for was older, more respectable, and had a more central position in journalism than *TheNotebook*. Yet content rotated so quickly on the newspaper's website that her articles only remained visible for a short amount of time. In contrast, her pieces stayed longer on *TheNotebook*'s homepage and were also more heavily promoted on social media platforms. According to Margaret, this exposure led to opportunities with other publications that paid her much better rates. Thus, for freelancers getting high traffic numbers turned into a key aspect of individual visibility.

Of course, such reputational strategies are far from new in creative occupations. As cultural sociologists have shown, most artistic fields and cultural worlds rely on prestige and reputation to anchor social hierarchies. As we saw earlier, Bourdieu further distinguished between two kinds of logics that structure artistic and cultural fields: an autonomous logic (based on prestige and recognition from one's peers) and a heteronomous logic (based on external criteria such as market success).[22] Interestingly, for freelance journalists, digital platforms are reconfiguring autonomous and heteronomous logics by conflating them: in online news, audience metrics often functioned as an indicator of professional recognition *and* market success. As Marie, in Paris, explained:

> Twitter is sooo important. Everybody is on Twitter. I mean, I got all of my jobs through Twitter. Two days ago, a guy I didn't know sent me an email, they're starting a website and they want to hire me.... I guess that the guy checked my profile, he noticed that I had many followers and everything. With Twitter now I have some influence, I have a network of people who follow me. It matters! I know that people also hired me for this reason! They think: "she's on Twitter, she has a large number of followers, so when-ever she tweets an article her followers will retweet it." Before, you had to send your CV or you depended on your friends or you had to shake hands with the right people. With Twitter, you enter the network of important people without having to send a CV.

For Marie, having a large number of followers on Twitter served two pur-poses. First, it was an indicator of a built-in audience that could follow her wherever she published. She believed that editors took these numbers into account when deciding to hire her because they knew that her large com-munity of followers could translate into more page views for her articles— and therefore for the website. (However, when I asked editors whether they did in fact check freelancers' number of followers, they all demurred, saying that they did not have enough time to do that.) Marie interpreted her metrics in a commercial sense, as a set of eyeballs that could be mone-tized through digital advertising and, therefore, should translate into higher pay and more work opportunities. Yet her second argument was more explicitly symbolic: Twitter, she said, was a tool to connect with peers. In-stead of relying on friends or shaking hands to make professional connec-tions, she could "enter the network of important people" through Twitter and use it to build her journalistic reputation. There, Marie's interpretation of her Twitter metrics was more explicitly professional: Twitter was about connecting with people who mattered in the journalistic field.[23] Patricia, another freelancer in New York, similarly viewed her social media follow-ing in terms of the economic and symbolic assets it represented:

> After the debate, I was so annoyed by Romney I wrote this piece and got 3,000 likes on Facebook—it's not bad, but it's depressing when I look at [the website of the magazine where I used to work], where it's more like 100,000 likes. It's frustrating because it's the same ideas, just fewer people read it. I have 2,000 followers on Twitter—I still don't know how to pass

the threshold and be followed massively. But now I'm followed by several editors, it's really important. It's a way to build my brand. That's what on-line journalism is about today: you have a brand and the people who read you follow you. Jimmy [a well-known blogger who writes for *TheNotebook*], for example, he moved four times, and people follow him everywhere. I want to get to that point.

Patricia described her reputation as a brand to be built, quantitatively and qualitatively. On the quantitative side, she complained about the low number of "likes" that her articles attracted on Facebook and lamented her small number of Twitter followers.[24] On the qualitative side, she mentioned that editors followed her on Twitter, which she saw as "really important" in order to "build her brand." Many freelancers similarly mixed quantitative and qualitative aspects in their quest for visibility: the kind of readers and followers that they attracted mattered at least as much as their absolute quantities, and sometimes more. Freelancers like Patricia and Marie drew clear distinctions between "lay" and "professional" readers: not only did articles need to be read by a large number of people; they also had to reach the *right* type of people—important journalists and editors.

Ultimately, however, freelancers on both sides of the Atlantic prioritized professional recognition over commercial success when thinking about the benefits of having a large number of followers on social media platforms. When freelancers agreed to write for little or no money in exchange for exposure, likes and clicks were a plus, but the real measure of success was how many new contacts and employment opportunities resulted from the effort. If no new leads materialized, they blamed the website for not attracting the *right* kind of readers. Nikos, who contributed an illustration blog for *LaPlace*, explained:

> It's true that I gained visibility—I don't even remember how many followers I have. Six months ago, I signed a contract with an advertising agency, they saw my drawings on *LaPlace* and liked them. But it's the first time that I got something out of this blog. So I tell myself that my investment had positive consequences.... But when Philippe tells me: "Congratulations! 3,000 clicks on your drawing," I want to tell him: "Wait ... I've been working for you for five years and nothing came out of it." The people who read my articles, they're internet users, not companies, and I don't need this kind of visibility, I mean, I do, but what I really need is to make a living!

Nikos eventually landed work with a firm that had learned about his work through *LaPlace*, so he believed that his investment had been profitable.

Yet he also remembered that for many years, "nothing came out" of his unpaid blog. In other words, clicks, likes, and retweets do not always translate into long-term rewards. As older freelancers know all too well, continued survival in journalism requires a strong network of professional relations. Building such a network takes considerable time and effort.[25]

Between Authenticity and "Personal Branding"

Overall, the similarities between the experiences of the freelancers working for *TheNotebook* in New York and *LaPlace* in Paris were striking: in both places, freelance journalists were willing to work for free as long as the publication provided good exposure. They carefully managed their visibility and their followers on Twitter and other social media platforms. They tracked both quantitative and qualitative exposure through audience metrics.

Yet the two groups differed in how they talked about their situation. First, the New York–based and Parisian freelancers had distinct conceptions of their position as independent workers. On the American side, freelancers did not seem to perceive negative stereotypes associated with their freelance status. Throughout the interviews, U.S. freelancers complained about their problems with health insurance—this was before the Affordable Care Act, or Obamacare—and real estate prices in New York City, but they were never pessimistic or discouraged about their situation as independent writers. Rather, they seemed to believe that freelancing was the most common way to start in journalism: they often used the metaphor of "hustling," explaining that they were doing what needed to be done in order to make a living out of their writing.

The situation was different in France. The Parisian freelancers I met often pointed out the hardships and discriminations they faced as independent workers. Gabriella's story was revealing in this respect: she started freelancing again in the early 2010s after several years as a salaried employee, first at *LaPlace*, where she was the managing editor, then at a prestigious culture magazine, where she wrote long-form articles. She soon realized that she was facing many unexpected difficulties as a freelance writer:

It's hard. What I hadn't anticipated before is the look of pity on journalists' faces. Parisian journalists are obsessed with salaried employment! A friend of mine told me, "You got fired?" No, actually, I resigned! This look of pity,

"Poor you, you don't have a real job ..." It's just hard. Also, in order to get interviews—if I go to a political meeting and I have a question, people ask for my name and my publication, and I don't have any, and often they refuse to answer. I think that it's not healthy to be that obsessed about salaried employment.

Freelancing has a bad reputation in France. As Gabriella put it, many editors and staff writers see freelancing as a sign of professional failure, to be viewed with pity. This lower prestige and perceived status of French freelancers may seem somewhat paradoxical, given the strong regulatory framework in place to protect and support freelancers, or *pigistes*. Indeed, for nearly eighty years, the French state has engaged in extensive efforts to provide a legal definition of freelance journalistic work. Since the 1974 Cressard Law, freelancers who meet the criteria for "professional journalists"—those who receive more than half of their income from one or several media companies—can claim severance packages, unemployment subsidies, paid leaves, and social security benefits including retirement subsidies and public health insurance.[26] According to many freelancers, however, the roots of the problem were deeper: employment in France remained structured around tenured positions (*contrat à durée indéterminée*), a system they criticized vehemently. As Valérie, a Parisian freelance writer twenty years younger than Gabriella, told me:

> People always assume that you're looking for salaried employment.... When you have a tenured position, it's like "Congratulations! You found the Holy Grail!" Well, no, I'm glad to be a freelancer. But each time I start a new shift in a newsroom, the bosses treat me like I'm an intern, like I'm incompetent. In France we're still in this system where freelancing is a fall-back option, where most people want to become salaried employees. But I think that younger people are starting to understand that we have nothing to expect from big companies.

Yet one should not overestimate the entrepreneurial zeal and rebellion of Parisian freelancers. This is where a second important difference between U.S. and French freelance journalists emerges. Though most of the French *pigistes* asserted that they loved their independent status, they were also deeply conflicted about its demands and the tolls that it took on their identity. Their doubts often crystallized around the notion of "personal branding," a term that many freelancers brought up on their own, without my asking, during the interviews. Behind this term, which comes from the self-help marketing literature, is the idea that workers need to consciously market their own reputations in order to be successful in the labor market.[27] Interestingly, freelancers in New York and Paris had different reactions to this idea. In New York, most freelance writers eagerly detailed the branding strategies they used to promote their work. This was the case for John, mentioned above:

> I try to promote myself. I know the importance of branding so I hired a friend to do these business cards for me. I left them everywhere. They're colorful and engaging. It's a way of keeping people interested. And my website is like an online portfolio that allows me to show editors, "Hey, look what I'm doing," but also to show my work to the rest of the world, with social media. So that's a way to get my name out there and my writing out there—for free, of course, but it's exposure.... I'm going to conferences, being persistent, meeting contacts, trying to get my ideas out there.

Like John, many freelancers in New York were very conscious of the fact that journalism was a marketplace. They knew that promoting their brand mattered, as did having a "portfolio" that they could use to get their name "out there." Most of them did not hesitate to use entrepreneurial metaphors to describe their efforts. The situation was different in Paris. The French freelancers I met only mentioned the notion of personal branding to criticize it seconds later. All were ambivalent about this entrepreneurial approach to journalism, Marie included:

> Networking ... I'm not very good at it. Once I know people, yeah, I'll follow them on Twitter and I'll try to stay in touch, but it's not systematic. I don't do *personal branding* [*in English*]—I'm trying to be myself. But then it's true that when I post one of my slideshows and tweet: "look at my latest slideshow," well ... I'm trying to sell myself [*j'essaie de me vendre*], it's true that I try to get attention. But I think that it's natural, I just finished a slideshow, it's natural, it's not strategic or mathematical.

French freelancers argued that it was normal to promote their work on Twitter because they were proud of what they had written or when they wanted their piece to circulate widely. Yet they were also deeply critical of what Marie called "strategic" behaviors or instrumental strategies such as following every single person one interacted with on Twitter, relentlessly promoting oneself on social media platforms, and being "inauthentic" or "superficial" online.[28] Personal branding appeared unnatural and morally tainted to Marie, who compared it to human trafficking ("selling oneself"). The Parisian freelancer ended up using a similar metaphor to *LaPlace*'s editors in chapter 4, when they compared the chase for traffic to prostitution. Indeed, French journalists—inside and outside of news organizations—relied on a morally charged repertoire in their criticism of instrumental behaviors oriented towards quantified forms of online visibility.

Conclusion

This chapter concludes the comparison of *TheNotebook* and *LaPlace* by focusing on the compensation and careers of freelance journalists. On both sides of the Atlantic, negotiations over who got paid and why mirrored the tension between click-based and editorial evaluation, but editors at the two sites put in place different systems to handle it. At *TheNotebook*, a hierarchical pay scale was installed—a ramification of the bureaucratic power structuring the U.S. newsroom. At *LaPlace*, formal equality prevailed, together with strong external boundaries and multiple exceptions—a system in line with the organization's disciplinary culture.

Overall, and in spite of these differences, freelancers in New York and Paris described their metrics-driven career strategies in strikingly similar ways. In both places, they relied on audience metrics not only as an indicator of popularity among lay readers but also as a tool to broaden one's reputation and reach senior editors. Social media metrics functioned both as a measure of their commercial success and—more importantly, for most of them—as a signal of their professional status. Yet American and French freelancers relied on different repertoires to make sense of their precarious and metrics-based reputations and identities. In Paris, freelancers perceived metrics-driven behaviors as a direct threat to their professional dignity, much more so than their American counterparts.

Such findings in turn strongly resonate with what sociologists Michèle Lamont and Laurent Thévenot describe as "national cultural repertoires." Lamont and Thévenot argue that the French are less likely than Americans to draw on market-based arguments and prefer to rely on "civic solidarity" arguments that emphasize nonmaterialist and egalitarian values. In line with these findings, French freelancers were less likely to describe themselves as rational maximizers on a competitive market. Instead, they criticized instrumental strategies as undermining the nonmaterialistic values that had attracted them to journalism in the first place.[29]

Nonetheless, these distinct reactions do not necessarily mean that French and American freelancers actually organized their careers differently. Whereas French freelancers had a more critical discourse about personal branding and metrics-driven behaviors than American writers, the two groups in fact described their career choices in strikingly similar ways. Parisian journalists were highly critical of instrumental approaches and asserted that they wanted to "be themselves," but they also engaged in the same strategic and metrics-oriented arbitrages as their New York–based counterparts. Thus, French freelancers drew on a somewhat inconsistent repertoire to describe their independent careers. In contrast, there was no such gap between the discourses and practices of American freelancers, who openly described themselves as rational maximizers on a competitive market *and* acted in decidedly instrumental ways to manage their employment relationships.

This dialectic relationship or "decoupling" between discourses and practices in turn resembles what we found earlier at the organizational level, in the comparison of *TheNotebook* and *LaPlace*.[30] As we saw throughout the book, *TheNotebook*'s editors talked about traffic numbers in ways that matched their daily use of web metrics. Similarly, the U.S. journalists who discursively professed their indifference towards numbers disregarded metrics in their daily work. In contrast, although *LaPlace*'s editors and journalists sarcastically dismissed audience metrics, they fixated on traffic numbers in their daily work. In other words, there was a marked disconnect at the Parisian website between what editors and journalists said they did and what they actually did with respect to the chase for clicks. Along similar lines, Parisian freelancers were more reluctant to rely on openly market-based repertoires to justify their actions, even when they did in fact work in a competitive market. American journalists did not have the same doubts: they switched in and out of market repertoires without missing a beat.

Like the organizations at the center of this comparison, the individual journalists we followed throughout the book faced strong pressures towards convergence. On both sides of the Atlantic, they encountered similar economic constraints, looked at the same audience and social media metrics, and made the same kinds of trade-offs between click-based imperatives—here, having one's articles reach a wider audience—and editorial ambitions. They used clicks and social media metrics as a signal of their relevance to a broad and ill-defined public encompassing both lay readers and professional peers.

At the same time, journalists relied on different discursive repertoires and sets of representations to make sense of their metrics-driven careers and identities.[31] In New York, freelance journalists embraced market-based descriptions of themselves as "personal brands," online and offline. In Paris, ambivalence and inconsistency prevailed, as journalists sought to reconcile the metrics-driven structures they experienced in their daily lives with the anti-commercial definition of professional dignity inherited from previous journalistic eras.

Conclusion

Things change rapidly in the world of online news. When I started my fieldwork in 2011, *TheNotebook* and *LaPlace* were both prospering. There was always a difference in scale between them—*TheNotebook* had a team of about forty journalists and attracted more than 4.5 million unique visitors per month, whereas *LaPlace* had fifteen journalists and attracted 2 million visitors per month. Over time, however, the two websites took different trajectories. Already, towards the end of my fieldwork in 2014, *TheNotebook* was growing, attracting about 30 million unique visitors, whereas *LaPlace* had declined to 1.5 million. In 2018, the fortunes of the two websites put them in entirely different categories. *TheNotebook*'s traffic numbers remained above 20 million unique visitors per month. It created a membership program, which attracted about 30,000 subscribers and $1.3 million in revenues per year. It also developed its audio presence through a podcast network. In contrast, *LaPlace* disappeared into the maw of its parent company. The website was absorbed into LeGroupeMag's main website, becoming a sub-site and later a simple "vertical" page. The journalists moved to LeGroupeMag's offices. After a larger French media company bought LeGroupeMag, *LaPlace*'s team was asked to develop a more specialized editorial line focusing on digital technologies. By 2018, there were only four journalists left in *LaPlace*'s newsroom.

Most of the people we followed throughout the book also moved on. On the East Coast, Sam, editor-in-chief of *TheNotebook*, became the CEO of an online project dedicated to visual exploration. Esther, the former culture editor, writes books. Jane, after several positions at major newspapers, took a position as a senior editor at a web magazine. Emma, one of the section editors, became a staff writer at a large newspaper. Noah and Sean, who had been on the staff during the early days of *TheNotebook* before turning to independent work, continued to freelance. In Paris, Philippe, *LaPlace*'s editor-in-chief, took a high executive position at LeGroupeMag. André became the president of an international NGO, while also hosting a radio show on a public channel. Marina, the former managing editor, turned to movie production. Gael became a consultant for digital news organizations. Alexandre and Gabriella worked as freelancers. On both sides of the Atlantic, almost everyone stayed in the world of online media.

· · ·

In the meantime, however, online media became a different place. Following the election of Donald Trump as the forty-fifth president of the United States, news organizations and digital platforms entered into a political and economic maelstrom. From the moral panic surrounding the uncovering of "content farms," organizations producing blatantly false stories, to the Russian interference in elections through the promotion of divisive political ads, the scandal of Cambridge Analytica's use of Facebook personal data, and the stream of tweets from the White House labeling mainstream news organizations as "fake news," the media ecosystem became the center of new controversies about the future of information and democracy.[1]

Metrics at Work shows that news websites bear some responsibility for these problematic developments. As we saw, when news organizations entered the chase for traffic, they began to publish more and faster. They relied on aggregation and clickbait headlines in order to increase their advertising revenues. They hired large numbers of flexible workers to keep their homepages "fresh." They engaged in relentless efforts to make their content more visible on Google, Facebook, and Twitter. These developments had editorial consequences—including an exponential increase in cat videos, scandal coverage, and contentious opinion pieces. Because of their heightened reliance on web analytics, news websites also contributed to the consolidation of the so-called "data economy": they made deals with social media platforms and search engines in order to monetize the fine-grained information they collected about their online readers. Over time, news websites started using more tracking software than any other category of website.[2] According Shoshana Zuboff, now that this tracking system is in place, "surveillance capitalism" seems here to stay: the future of the knowledge economy will most likely be based on individual targeting and personalization—an infrastructure that raises serious concerns about privacy encroachments, political manipulation, and the automated reproduction of social, racial, and economic inequality.[3]

Yet these worrisome developments are only part of the picture. In this book, I seek to change how we think about data, metrics, and algorithms. In order to capture the complex social and political changes that stem from these digital systems, we need to go beyond conceptualizing metrics as mere vehicles of rationalization, convergence, and surveillance. To that end, I show that metrics should be understood as contested symbolic objects. The case of online news illustrates that how metrics can take a variety of meanings and be used in radically different ways depending on the meso- and macro-level features of the institutional contexts in which they are deployed. Specifically, the book makes several points that go against conventional wisdom regarding online news and digital metrics.

Against Standardization

First, *Metrics at Work* argues against the deterministic idea that journalistic work is becoming standardized at the lowest common denominator in the same way around the world. Instead, I document how workers can reproduce cultural difference within a larger process of economic and technological convergence.

Overall, it is true that web newsrooms around the world face strong pressures towards convergence. Digital technologies facilitate the movement of news content across borders, and journalism has become a more cosmopolitan occupation. This makes journalists more likely to imitate some of the innovations taking place in other countries, especially when these come with a high level of prestige. We saw how this process played out as *LaPlace*'s founders consciously replicated the business strategies and editorial formats of *TheNotebook* in order to gain legitimacy—a process I analyzed as a case of transnational circulation between national fields.

In addition, news websites operate in a highly unstable and unpredictable market. Not knowing which innovations would turn out to be successful, they often end up adopting the same strategies—publishing more, faster, and promoting clickbait content—in hopes of attracting traffic. As we saw, in spite of the different economic systems of public subsidies in place in the United States and France, web newsrooms in the two countries started using similar analytics tools to get detailed data about the behavior and preferences of their online readers. Both newsrooms relied on similar data-driven strategies in order to manage their homepages, tweak their headlines, and optimize their content—an evolution I analyze as a form of isomorphic convergence.

Over time, this led to the emergence of similar tensions between competing modes of evaluation, which I called editorial and click-based, in the offices of *TheNotebook* and *LaPlace*. Where editorial evaluation prioritizes the internal quality of news articles and the judgment of peers, click-based evaluation focuses on the quantitative success of news articles in terms of audience metrics. As we saw, the two definitions often clash. In an ideal world, all authors and articles scoring high in terms of editorial evaluation would also be successful in the click-based framework. Yet

I found that was the exception, not the rule. In most newsrooms, the individualization and ubiquitous presence of web analytics made the tension between these modes of evaluation particularly acute.

If the analysis stopped here, it would be a somewhat deterministic story of quantification, standardization, and editorial decline across national borders. In spite of these multiple pressures towards convergence, however, I have documented how the subset of journalists at the center of this book reproduced national traditions in navigating the tension between editorial and click-based evaluation. We saw how journalists in the United States and France interpreted audience metrics and understood their algorithmic publics in strikingly different ways. At *TheNotebook*, a strong division of labor prevailed: editors were in charge of click-based evaluation, whereas staff writers focused on editorial goals. In contrast, at *LaPlace*, everyone did a bit of everything: editors and staff writers alike handled click-based imperatives and editorial concerns.

To compare how metrics were integrated into these organizational structures, I have developed a theoretical framework contrasting the concepts of bureaucratic and disciplinary power. *TheNotebook* relied on a bureaucratic system based on clear hierarchies and marked internal boundaries. In contrast, disciplinary control reigned at *LaPlace*, with flatter hierarchies, a relative lack of specialization, and fuzzy internal boundaries. These distinct kinds of organizational power in turn came with different uses of digital metrics. In the bureaucratic regime, metrics were typically mobilized for predefined rewards and penalties, and their meanings were unambiguous. In the disciplinary regime, metrics were omnipresent but came with more ambiguous meanings. Workers internalized them, usually experiencing strong emotions based on their numbers.

I find that these distinct organizational structures were inherited from previous eras of the U.S. and French journalistic fields, which the editors and journalists of the two websites reproduced when they came up with recipes for news production in a competitive digital landscape. Ironically, the French website's founders sought to create a more egalitarian workplace, but their staff writers experienced greater stress from the metrics that managers liked to critique. In a paradoxical twist, the liberatory rhetoric and countercultural legacy of *LaPlace*'s early years led to weak institutional buffers against the individualizing pressure of clicks.[4]

The strikingly different effects of metrics in the organizations studied in this book raise a number of questions about how managerial power will evolve in the age of algorithms. Across sectors, organizations are developing increasingly sophisticated analytics and algorithms to control their workers. From policing to healthcare, higher education, transportation, criminal justice, academia, finance, credit, retail, and nongovernmental organizations, managers collect, store, and analyze growing amounts of data with the goal of improving how they direct, evaluate, and discipline their employees. Yet we still know little about how organizations incorporate this data in their production process and how this varies across fields. What will the future of workplace metrics look like? Will they be integrated into bureaucratic power, disciplinary dynamics, or something else? And how will these changes affect the working conditions of employees and contract workers? The findings of *Metrics at Work* caution against technological determinism, showing that the answers should emerge from empirical analyses of how digital metrics become intertwined with existing organizational dynamics and professional cultures, within and across industries.[5]

Clicks, Field Trajectories, and the Future of News

Second, *Metrics at Work* documents how the meanings of digital metrics— even when presented through identical software programs—can vary across national borders. When American and French journalists looked at audience metrics, they *saw* different things. In New York, journalists understood web analytics as a clear signal of market pressures. As such, metrics were either actively optimized (by editors) or rejected (by staff writers) as a commercial encroachment on journalistic autonomy. In contrast, traffic numbers came with multifaceted meanings in the Parisian newsroom: *LaPlace*'s editors and staff writers criticized metrics as an indicator of market forces and at the same time valued those metrics as a measure of their public relevance. I find that these representations were shaped by the trajectories of the journalistic field in the two countries. In the United States, strong professionalization in the face of early market pressures came with a notable distance between journalists and their readers. In contrast, since the Dreyfus Affair, French journalists have defined themselves as intellectuals in charge of shaping public opinion. Such trajectories had an enduring influence on the discourses and practices of journalists working at *TheNotebook* and *LaPlace*.

Are these findings representative of the U.S. and French journalistic fields as a whole? As we saw, *TheNotebook* and *LaPlace* are somewhat idiosyncratic organizations: both are hybrid publications, in the sense that they operate online, but were founded by journalists who had spent most of their careers working for print publications. This hybrid status provides a unique opportunity to study how journalists reproduced cultural difference at a time of convergence. Over the years, Sam, Philippe, Emma, and Marina faced the same dilemmas (how to maximize traffic, continue publishing quality content, pay their contributors a living wage, and so on) as their publications grew and the market for online news evolved. When trying to address these dilemmas, the journalists relied on the representations, discourses, and routines that they had developed during the early parts of their careers in print newsrooms. The national differences in these institutionalized recipes turned out to be markedly different.

Yet this does not mean that all news organizations in the United States and France present such differences, nor does it entail that the future of news production in the two countries will resemble the distinct paradigms analyzed here. In fact, both legacy news organizations and "digital native" websites appear to be more similar across the Atlantic Ocean than what we saw at *TheNotebook* and *LaPlace*. In the United States and in France, legacy news organizations (websites with a print counterpart, such as *The New York Times*, *The Washington Post*, *Le Monde*, and so on) tend to rely on bureaucratic systems for handling metrics, in which specific editors and data specialists are in charge of traffic, whereas staff writers are buffered from the pressure of having to maximize clicks. Similarly, in New York and in Paris, "digital natives" (websites dedicated to news aggregation and traffic maximization, staffed by journalists who spent most of their careers online, such as *The Huffington Post* and *Buzzfeed* in the United States and France) typically rely on disciplinary dynamics: in these newsrooms, audience metrics become an integral part of the journalists' status and emotional well-being. In other words, as the field of online news becomes more complex and specialized, specific managerial paradigms regarding metrics spread within subfields, across national borders.[6]

On top of this, the types of audience metrics used in web newsrooms are also changing. Indeed, since the end of my fieldwork, the chase for traffic has evolved. Instead of the war of all against all recounted in this book, many newsrooms have started thinking more strategically about traffic. Though off-the-shelf tools like Chartbeat are still popular, news organizations have also developed in-house software programs in order to better understand their online traffic. Publications relying on pay walls and subscription systems are now implementing metrics more carefully to attract and measure loyalty. Others—including newsrooms that use

Chartbeat—have turned to more qualitative indicators, such as the measure of "time engaged" on each article.[7]

Audience analytics and the chase for traffic are no longer a novelty in the journalistic field. Hence, the specific dynamics we saw at *TheNotebook* and *LaPlace* may soon be a thing of the past. As more complex and specialized arrays of metrics-oriented strategies unfold, further research should continue to explore how they are used and understood by journalists, and what this means for the future of news production.[8]

The Power of Algorithmic Publics

Finally, beyond the case of journalism, *Metrics at Work* reveals how new types of publics are materialized through algorithmic technologies. It is common to lament the amount of time we spend looking at screens. Scholars highlight the alienating and isolating potential of digital technologies, arguing that we should "reclaim the power of conversation."[9] Observers decry the distraction and loss of concentration that stem from switching constantly between websites and internet browser windows. There are regular moral panics about the effects of screen time on sociability and mental health, especially where teenagers and young adults are concerned.

Yet screens, software programs, and digital metrics also materialize new kinds of social presences in our daily lives. Facebook brings us updates, posts, and pictures from our "friends" past and present, giving them some modicum of presence in our lives.[10] Streaming programs from YouTube to Twitch allow us to connect with other online viewers in following the daily activities and updates posted by influencers and entertainers.[11] Dating websites bring potential romantic partners to our profiles and inboxes, giving us the option of "swiping" or messaging far beyond our conventional social circles.[12] E-commerce platforms like Amazon display listings of all the different companies providing versions of the goods and products we are searching for. In addition to individual, romantic, or commercial interactions, algorithmic technologies can also bring broader civic and professional communities to our screens.

Indeed, *Metrics at Work* shows that audience metrics always stand for the larger entity of algorithmic publics—collectives of online readers that are mediated and represented through computational procedures. Publics have always been complex social constructs; algorithmic publics are even more so. Thus, in spite of the multiplication of analytics providing detailed information about reader behavior, algorithmic publics remain contested entities. At *TheNotebook*, journalists and editors understood their algorithmic publics as commodified, segmented, and largely passive. At *LaPlace*, journalists both endowed their algorithmic publics with civic potential and criticized them as vehicles of market pressure, comparing the chase for clicks to prostitution.

Regardless of the journalists' orientations towards them, it was striking how *present* these algorithmic publics were in the daily lives of the journalists I interviewed. Algorithmic publics were a palpable force in web newsrooms. Compared to print journalists, who only had high-level statistics (marketing surveys), anecdotal evidence (letters to the editors), and their own imagination to create a representation of their publics, web journalists used the trove of information provided by analytics software programs to visualize their publics in far more detail. Web analytics dashboards put these complex collectives at the center of the everyday experiences of web journalists, on the computer screens they looked at, through dials and numbers moving in real time.

This algorithmically mediated presence of distributed publics endowed with multiple meanings raises questions that go beyond the case of journalism. One can think of other fields where previously poorly documented publics are now represented through digital metrics and algorithms. For writers, musicians, visual artists, fashion models, and chefs, platforms such as Goodreads, Twitter, Facebook, Instagram, and Yelp have become inescapable infrastructures for the promotion of their careers and "personal brands," where they can track the diffusion and popularity of their activities among different publics, from fans to peers to larger collectives. How do they react to the judgment of these newfound publics? How do they envision their algorithmic publics? When and why do they resist?[13]

Another intriguing case is the one of academia. Traditionally, academics have learned about the reception of their work in oblique and indirect ways—through in-person or written exchanges with other academics, footnotes, and reviews by peers and journalists. Academics have long contrasted the short-term and long-term impact of their production, usually hoping that one's "vocation" would end up being appreciated by posterity, one way or another.[14] Yet the contemporary academic field is quite different from these canonical descriptions. Across disciplines, academics are now encouraged to publish in journals with high impact factors, maximize their "h-index," track their number of citations through Google Scholar alerts, and connect with peers on Twitter, Facebook, Academia .edu, and so on. Through all these sources of data, academics receive more information than ever before about their algorithmic publics, made up of readers who are similarly connected and represented through computational procedures.

Whether they like it or not, academics now have to take these publics into account. Universities depend on the quantified productivity and prestige of their scholars to maintain their position in national and international rankings. Consequently, some now organize workshops to help faculty members optimize their social media "exposure." Academic journals are not immune either, since their continued existence often depends on their resonance and popularity within the disciplines they publish. Thus, not unlike news websites, academic journals increasingly display "top ten" lists of most-downloaded articles, lists of their most-cited articles, as well as broader metrics of impact, including "altmetrics" based on social media mentions and online news coverage.[15]

Like the clicks discussed throughout this book, there are several ways to make sense of these evolutions. One can criticize these changes as an encroachment of market pressures and instrumental rationality on academic autonomy. Such a perspective usually goes hand in hand with a broader critique of neo-liberal forces in modern-day academia. Yet one can also argue that these algorithmically connected collectives and the digital metrics that come with them have a strong symbolic potential. Perhaps these new metrics will afford visibility to scholars or fields that were previously less prominent; perhaps they will create a sense of shared accountability in places where it is currently missing. These different aspects of metrics help to understand their appeal for individual academics as well as for institutions of higher education.

Expanding further beyond the cases of journalism, cultural production, and academia, the multiplication of digital metrics brings with it new social, professional, and economic spaces where people are primarily working with and for algorithmic publics. To take but a few examples, Wikipedia editors, YouTube creators, and ad tech developers all publish content across multiple digital platforms.[16] Like web journalists, these actors desperately want to reach larger publics. Like web journalists, they collect, store, and analyze digital data in order to influence online users. Yet they are not necessarily bound by the professional norms and institutional structures that have defined news production over the course of the past century and a half. We need to take these emerging fields seriously in order to understand how the information we consume is changing, and why. We also need to think about our responsibility as online readers. Like it or not, we are momentarily part of numerous algorithmic publics as we flip idly between apps and websites on our phones and computers every day. This makes our eyeballs valuable for the industries that seek to target us, measure our attention, and nudge us into clicking. It also means that each of our clicks counts in shaping the future of public debate.

A Fly on the Screen?

Behind the Scenes in the (Digital) Field

In this appendix, I reflect on what it means to do ethnographic fieldwork in highly connected web newsrooms located on different sides of the Atlantic. Like other ethnographers, I believe it is important to include methodological reflections on the process of doing fieldwork in order to interrogate how our presence and perspective situate our findings. Moreover, I hope that it will be a useful addition to the dynamic literature on digital ethnography. The first part discusses the strategies I used to get access to news organizations and how my research question evolved over time. The second part turns to my position in the field, both as a French woman living in the United States and as a junior academic studying the "rival" field, so to speak, of journalism. In the final section, I introduce the idea of being a "fly on the screen" to describe the toolkit of offline and online tactics I developed to study the world of digital news.

Entering the Field

Some ethnographic studies stem from a profound personal engagement with the subject at hand. Others seem more accidental, though they are never completely so. Here I introduce the far from linear path that led me to studying digital metrics and web journalism.

In 2008, I began a PhD in Sociology at Princeton University. I knew that I wanted to study a field undergoing profound economic and organizational changes; I was also interested in studying digital technologies. As an undergraduate student in France, I had not interacted much with the internet; I had mostly used email and word processors. In the suburban and well-connected depths of the Princeton campus, I discovered the pleasures of Netflix, Skype, eBay, Amazon, Facebook, and Yelp, which became part of my everyday life. I was interested in observing the effects of digital platforms on social processes.

I soon decided to focus on web journalism. The media industry, I thought, was going through exceptional changes: advertising revenues were crashing, news organizations were firing large chunks of their work-force, and there was no clear business model in sight, in large part be-cause of the transition to online publishing. At the same time, there was also a lot of experimentation taking place, from blogging to multimedia content or crowdfunded projects. I knew that I wanted to spend time in Paris, which I missed, and looked into the different regulations of jour-nalism in the United States and France.

Such were the vague thoughts that guided my first months of research. In mid-2011, I wrote a dissertation prospectus on the rise of contingent work in web journalism and its consequences on news content in the United States and France. I decided to rely on written consent in order to make it clear to journalists that this was a long-term academic project and that I was not planning to steal their scoops.[1] I wanted to be part of the French intellectual community during my fieldwork and registered for a joint dissertation at the Ecole des Hautes Etudes en Sciences Sociales.

Several months later, I moved to the eleventh arrondissement, in the northeast of Paris, and started conducting preliminary interviews with web journalists, whom I contacted through interpersonal contacts and snowball sampling, asking friends, friends of friends, and interviewees whether they could put me in touch with other web journalists. Yet I soon became frustrated with these interviews. Journalists seemed to have little agency: when they talked about their work, everything appeared to be dictated by their editors' demands. In the interviews, newsrooms emerged as mythical places endowed with high emotional energy and dense net-works of interactions. I felt that I was missing the full picture by not spending time there.

I was also starting to take the journalists' discourses with a grain of salt. The reason for that, I morosely wrote in my notebook on a rainy Parisian afternoon, was that journalists are professional communicators: they are used to describing the world through words. They talk about it, they write stories about it, and—like most social scientists—they believe that they know why things are changing. More often than not, my ques-tions received boilerplate answers: journalists predictably lamented the rise of commercial pressures in the news business, criticized the decline of shoe-leather journalism, and worried about the multiplication of bloggers willing to write for free. "Talk is cheap," noted Colin Jerolmack and Shamus Khan in the context of another study. At that point, I could not have agreed more.[2]

Therefore, I changed tactics and sought to get access to web news-rooms. What followed was a frantic quest to be referred to editors-in-chief to get permission to spend time in their offices. In December 2011,

I interviewed Lise, a journalist from *LaPlace*, whom I had met through a friend. She agreed to ask Philippe and André, respectively editor-in-chief and CEO of *LaPlace*, if I could conduct fieldwork in the newsroom. They agreed, quite informally.[3] In January 2012, I started spending two days a week at *LaPlace*, transcribing my notes and conducting interviews outside of the newsroom during the rest of the week. In April, I flew back to New York. I primarily contacted journalists working for *TheNotebook*, which *LaPlace*'s journalists had mentioned as one of their models. Eventually, I met with Sam, *TheNotebook*'s editor-in-chief, who gave me permission to observe the newsroom for a week. I started with two segments of fieldwork at *TheNotebook*, one in September 2012, the other in February 2013. To complement these short periods of official fieldwork, I returned to the *TheNotebook*'s offices multiple times, usually for specific reasons—to conduct interviews with journalists or observe a given meeting. I would then stay for several hours after the interviews or observations, and sit with the journalists at their desk or hang out in the open space.

At that point, I started thinking about the comparability of the material I was gathering in New York and Paris. On the French side, *LaPlace* had imitated *TheNotebook* from the start: they wanted to be the French version of *TheNotebook*; the two editors-in-chief, Philippe and Sam, knew each other (see chapter 2). With that anchor in mind, it made sense to focus on *TheNotebook* in New York. By then, however, *TheNotebook* had established an official partnership with another website in Paris, which I will call *TheNotebook.fr*. After interviewing *TheNotebook.fr*'s editor-in-chief, I got the permission to conduct a week of observation in their newsroom and interviewed six journalists there. This data made me realize that *TheNotebook* and *TheNotebook.fr* had in fact different dynamics: *TheNotebook.fr* was smaller, slow paced, and magazine-oriented compared to *TheNotebook*.

By contrast, the similarities between *LaPlace* and *TheNotebook* became clearer. The two websites had been founded by print journalists who had previously worked for prestigious print publications. Both had been created relatively early in the history of stand-alone news websites. Both had a liberal editorial line, mixed commentary and breaking news, had received major journalistic awards, and relied on advertising revenue as their main source of income. Both were owned by larger media companies and were trying (not always successfully) to be profitable. Last but not least, *LaPlace* had explicitly modeled itself on *TheNotebook*, both editorially and economically. In consequence, I decided to focus my analysis on *TheNotebook* and *LaPlace*—two organizations that I expected to converge.[4]

As is often the case in ethnographic projects, my research question evolved over time in what Iddo Tavory and Stefan Timmermans describe as an "abductive" process.[5] Based on the fieldwork I had conducted, I became particularly interested in the question of audience metrics. All of the websites I had observed used analytics software programs. During the interviews, most of the editors and the journalists brought up the subject of clicks, tweets, and audience analytics, even without my asking. Yet in spite of the fact that the same kind of audience data was available on both sides of the Atlantic, journalists used it very differently depending on the newsroom. In some places, Chartbeat was ubiquitous; in others, it was absent. I decided to focus on the uses and interpretations of audience data, keeping a toolkit of different theoretical frameworks at hand (field theory, economic sociology, science and technology studies, and so on) to make sense of these findings. In an effort to achieve theoretical sampling, I continued my fieldwork with the explicit goal of getting as much variation as possible in how news organizations and journalists used web metrics.[6] I conducted additional fieldwork and interviews at *TheNotebook* in February-March 2013 and at *LaPlace* in April-May 2013. In parallel, I studied several other websites that journalists often described as "competitors" of *TheNotebook* and *LaPlace*.[7]

All in all, I conducted more than 500 hours of observations in eight web newsrooms. I did 101 interviews for this project: 45 in the United States, 56 in France. Of the 45 interviews conducted in the United States, 28 were with journalists, editors, managers, data specialists, and freelancers working for *TheNotebook*. Of the 56 interviews I did in Paris, 33 were with journalists, editors, managers, freelancers, and bloggers working for *LaPlace*. Of all the interviews, 34 were with women; the rest were men. I interviewed 22 journalists who were under 30 years old, 58 journalists who were between 30 and 45 years old, and 21 journalists who were above 45 years old. Seven interviewees were racial or ethnic minorities; 38 were freelancers at the time of the interview; 38 journalists had a journalism degree. The main differences between the French and American interviewees were the proportion of women (25 percent in the United States against 40 percent in France) and the percentage of people who had a journalism degree (11 percent in the United States, 58 percent in France).[8] I recorded all the interviews, transcribed, and translated them myself. I stopped doing intensive fieldwork in the fall of 2014, but did follow-up interviews and occasional observations until the fall of 2015.

Two days before my dissertation defense, in July 2014, an interview about my research was published on a French news website, with the following headline (which I had not chosen): "Chasing the audience, uniformizing the news, web journalism in a race to the bottom."[9] The article was read in many French newsrooms. Journalists wrote about it on Twitter, discussing and sometimes contesting my findings. I received multiple emails asking for my dissertation. This was somewhat terrifying. "Giving back" to the people one studies is standard practice in ethnography. In this case, however, the process through which many of my French interviewees learned about my findings was probably the worst possible way. Over time, I developed better strategies for presenting my research to the journalists who had generously given me time, access, and information.[10]

Since then, I kept up with many of them. I met them for coffees and lunches, in New York and Paris. I followed their careers and writings. I ran into them at conferences at Stanford University, the Data & Society Institute, the Knight Foundation, The New School for Social Research, Sciences Po, and other places. I keep reading the websites they write for. And every single day, for better or for worse, I follow what they post on Twitter. I will return to this point later.

Experiencing the Field

One's position in the field is never neutral, as we know from ethnographic scholarship. From the colonial underpinnings of classical anthropology to the deeply embodied experiences that come with most fieldwork sites, understanding the position from which one speaks is essential in order to better situate the material collected and analyzed.[11] Reflecting on my position as an observer in web newsrooms in New York and Paris, several points come to mind.

I was born and raised in Paris, where I also did my undergraduate studies. This affected my research project—I wanted to spend time there—but also the kind of access I had in the two countries. In France, getting in touch with journalists was easy. Paris is a small world for elites. Power networks are highly concentrated, and journalists, politicians, and academics share multiple ties. Through friends and colleagues, I found many contacts in the web newsrooms I wanted to study. Whenever I interviewed French journalists, the interview typically started with a ritual couple of minutes figuring out how many people we knew in common.[12]

In contrast, getting access to journalists and newsrooms in New York was a more complicated endeavor. I started by asking graduate school friends, colleagues, and professors to refer me to people they knew; I met several journalists that way. Yet my main strategy was mass cold email-ing. Whenever I identified a journalist who regularly wrote for one of the online publications I was interested in, I would search for their email ad-dress online. I would then send them one, two, or up to three emails asking for an interview. Most of these emails never received a response; others did. Overall, I was very grateful to all the journalists and editors who took the time to meet with me.

This difference in familiarity was somewhat mirrored in the kind of access I obtained at *TheNotebook* and *LaPlace*. Indeed, my position as an observer starkly differed at the two websites. Overall, *TheNotebook*'s management was very cautious about letting observers enter their offices. Akin to a technology company, they seemed to fear divulging their "secret sauce" to outsiders. They saw their newsroom as a space that needed to be protected from external interference. Thus, the top editors met my request to conduct observation in the newsroom with care and set strict rules for my presence. They sent emails to the whole staff that introduced me, summarized my project, and mentioned the duration of my stay. They carefully inspected the consent forms that I handed them. Staffers them-selves were often surprised and cautious when they saw me, sometimes double-checking with their superiors whether they were allowed to share a bit of information with me (see chapter 6). They made jokes about being interviewed, which they found unusual. They asked about my project and how long it would take to publish it.

At *LaPlace*, in contrast, the team took little notice of me. The news-room was almost like a public space: there would often be people visiting—observers, academics, or other journalists. "The bosses" (*les chefs*) accepted my presence in the newsroom without questions and immediately signed the consent forms. They never asked how long or how often I would come. They never formally introduced me to the team. I tried to create a regular routine, such as coming on specific days per week. Each time, the editors' response was, "Sure, just send us an email in the morning when you're coming." At the time, I surmised that this absence of curiosity was a consequence of the other research projects that had already been con-ducted at *LaPlace*. Indeed, several sociologists had already done fieldwork in the newsroom before I started my project.[13] Thus, I was "old news" for the Parisian journalists, who were nonetheless generous with their time: they met with me for interviews, invited me to join them for their cigarette and lunch breaks, and sent me information over email that they thought might be useful for my research.

Overall, during my days of fieldwork, I noticed that I had stronger affinities with younger journalists, and with journalists who had a more intellectual profile, both in Paris and in New York. They were usually more educated: French journalists had studied in *classes préparatoires*; American journalists had attended a Master's program. These journalists were mostly women and were more likely to write for the "soft" part of news websites: culture and the arts, gender and sex, work and employment, health, and justice. They often witnessed the growing role of web metrics firsthand (see chapter 4) and found my project interesting for that reason. The strong ties that I established with them—they "vouched" for me in the office and were the ones who invited me to join the informal events organized by the journalists—shaped the kind of material I was able to collect, as well as my analysis and interpretation of the findings.

Interactions could be more complicated with male journalists covering traditionally prestigious beats such as politics, economy and finance, international news, and so on. Many of them adhered to a more competitive view of journalism being about breaking news, high-stakes investigative reporting, and scooping one's rivals.[14] These journalists did not particularly enjoy being interviewed. In fact, they often actively subverted the interview situation, turning it into one of the two scenarios they seemed to be more comfortable with: flirting, or meeting with potential sources. This happened several times in Paris, where male political journalists would agree to meet for interviews but only at night and in bars, even though I told them that loud settings made it harder to record and transcribe interviews.

For instance, I remember a Parisian political journalist in his forties who kept calling me "the spy," chuckling each time he passed me by in the office of newsroom. One day, during an editorial meeting, I was sitting in the back of the room taking notes. The journalists—most of whom were men—were discussing a piece of political gossip, disagreeing about whether to publish it or not. At some point, the journalist in question addressed me (in front of a room of thirty people), shouting "hey, be careful about what you write, this information shouldn't leave the room!" I mumbled that I had no intention of sharing the news. When I finally met him for an interview, a week later, he set our appointment at a bar. He refused to answer most of my questions. When he did answer, he kept telling me that things were "off the record." He also repeatedly reversed the interview situation, asking me questions about my background, project, and personal life. This made me realize that my presence could be perceived as a threat—as a woman connected to an Ivy League university, asking questions not about the noble parts of their job but about the "dirty" topic of audience metrics. Situations like these occurred less often in New York, where male political journalists were more often indifferent than aggressive in my presence.[15]

These distinct modalities of access made me notice how different the relationship between journalists and academics continues to be in the two countries. Overall, I felt that the close connections between academia and journalism that developed during and after the Dreyfus affair had an enduring legacy in France (see chapter 1). This was in part due to broader forces, such as the tight structure of elite higher education and the small network of *classes préparatoires* and *grandes écoles* in Paris. Conversely, my lack of journalistic connections on the East Coast of the United States made me think in a more analytical way about the separation between academia and journalism in the American context. Of course, this feeling of estrangement could also have been an effect of my position as a freshly arrived international student, as a nonnative English speaker with a marked accent, and as someone raised in another country. Regardless, these differences, as well as my built-in familiarity with the French context, informed the nature of my relationship with journalists in the two countries, as well as my understanding of the connections between journalists, academics, and intellectuals at the center of this book.

A "Fly on the Screen"? Studying Digital Workplaces

Web journalists spend most of their waking lives online. They switch between screens constantly, moving between their desktop computers, laptops, tablets, and smartphones. They publish articles, tweet, answer comments, write for personal blogs and for other publications. They are also active consumers of digital content, doing background research, searching for information, conducting interviews on Skype, and taking photos and videos with their smartphones for their articles. They communicate with colleagues and friends through multiple digital channels, including emails, group chats, text messages, tweets, and Facebook posts. They organize their time and schedule meetings through online calendars and shared invitations. In short, more often than not, they are looking at screens.[16]

How can ethnographers study people who are constantly connected to the internet? Ethnographic methods were first developed for the study of remote and bounded communities. In anthropological classics such as

Bronislaw Malinowski's analysis of Trobriand islanders or Claude Levi-Strauss's fieldwork with Amazonian tribes, the anthropologist travels to a remote country and encounters a relatively untouched, homogeneous social group. Research questions changed over time, but ethnographic methods have remained more or less the same. Ethnographers frequently explain that they rely on a "fly on the wall" strategy, "hanging out" and "going along" with the groups and communities they are studying, with little overt or explicit intervention.[17] This framework also informs recent ethnographic approaches focusing on complex and distributed forms of social organization, from the study of scientific laboratories and hierarchical firms to postcolonial, global, and multisited processes.[18]

The development of online technologies poses unique challenges and opportunities for ethnographers. Here I use the metaphor of a "fly on the screen" to describe the toolkit of tactics I developed to analyze web journalists and their work in New York and Paris.[19] These include in-depth ethnographic observations of digitally mediated workplaces, interviews complemented by Twitter traces, and a quantitative study of several large data sets based on web crawls. These different approaches allowed me to triangulate the journalists' discourses in ways that would not have been possible had I not used all these types of data.

Observations and the "Rotation" Tactic

The first strategy in my toolkit was observation. I wanted to get a sense of journalists' work practices, professional norms, and occupational communities in action. I had planned to rely on the method of "shadowing" web journalists throughout their workdays.[20] After a couple of weeks doing fieldwork, however, I realized that this was not quite working in web newsrooms, for several reasons. First, many of the journalists I studied remained largely silent throughout the day: they mostly communicated with their colleagues through emails, texts, or chat tools. I could not really follow them around unobtrusively: they usually stayed at their desk, only leaving to make phone calls or interviews with sources for their articles.

In addition, the journalists often felt uncomfortable having me stay with them for long periods of time. The main reason was that—like most of us—they were constantly multitasking.[21] Journalists always had multiple windows opened on their computer screens. Some of these windows were work-related: journalists would have a Word document where they would write their articles, a tweet deck (a desktop program compiling information from Twitter) where they would follow what other journalists were posting, a group chat where they would interact with their colleagues, a content management system to upload articles, and so on. But they also had other windows open that did not necessarily relate to their work. These included private text message threads, online shopping searches, travel booking webpages, pictures of parties or family, etc. Many journalists felt self-conscious about these activities. Whenever I asked them whether I could observe their work, they often started by hurriedly closing several windows, making jokes and telling me that they were not watching pornography.

The strategy I developed to make my presence less intrusive was to adopt what I came to call the "rotation" method. Whenever I arrived in a newsroom, I would start at the first table on one side of the room, asking the closest journalist whether I could sit with them for an hour. If they agreed (they almost always did, except when they were about to go out for an interview), I pulled an office chair—preferably one with wheels, so that I could roll around—and sat down slightly behind them, in a way that made it possible for me to look at their screen without interfering with their work. For the next sixty minutes, I would take notes on what they were doing, copying what they were writing, what kind of messages they were exchanging, and which windows they were opening. When I did not understand what they were doing, I asked them about it. After an hour, I would move to the next closest journalist. Once I was done with the first table, I would move to the next table. The next day, I would start where I left off. When I was done with the tour of the office, I would start over at the first table.

This rotation method had several advantages. First, by telling journalists that I would only be there for an hour, I gave them a manageable timeframe: most journalists seemed fine avoiding private browsing for sixty minutes. At the same time, an hour was long enough that many of them would—to some extent—forget my presence. They would act self-consciously for the first fifteen minutes, turning around frequently to ask me questions or explain what they were doing, but after a while they would stop caring and go back to work. In addition, the rotation method structured expectations in the newsrooms. Journalists knew that I was going around the tables, one workstation at a time. They were not surprised when I came and asked if I could sit with them. In fact, many complained when for some reason I had to change my routine, joking that they were not interesting enough for me to observe their work.

Offline and Online: Combining Interviews and Twitter Traces

In parallel, I relied on interviews to understand how journalists made sense of their work. But I adjusted the interview method to account for the online activities of web journalists, complementing it with a systematic analysis of their online traces on Twitter and other platforms.

The interview process almost always started with an email exchange in which I would introduce my project and ask to meet for an interview at a place of their choice (cafes, sometimes bars, less often offices or apartments).[22] I would always let them pick the place, simply mentioning that I would record the interview and that I would prefer a somewhat quiet place. The interviews were semi-structured. I typically began by asking about their motivation for becoming a journalist. I then retraced their career before focusing on their current job. I asked about their traffic numbers, often focusing on a specific article with either high or low numbers. This was useful to get a better sense of how closely they followed audience metrics. When it seemed as though the interview was about to end, I asked about the "best" and "worst" articles that they had ever published, asking why they had picked them. I concluded the interview with socioeconomic and demographic questions.

Following the interviews, I would search for information online about the journalists and their production. I looked at how successful the articles the journalists had designated as their "best" and "worst" ones had been in terms of traffic, to see whether they adhered to editorial or click-based evaluation. I also usually followed up by sending them an email asking whether they could send me further information about some subject we had talked about. Through this follow-up method, I was given access to several internal emails (with the promise that I would anonymize them), screenshots, access codes to web analytics software programs and chat tools that newsrooms were using, and so on.

In parallel, I systematically followed journalists on Twitter. Almost all of them had a profile on the social networking site. Most were very active, tweeting, retweeting, and liking posts multiple times a day. As we saw in chapter 3, news websites also use Twitter to promote their content. I followed their pages as well. Consequently, over the course of my project, Twitter became an essential source of information about the journalists and newsrooms I was studying. In particular, it is an excellent tool to better understand the boundaries that journalists established between different kinds of publications, in New York and in Paris (see chapter 5).

From endorsements and retweets to "clashes" and disputes, web journalists often made their professional values and preferences visible on Twitter.

One incident may give a sense of what these disputes looked like and what they meant regarding the structure of the field. In April 2013, I was conducting observations at *FrenchMag*, a website that was often described as one of *LaPlace*'s rivals. That afternoon, *FrenchMag* had posted an article about the singer Beyoncé, who had been seen wearing a revealing costume. The headline of the article was a pun based on a slang word to describe women's breasts. Right after the article was published, *FrenchMag*'s managing editor sneered: "Gael [from *LaPlace*] just tweeted that our Beyoncé article is '*degrading*.' ... That this is not '*his* vision of journalism ...' [*his emphasis*]." The staffers took a couple of seconds to look at the incriminating tweet. One of them commented: "What a hypocrite.... It means that he clicked on the article! Such bad faith!" Another writer concurred: "They pick the wrong battle at *LaPlace*.... I mean, I never check their website, I don't find it interesting, so why do they keep checking our site?" When I went back home, I took a screenshot of Gael's tweet. Several journalists I knew had reacted to the post during the day, discussing whether the pun was vulgar or not. Episodes like this one provided data on the position-takings between different websites that I used to complement my analysis.[23]

Long after I was done with my fieldwork, I continued to rely on Twitter to keep up with the world of online news. As I write this manuscript, I continue to check Twitter multiple times a day. Through the algorithmic sorting of the social media platform, I learn about the publications and career updates of the web journalists I interviewed. Journalists usually publicize their articles there; other journalists then "retweet" the articles, effectively rebroadcasting them, often with a comment. Over the years, I have been taking screenshots of these exchanges whenever they involve journalists I met for this project. This has been incredibly helpful for identifying networks of like-minded writers. Journalists also usually post significant career changes on Twitter, announcing new positions, sometimes detailing what they hope to achieve there. I have used this data to map evolving connections between news organizations. In network terms, whenever a journalist moves from one newsroom to another, she or he creates a tie between two nodes. Thus, newsrooms that "exchange" many journalists can be described as close, whereas newsrooms that do not exchange journalists are more distant. This data helped me map the fields of *TheNotebook* and *LaPlace*, as well as their evolutions over time.

This use of social media data to complement interviews and observations constitutes a major change for ethnographic research in a data-saturated world.[24] In particular, it transforms the kind of rapport ethnographers have with the people they study. Traditionally, scholars would leave the field after an intense period of embedded ethnographic research. They would rarely go back to the places and communities they had studied—a mechanism called the "disengagement process" in ethnographic methods.[25] In the brave new world of digital technologies, however, ethnographers can never fully "disengage." Every day, I see what the journalists I interviewed and spent time with for this project are publishing. I read their jokes and follow their interactions with colleagues. I "like" and "retweet" their posts; they sometimes do the same for mine. In other words, and to use a concept from this book, we remain part of each other's algorithmic publics.

This algorithmically gathered information provides a more complete understanding of how journalistic careers and networks evolve over time, but it also comes at a price. The past and the present of ethnographic observations are forever connected. Instead of relying on a settled standpoint to interpret the qualitative data I gathered in 2011–2015, my analysis is guided by a more fluid understanding of the journalists' positions and identities over time. For better or for worse, this week's Twitter feed continues to affect how I make sense of the ethnographic data I collected years ago.

Web Crawls and Large Data Sets

To complement this ethnographic data and Twitter traces about journalists and news organizations, I worked with several computer scientists to collect large data sets based on the online content published by *TheNotebook* and *LaPlace*. I wanted to check whether the discourses of staff writers and editors about the chase for clicks actually matched the evolution of publication rhythms and traffic numbers for the two websites over time.

With the assistance of a computer scientist in Paris, I first did a pilot study in which we devised a web crawl to collect all the articles published in the central column of *LaPlace*'s website between May 2007 and September 2012—a total of 13,159 articles. We then gathered information on the characteristics of the articles themselves: the time of publication, the number of words, quotes, images, and hyperlinks present in the text, and the "tags" of the article. We also gathered data on the articles' online popularity, including the number of visitors, number of times the article was mentioned on Twitter, the number of times the article was "liked" on Facebook, and the number of comments left by readers. I manually collected and coded information about the authors, such as their name, the number of authors, their status (staffer, freelancer, or blogger), and the gender of the author.

I conducted a statistical analysis of this data set to trace the determinants of online popularity, the results of which were published in 2015.[25] Yet this pilot data was problematic, for several reasons. First, articles that were never published on the homepage of the website were not included in the sample. Second, the sample did not include a type of article informally called "HuffPos"—short rewrites of external web content that became an important part of the Parisian website's strategy in the chase for clicks (see chapter 5). Last but not least, it was impossible to collect equally detailed data for *TheNotebook*: the New York website did not have the same structure and did not make its traffic numbers public.

Thus, in 2017, I decided to collect new data about *TheNotebook* and *LaPlace*. In collaboration with two Stanford students, we collected all the articles published by *TheNotebook* and *LaPlace* between 2009 and 2015—a total of 91,270 articles for *TheNotebook* and 60,816 articles for *LaPlace*. For *TheNotebook*, we used the website search feature and collected each article's URL, title, description, the URL of the image featured with the article (when available), the section of the article, the rubric, the publication date and time, the author's name, and the word count. We gathered comparable data for *LaPlace*, going through the articles' URLs and collecting data about the time and date of publication, section, title, and word count.

Overall, the statistical analysis of this new data supported most of the qualitative discourses provided by editors and staff writers. But it also raised interesting questions whenever the numbers did not quite match what journalists were saying. In some cases, the reason for the discrepancy made sense. For example, *TheNotebook*'s editor-in-chief said in an interview that the number of articles published on the website had tripled under his tenure. The statistical analysis revealed that it had in fact been multiplied by about 2.5. "Triple" sounds better than "2.5," especially when one is an editor-in-chief. In that case, the gap between our data and the journalists' discourses was not particularly surprising.[26]

In other cases, the statistical data provided more intriguing results, which reoriented my analysis. For instance, I realized that the average length of the articles published on *TheNotebook* and *LaPlace* evolved in different directions over time. Overall, the mean length of articles remained stable at *TheNotebook* between 2009 and 2015, around 660 words. In contrast, the mean length of *LaPlace*'s articles increased from about 400 in 2009 to 700 in 2015. This was surprising, since the journalists working for *TheNotebook* and *LaPlace* had similarly complained during my fieldwork about the decreasing length and depth of the articles they were writing (see chapters 3 and 5). This made me look more closely at the different types of articles being published on the two websites. It turned out that most of the evolution on the French side was driven by the increasing number of words in the short "HuffPos," whereas the length of the "fast" aggregation-based articles published on *TheNotebook* remained relatively stable over time.

I used this statistical analysis to better contextualize the ethnographic material I had collected in web newsrooms. This tactic allowed me to go beyond the discourses and representations of journalists. Similar mixed-method and multimedia approaches could be used beyond the case of web journalism. Indeed, given the sheer amount of information we leave through digital footprints, scholars can complement ethnographic material with qualitative and quantitative analyses of the online traces of the people and communities they study.[27] This provides new opportunities for the triangulation and cross-verification of ethnographic material through multiple sources. At the same time, it raises important questions about privacy, informed consent, and the right to exploit online information for research at a time when most of our data is harvested by for-profit companies for advertising purposes.[28]

Conclusion

A "fly on the screen" is how I described to journalists the toolkit of strategies I developed over time to study highly connected web newsrooms. Ethnographic "rotations" and observations, interviews complemented by Twitter traces, and large data sets based on online content together constituted my approach for studying the rapidly changing routines of web journalists in the digital era. This appendix includes reflections on some of the challenges associated with this kind of research. I described my trajectory, in between Paris and New York, and contextualized the ethnographic material I collected for this book based on my position in the field.

Spending time in web newsrooms has made me particularly conscious of the privilege that comes with being an academic, especially one working at a research institution such as Stanford University. It took me eight years from the beginning of my dissertation research to write this book. Each chapter, concept, and ethnographic note went through multiple iterations and rounds of feedback. In contrast, web journalists generally write their stories in a few hours, or at most several days. This hurried pace does not only characterize journalistic work; it is also constitutive of the market for online content more generally. Overall, web journalism is transforming so quickly that the findings of this book may already be describing a discrete historical moment, far removed from the current preoccupations of web journalists. Yet the broader argument developed here about the meanings of digital metrics is applicable beyond the specific case of web newsrooms in New York and Paris. Given the rapid transformations of the news ecosystem, I also hope that journalists will recognize in this book a version of their voices and dilemmas, transcribed back from the seemingly distant past of the early 2010s.

NOTES

·········

Introduction

1. See Angwin, Julia, 2014, *Dragnet Nation: A Quest for Privacy, Security, and Freedom in a World of Relentless Surveillance*, New York: Times Books, Henry Holt and Company; Pariser, Eli, 2011, *The Filter Bubble: How the New Personalized Web Is Changing What We Think and How We Read*, London: Penguin; Bakshy, Eytan, Solomon Messing, and Lada A. Adamic, 2015, "Exposure to Ideologically Diverse News and Opinion on Facebook," *Science* 348 (6239): 1130–1132; Barocas, Solon, and Andrew D. Selbst, 2016, "Big Data's Disparate Impact," *California Law Review* 104: 671–732. On the metaphor of data as the new oil, see Tarnoff, Ben, 2017, "Silicon Valley Siphons Our Data Like Oil. But the Deepest Drilling Has Just Begun," *The Guardian*, August 23, retrieved: https://www.theguardian.com/world/2017/aug/23/silicon-valley-big-data-extraction-amazon-whole-foods-facebook.

2. For overviews, see Scholz, Trebor, 2012, *Digital Labor: The Internet as Playground and Factory*, New York: Routledge; Graham, Mark, and Mohammad Amir Anwar, 2018, "Digital Labour," in *Digital Geographies*, edited by J. Ash, R. Kitchin, and Leszczynski, London: Sage; Rosenblat, Alex, Tamara Kneese, and danah boyd, 2014, "Workplace Surveillance," *SSRN Electronic Journal*, retrieved: https://repository.usfca.edu/cgi/viewcontent.cgi?article=1021&context=ms.

3. On quantification before and after digitization, see Desrosières, Alain, 2000, *La politique des grands nombres. Histoire de la raison statistique*, Paris: La Découverte; Hacking, Ian, 1990, *The Taming of Chance*, Cambridge; New York: Cambridge University Press; Carruthers, Bruce G., and Wendy N. Espeland, 1991, "Accounting for Rationality: Double-Entry Bookkeeping and the Rhetoric of Economic Rationality," *American Journal of Sociology* 97 (1): 31–69; Deringer, William, 2018, *Calculated Values: Finance, Politics, and the Quantitative Age*, Cambridge, MA: Harvard University Press; Bouk, Dan, 2015, *How Our Days Became Numbered: Risk and the Rise of the Statistical Individual*, Chicago: University of Chicago Press; Espeland, Wendy Nelson, and Mitchell L. Stevens, 1998, "Commensuration as a Social Process," *Annual Review of Sociology* 24 (1): 313–343; Porter, Theodore M., 1996, *Trust in Numbers. The Pursuit of Objectivity in Science and Public Life*, Princeton: Princeton University Press; Zelizer, Viviana, 1994, *Pricing the Priceless Child: The Changing Social Value of Children*, Princeton: Princeton University Press; Brubaker, Rogers, 1984, *The Limits of Rationality: An Essay on the Social and Moral Thought of Max Weber*, London; Boston: Allen & Unwin; Fourcade, Marion, 2010, *Economists and Societies: Discipline and Profession in the United States, Britain, and France, 1890s to 1990s*, Princeton: Princeton University Press; Igo, Sarah, 2008, *The Averaged American*, Cambridge, MA: Harvard University Press; Rottenburg, Richard, Sally E. Merry, Sung Joon Park, and Johanna Mugler, eds., 2015, *The World of Indicators. The Making*

of Governmental Knowledge through Quantification, Cambridge: Cambridge University Press; Bucher, Taina, 2018, *If … Then. Algorithmic Power and Politics*, Oxford: Oxford University Press. On data, mechanization, and automation, see Zuboff, Shoshana, 1988, *In the Age of the Smart Machine: The Future of Work and Power*, New York: Basic Books; Noble, David F., 1984, *Forces of Production: A Social History of Industrial Automation*, New York: Knopf. Zelizer, Viviana A., 1997, *The Social Meaning of Money*, Princeton: Princeton University Press. Note that techniques of quantification and worker surveillance in the U.S. context and elsewhere cannot be separated from the history of slavery and the tracking of African Americans. See Browne, Simone, 2015, *Dark Matters. On the Surveillance of Blackness*, Durham: Duke University Press Books; Noble, Safiya U., 2018, *Algorithms of Oppression: How Search Engines Reinforce Racism*, New York: NYU Press; Cottom, Tressie McMillan, 2017, "Black Cyber Feminism: Intersectionality, Institutions, and Digital Sociology," in *Digital Sociologies*, edited by J. Daniels, K. Gregory, and T. McMillan Cottom, Bristol, UK: Policy Press, 211–232; Benjamin, Ruha, 2019, *Race after Technology*, New York: Polity Press; Desmond, Matthew, 2019, "If You Want to Understand the Brutality of American Capitalism, You Have to Start on the Plantation," *New York Times*, Aug. 14, retrieved: https://www.nytimes.com/interactive/2019/08/14/magazine/slavery-capitalism.html.

4. See Boczkowski, Pablo J., 2005, *Digitizing the News: Innovation in Online Newspapers*, Cambridge: MIT Press; Anderson, Chris, 2013, *Rebuilding the News: Metropolitan Journalism in the Digital Age*, Philadelphia: Temple University Press; Usher, Nikki, 2014, *Making News at The New York Times*, Ann Arbor: University of Michigan Press; Ryfe, David M., 2012, *Can Journalism Survive? An Inside Look at American Newsrooms*, London: Polity; Nielsen, Rasmus Kleis, 2016, "The Many Crises of Western Journalism: A Comparative Analysis of Economic Crises, Professional Crises, and Crises of Confidence," pp. 77–97 in Alexander, Jeffrey C., Elizabeth Butler Breese, and Maria Luengo, eds., 2016, *The Crisis of Journalism Reconsidered*, New York: Cambridge University Press; Cagé, Julia. 2015. *Sauver les médias. Capitalisme, financement participatif et démocratie*, Paris: Le Seuil, La Républiquedes idées; Downie Jr., Leonard, and Michael Schudson, 2009, "The Reconstruction of American Journalism," *Columbia Journalism Review*, October 19, retrieved: https://archives.cjr.org/reconstruction/the_recon struction_of_american.php. For recent data on the sources of revenues of news organizations in the United States, see Pew Research Center's Project for Excellence in Journalism, 2016, *The State of the News Media 2016*, retrieved: http://assets .pewresearch.org/wpcontent/uploads/sites/13/2016/06/30143308/state-of-the -news-media-report-2016-final.pdf. On audience metrics, see Anderson, Chris W., 2011, "Between Creative and Quantified Audiences: Web Metrics and Changing Patterns of Newswork in Local US Newsrooms," *Journalism* 12 (5): 550–566; Usher, Nikki, 2013, "Al Jazeera English Online: Understanding Web Metrics and News Production When a Quantified Audience Is Not a Commodified Audience," *Digital Journalism* 1 (3): 335–351; Petre, Caitlin, 2015, "The Traffic Factories: Metrics at Chartbeat, *Gawker Media*, and *The New York Times*," Tow Center for Digital Journalism, Columbia University School of Journalism; Christin, Angèle, 2018, "Counting Clicks. Quantification and Variation in Web Journalism in the United States and France," *American Journal of Sociology*, 123 (5): 1382–1415.

5. See, for instance, Edmonds, Rick, 2014, "Time to Ditch Uniques and Page Views for Engagement in Measuring Digital Audiences," *Poynter*, March 17, retrieved: https://www.poynter.org/reporting-editing/2014/time-to-ditch-uniques-and -page-views-for-engagement-in-measuring-digital-audiences/; Foer, Franklin, 2017, "When Silicon Valley Took over Journalism," *The Atlantic*, September, retrieved: https://www.theatlantic.com/magazine/archive/2017/09/when-silicon-valley -took-over-journalism/534195/; Chin, Jeff, 2018, "We Detox from Chartbeat," *NiemanLab*, Predictions of Journalism 2019, retrieved: https://www.niemanlab .org/2018/12/we-detox-from-chartbeat/; Schmidt, Christine, 2019, "How to Build a Newsroom Culture That Cares about Metrics Beyond Pageviews," Nieman Lab, March 13, retrieved: https://www.niemanlab.org/2019/03/how-to-build-a -newsroom-culture-that-cares-about-metrics-beyond-pageviews/; Kramer, Melody, 2019, "How to Build a Metrics-Savvy Newsroom," American Press Institute, March 13, retrieved: https://www.americanpressinstitute.org/publications/how -to-build-a-metrics-savvy-newsroom/single-page/. For a broader analysis, see McChesney, Robert W., and Victor W. Pickard, eds., 2011, *Will the Last Reporter Please Turn out the Lights: The Collapse of Journalism and What Can Be Done to Fix It*, New York: New Press. For a rare positive take on metrics (by *The Guardian*'s editor for strategic projects and former audience editor), see Moran, Chris, 2019, "You May Hate Metrics, But They're Making Journalism Better," *Columbia Journalism Review*, April 2, retrieved: https://www.cjr.org/innovations /you-may-hate-metrics-guardian-audience-twitter-images.php.

6. Starkman, Dean, 2010, "The Hamster Wheel," *Columbia Journalism Review*, September 14, retrieved: http://archives.cjr.org/cover_story/the_hamster_wheel.php.

7. Silverman, Craig, 2016, "This Analysis Shows How Viral Fake News Stories Outperformed Real News on Facebook," *BuzzFeed*, November 16; boyd, danah, 2016a, "Reality Check: I Blame the Media," *Points*, November 9, retrieved: https:// points.datasociety.net/reality-check-de447f2131a3.

8. See Lamont, Michèle, 1992, *Money, Morals, and Manners: The Culture of the French and American Upper-Middle Class*, Chicago: University of Chicago Press; Lamont, Michèle, and Laurent Thévenot, eds., 2000, *Rethinking Comparative Cultural Sociology: Repertoires of Evaluation in France and the United States*, Cambridge: Cambridge University Press; Tocqueville, Alexis de, 2003, *Democracy in America*, London: Penguin. Regarding the distinct journalistic traditions in the two countries, see Benson, Rodney, 2013, *Shaping Immigration News: A French-American Comparison*, Cambridge: Cambridge University Press; Padioleau, Jean G., 1985, *"Le Monde" et le "Washington Post": Précepteurs et mousquetaires*, Paris: Presses Universitaires de France. We will return to these differences in chapter 1.

9. On Big Data, see Mayer-Schönberger, Viktor, and Kenneth Cukier, 2013, *Big Data: A Revolution That Will Transform How We Live, Work, and Think*, Boston: Houghton Mifflin Harcourt; boyd, danah, and Kate Crawford, 2012, "Critical Questions for Big Data: Provocations for a Cultural, Technological, and Scholarly Phenomenon," *Information, Communication, and Society* 15 (5): 662–679. On algorithms, Mazzotti, Massimo, 2017, "Algorithmic Life," *Los Angeles Review of Books*, January 22, retrieved: https://lareviewofbooks.org/article/algorithmic-life/; Seaver, Nick, 2017, "Algorithms as Culture. Some Tactics for the

Ethnography of Algorithmic Systems," *Big Data & Society* 4 (2); Ziewitz, Malte, 2016, "Governing Algorithms: Myth, Mess, and Methods," *Science, Technology, & Human Values* 41 (1): 3–16.

10. This definition draws on Barocas, Solon, Alex Rosenblat, danah boyd, Seeta Pena Gangdharan, and Corrine Yu, 2014, "Data & Civil Rights: Technology Primer," *Data & Civil Rights Conference*, October, retrieved: https://papers.ssrn.com/sol3/papers.cfm?abstract_id=2536579.

11. This distinction between algorithms on the one hand and metrics and analytics on the other hand echoes the one developed by Karin Knorr-Cetina between algorithms and what she analyzes as "scopic systems." See Knorr-Cetina, Karin, 2003, "From Pipes to Scopes: The Flow Architecture of Financial Markets," *Distinktion* 2: 7–23. On data visualization, see Kennedy, Helen, Rosemary Lucy Hill, Giorgia Aiello, and William Allen, 2016, "The Work That Visualisation Conventions Do," *Information, Communication & Society* 19 (6): 715–735; Healy, Kieran, 2018, *Data Visualization: A Practical Introduction*, Princeton: Princeton University Press.

12. See, for instance, Miller, Alex P., 2018, "Want Less-Biased Decisions? Use Algorithms," *Harvard Business Review*, July 26, retrieved: https://hbr.org/2018/07/want-less-biased-decisions-use-algorithms; Anderson, Chris, 2008, "The End of Theory: The Data Deluge Makes the Scientific Method Obsolete," *Wired*, June 23, retrieved: https://www.wired.com/2008/06/pb-theory/.

13. See O'Neil, Cathy, 2016, *Weapons of Math Destruction: How Big Data Increases Inequality and Threatens Democracy*, New York: Crown; Pasquale, Frank, 2015, *The Black Box Society: The Secret Algorithms That Control Money and Information*, Cambridge, MA: Harvard University Press; Barocas and Selbst, "Big Data's Disparate Impact"; Broussard, Meredith, 2018, *Artificial Unintelligence. How Computers Misunderstand the World*, Cambridge, MA: MIT Press; Noble, *Algorithms of Oppression*; Couldry, Nick, and Ulises A. Mejias, 2019, *The Costs of Connection. How Data Is Colonizing Human Life and Appropriating It for Capitalism*, Stanford: Stanford University Press; Beer, David, 2016, *Metric Power*, London: Palgrave Macmillan; Muller, Jerry Z., 2018, *The Tyranny of Metrics*, Princeton: Princeton University Press. For analyses of quantification as a form of surveillance, discipline, and control, see Foucault, Michel, 2010, *The Birth of Biopolitics: Lectures at the Collège de France, 1978–79*, edited by M. Senellart, first paperback edition [repr.], New York: Picador; Foucault, Michel, 1995, *Discipline and Punish: The Birth of the Prison*, Second Vintage Books edition, New York: Vintage Books; Sauder, Michael, and Wendy Nelson Espeland, 2009, "The Discipline of Rankings: Tight Coupling and Organizational Change," *American Sociological Review* 74 (1): 63–82; Zuboff, Shoshana, 2019, *The Age of Surveillance Capitalism. The First for a Human Future at the New Frontier of Power*, New York: Public Affairs; Mau, Steffen, 2019, *The Metric Society: On the Quantification of the Social*, New York: Polity.

14. Zuboff, *Smart Machine*.

15. Christin, Angèle, 2017, "Algorithms in Practice: Comparing Web Journalism and Criminal Justice," *Big Data & Society* 4 (2): 1–14.

16. Note that this is largely due to methodological choice. When relying on ethnographic methods, one is often bound to study uses and practices. For a discussion, see Christin, "Algorithms in Practice"; Seaver, "Algorithms as Culture."

17. This is not to say that metrics perfectly or objectively represent the world that they bring in numbered form. On the social construction of representation, see Daston, Lorraine, and Peter Galison, 2007, *Objectivity*, Cambridge, MA: Zone Books; Coopmans, Catelijne, Janet Vertesi, Michael E. Lynch, and Steve Woolgar, 2014, *Representation in Scientific Practice Revisited*, Cambridge, MA: The MIT Press. On the "reactive" effects of metrics, see Espeland, Wendy Nelson, and Michael Sauder, 2007, "Rankings and Reactivity: How Public Measures Recreate Social Worlds," *American Journal of Sociology* 113 (1): 1–40.

18. My approach in turn participates in and draws on a growing and exciting body of ethnographic and qualitative research examining the practices and representations related to algorithmic systems. See, for instance, Brayne, Sarah, 2017, "Big Data Surveillance: The Case of Policing," *American Sociological Review* 82,5): 977–1008; Levy, Karen E. C., 2015, "The Contexts of Control: Information, Power, and Truck-Driving Work," *Information Society* 31 (2): 160–174; Ticona, Julia, and Alexandra Mateescu, 2018, "Trusted Strangers: Cultural Entrepreneurship on Domestic Work Platforms in the On Demand Economy," *New Media & Society* 20 (11): 4384–4404; Shestakofsky, Benjamin, 2017, "Working Algorithms: Software Automation and the Future of Work," *Work and Occupations* 44 (4): 376–423; Rosenblat, Alex, and Luke Stark, 2016, "Algorithmic Labor and Information Asymmetries. A Case Study of Uber Drivers," *International Journal of Communication* 10: 3758–3784; Bucher, Taina, 2017, "The Algorithmic Imaginary: Exploring the Ordinary Affects of Facebook Algorithms," *Information, Communication & Society* 20 (1): 30–44; Duffy, Brooke Erin, and Emily Hund, 2015, "'Having it All' on Social Media. Entrepreneurial Femininity and Self Branding Among Fashion Bloggers," *Social Media + Society*, 1–15; Petre, Caitlin, 2018, "Engineering Consent: How the Design and Marketing of Newsroom Analytics Tools Rationalize Journalists' Labor," *Digital Journalism* 6 (4): 509–527; Lane, Jeffrey, 2018, *The Digital Street*, New York: Oxford University Press; Ziewitz, Malte, 2019, "Rethinking Gaming: The Ethical Work of Optimization in Web Search Engines," *Social Studies of Science*, 1–25; Seaver, "Algorithms as Culture"; Ames, Morgan G., 2019, *The Charisma Machine. The Life, Death, and Legacy of One Laptop Per Child*, 2019, Cambridge: MIT Press; Gillespie, Tarleton, 2018, *Custodians of the Internet: Platforms, Content Moderation, and the Hidden Decisions That Shape Social Media*, New Haven: Yale University Press. These recent approaches in turn are profoundly informed by groundbreaking ethnographic work on the uses and practices connected to digital technologies. See boyd, danah, 2014, *It's Complicated: The Social Lives of Networked Teens*, New Haven: Yale University Press; Marwick, Alice E., 2013, *Status Update: Celebrity, Publicity, and Branding in the Social Media Age*, New Haven: Yale University Press; Neff, Gina, 2012, *Venture Labor: Work and the Burden of Risk in Innovative Industries*, Cambridge: MIT Press; Nelson, Alondra, 2016, *The Social Life of DNA: Race, Reparations, and Reconciliation after the Genome*, New York: Beacon Press.

19. This argument about the symbolic role of metrics is not limited to highly skilled, high-status occupations. For analyses of resistance and manipulation in blue-collar and service work, see Ticona and Mateescu, "Trusted Strangers"; Levy, "Contexts of Control"; Rosenblat, Alex, 2018, *Uberland: How Algorithms Are Rewriting the Rules of Work*, Berkeley: University of California Press; Adler-Bell,

Sam, 2019, "Surviving Amazon," *Logic*, Bodies, 8, retrieved: https://logicmag.io /bodies/surviving-amazon/.

20. Note that there are several other sets of analytics and algorithms currently being deployed in web newsrooms. First, machine-learning and data-mining models are used to find stories and strengthen accountability reporting by analyzing large data sets—this set of algorithms is designated through the term "data journalism" or "computational journalism." Second, algorithmic programs are also developed to automate the production of news articles (especially in sports or financial news), content moderation, and online distribution in what is often called "automated journalism." In this book, I do not analyze these distinct types of algorithms, which were not used in the newsrooms I studied, and which raise differently different questions than the analytics software programs and traffic metrics at the center of this study. For analyses of data and automated journalism, see Diakopoulos, Nicholas, 2019, *Automating the News: How Algorithms Are Rewriting the Media*, Cambridge, MA: Harvard University Press; Anderson, Chris W., 2018, *Apostles of Certainty: Data Journalism and the Politics of Doubt*, Oxford: Oxford University Press; Carlson, Matt, 2014, "The Robotic Reporter. Automated Journalism and the Redefinition of Labor, Compositional Forms, and Journalistic Authority," *Digital Journalism* 3 (3): 416–431; Lewis, Seth C., and Oscar Westlund, 2015, "Big Data and Journalism: Epistemology, Expertise, Economics, and Ethics," *Digital Journalism* 3 (3): 447–466.

21. The concept of "evaluation," which I use in the book and which is further developed in chapter 3, differs from the more widely used concept of "logic" insofar as it hopes to avoid reifying the set of cognitive and practical operations that are used in evaluating ideas, objects, and people under an overarching umbrella term. For a discussion of the idea of evaluation, see Lamont, Michele, 2012, "Toward a Comparative Sociology of Valuation and Evaluation," *Annual Review of Sociology* 38 (1): 201–221. For an overview of the concept of logic in organizational analysis and management research, see Thornton, Patricia H., William Ocasio, and Michael Lounsbury, 2012, *The Institutional Logics Perspective: A New Approach to Culture, Structure, and Process*, Oxford: Oxford University Press. For a critical appraisal of the concept of logic, see Swidler, Ann, 2003, *Talk of Love: How Culture Matters*. Chicago: University of Chicago Press.

22. Theoretically, this approach in terms of conflicting modes of evaluation draws on what has been labelled the valuation/evaluation perspective, which emphasizes the tension and conflicts that arise between different modes of valuation, for example, between moral, aesthetic, and economic understandings of "what counts." See Boltanski, Luc, and Laurent Thévenot, 2006, *On Justification: Economies of Worth*, Princeton: Princeton University Press; Stark, David, 2011, *The Sense of Dissonance: Accounts of Worth in Economic Life*, Princeton: Princeton University Press; Lamont, "Evaluation"; Swidler, *Love*; Fourcade, Marion, 2011, "Cents and Sensibility: Economic Valuation and the Nature of 'Nature,'" *American Journal of Sociology* 116 (6): 1721–1777; Anteby, Michel, 2008, *Moral Gray Zones: Side Productions, Identity, and Regulation in an Aeronautic Plant*, Princeton: Princeton University Press; Vatin, François, ed., 2009, *Évaluer et valoriser: Une sociologie économique de la mesure*, Toulouse: Presses Universitaires du Mirail; Beckert, Jens, and Patrik Aspers, 2011, *The Worth of Goods: Valuation and*

Pricing in the Economy, New York: Oxford University Press; Childress, C. Clayton, 2017, *Under the Cover: The Creation, Production, and Reception of a Novel*, Princeton: Princeton University Press; Gerber, Alison, 2017, *The Work of Art. Value in Creative Careers*, Stanford: Stanford University Press; Lena, Jennifer C., 2019, *Entitled: Discriminating Tastes and the Expansion of the Arts*, Princeton: Princeton University Press; Leschziner, Vanina, 2015, *At the Chef's Table. Culinary Creativity in Elite Restaurants*, Stanford: Stanford University Press; Chong, Phillipa K., 2019, *Inside the Critics' Circle. Book Reviewing in Uncertain Times*, Princeton: Princeton University Press.

23. Ibsen, Henrik, 1882, *An Enemy of the People*, retrieved: http://www.guten berg.org/files/2446/2446-h/2446-h.htm.

24. This would be in line with Bourdieu's analysis of journalism, for instance, when he writes that "the forces of commercial heteronomy ... are progressively gaining ground to such an extent that all fields—journalism, publishing, etc.—are governed by what could be called an 'audience ratings mentality,'" p. 43 in Bourdieu, Pierre, 2005, "The Political Field, the Social Science Field, and the Journalistic Field," pp. 30–47 in *Bourdieu and the Journalistic Field*, edited by R. Benson and E. Neveu, Cambridge, UK: Polity Press; Champagne, Patrick, and Dominique Marchetti, 2005, "The Contaminated Blood Scandal: Reframing Medical News," pp. 113–134 in Benson and Neveu, *Bourdieu and the Journalistic Field*; Duval, Julien, 2004, *Critique de la raison journalistique: Les transformations de la presse économique en France*, Paris: Seuil; Krause, Monika, 2011, "Reporting and the Transformations of the Journalistic Field: US News Media 1890–2000," *Media, Culture & Society* 33 (1): 89–104

25. On the "Americanization" approach, see Ritzer, George, 2011, *The McDonaldization of Society 6*, sixth edition, Los Angeles, London: Pine Forge, SAGE Publications. For the "hybridity" approach, see Hannerz, Ulf, "Scenarios for Peripheral Cultures," in *Culture, Globalization, and the World-System: Contemporary Conditions for the Representation of Identity*, edited by A. D. King, Minneapolis: University of Minnesota Press; Appadurai, Arjun, 1996, *Modernity at Large: Cultural Dimensions of Globalization*, Minneapolis: University of Minnesota Press; Sousa Santos, Boaventura, 2006, "The Heterogeneous State and Legal Pluralism in Mozambique," *Law & Society Review* 40: 39–76.

26. Important exceptions include Chen, Julie Y., 2018, "Thrown under the Bus and Outrunning It! The Logic of Didi and Taxi Drivers' Labour and Activism in the On-Demand Economy," *New Media & Society* 20 (8): 1–21; Wood, Alex J., Vili Lehdonvirta, and Mark Graham, 2018, "Workers of the Internet Unite? Online Freelancer Organization Among Remote Gig Economy Workers in Six Asian and African Countries," *New Technology, Work and Employment* 33 (2): 95–112; Irani, Lilly, 2019, *Chasing Innovation. Making Entrepreneurial Citizens in Modern India*, Princeton: Princeton University Press; Takhatev, Yuri, 2012, *Coding Places. Software Practice in a South American City*, Cambridge: MIT Press; Burrell, Jenna, 2012, *Invisible Users: Youth in the Internet Cafés of Urban Ghana*, Cambridge: MIT Press. See also Bozckowski, Pablo J., and Ignacio Siles, 2014, "Steps Toward Cosmopolitanism in the Study of Media Technologies," *Information, Communication & Society* 17 (5): 560–571; Wimmer, Andreas, and Nina G. Schiller, 2003, "Methodological Nationalism, the Social Sciences, and the Study

of Migration: An Essay in Historical Epistemology," *International Migration Review* 37 (3): 576–610; Christin, Angèle, 2016, "Is Journalism a Transnational Field? Asymmetrical Relations and Symbolic Domination in Online News," *The Sociological Review* 64 (2): 212–234.

27. Champagne, Patrick, 1995, "La double dépendance. Quelques remarques sur les rapports entre les champs politique, économique et journalistique," *Hermès* 17–18: 215–229; Bourdieu, Pierre, 1993, *The Field of Cultural Production*, New York: Columbia University Press; Bourdieu, Pierre, 1999a, *On Television*, New York: The New Press; Bourdieu, Pierre, and Loïc J. D. Wacquant, 1992, *An Invitation to Reflexive Sociology*, Chicago: University of Chicago Press; Benson and Neveu, *Bourdieu and the Journalistic Field*; Benson, Rodney, and Abigail C. Saguy, 2005, "Constructing Social Problems in an Age of Globalization: A French American Comparison," *American Sociological Review* 70 (2): 233–259; Christin, "Transnational Field." Note that there are other meso-level approaches to make sense of the journalistic landscape, including "media systems" as well as different interpretations of the concept of "fields." See Hallin, Daniel C., and Paolo Mancini, 2004, *Comparing Media Systems. Three Models of Media and Politics*, Cambridge, UK: Cambridge University Press; Ryfe, David, 2016, *Journalism and the Public*, New York: Polity. For the sake of the argument developed here, however, the Bourdieuian concept of the journalistic field turned out to be the most useful, for three reasons. First, at the macro- and global level, it makes it possible to compare not fixed entities but instead systems of relations between autonomous and heteronomous forces in the United States and France. Second, at the national level, it affords a relational view of the connections between news organizations and individual journalists. Third, at the micro-level, it provides a template (in terms of autonomous and heteronomous logics) for understanding the tension between editorial and click-based evaluation. These connections between the macro-, meso-, and micro-level are less developed in alternative frameworks (see Ryfe, *Journalism and the Public*, 11–12, for a discussion). That said, the perspective developed in *Metrics at Work* also expands field theory by putting at the center of the analysis the relationship of journalists and news organizations with their publics—a concept that remains somewhat missing from most field-based approaches (see Ananny, Mike. 2018, *Networked Press Freedom: Creating Infrastructures for a Public Right to Hear*, Cambridge: MIT Press). By focusing on the relationship between journalists and algorithmic publics, this book draws on a relational approach of occupations and professions. It bridges the production side (here, journalism) and the consumption side (here, the algorithmic publics). See Anteby, Michel, Curtis Chan, and Julia DiBenigno, 2016, "Three Lenses on Occupations and Professions in Organizations: Becoming, Doing, and Relating," *Academy of Management Annals* 10 (1): 183–244. Note that a more exhaustive relational analysis would also include sources, public officials, and sources—the "content," so to speak, of journalistic work. For an analysis of the triangular relationship between media, publics, and celebrities, see Marcus, Sharon, 2019, *The Drama of Celebrity*, Princeton: Princeton University Press.

28. See Ryfe, *Journalism and the Public*; Schudson, Michael, 2005, "Autonomy from What?" in Benson and Neveu, *Bourdieu and the Journalistic Field*, 214–223.

29. For comparative approaches of journalistic production in the United States and France, see Benson, *Shaping Immigration News*; Hallin and Mancini, *Comparing Media Systems*; Padioleau, *Précepteurs et mousquetaires*. On the American side, see Schudson, Michael, 1978, *Discovering the News: A Social History of American Newspapers*, New York: Basic Books; Starr, Paul, 2005, *The Creation of the Media: Political Origins of Modern Communications*, New York: Basic Books; Hamilton, James T., 2006, *All the News That's Fit to Sell. How the Market Transforms Information into News*, Princeton University Press; Haveman, Heather A., 2015, *Magazines and the Making of America: Modernization, Community, and Print Culture, 1741–1860*, Princeton: Princeton University Press. On the French side, see Ferenczi, Thomas, 1993, *L'invention du journalisme en France*, Paris: Plon; Charle, Christophe, 1990, *Naissance des "Intellectuels," 1880–1900*, Paris: Editions de Minuit; Ory, Pascal, and Jean-François Sirinelli, 1986, *Les intellectuels en France: De l'affaire Dreyfus à nos jours*, Paris: Armand Colin. More generally, the United States and France also have distinct ways of assessing value and legitimacy—in other words, different definitions of "what counts." Attention to these differences goes back to Alexis de Tocqueville, who first contrasted the democratic spirit of the United States with the aristocratic tradition in France. See Tocqueville, *Democracy in America*. More recently, scholars have compared the role of highbrow culture in France, where "distinction" retains its primacy, to the case of the United States, where knowledge of high culture matters relatively less than monetary or moral worth. See Lamont and Thévenot, *Rethinking Comparative Cultural Sociology*; Lamont, *Money, Morals, and Manners*.

30. Cited on p 11 in Alexander, Breese, and Luengo, *The Crisis of Journalism Reconsidered*. See also Ryfe, *Journalism and the Public*.

31. There is a large literature on "publics" that relates the concept to different types of political dynamics—from "deliberative" politics to "agonistic" publics or "counter" publics. Here I do not adopt a normative approach but instead rely on the concept of public in order to refer to the civic representations that journalists often have of their readers and impact on social and political collectives in democratic societies—here the United States and France. For normative approaches, see Habermas, Jürgen, 1989, *The Structural Transformation of the Public Sphere: An Inquiry into a Category of Bourgeois Society*, Cambridge, MA: MIT Press, 27; Fraser, Nancy, 1990, "Rethinking the Public Sphere," *Social Text* 25/26: 56–80. Mouffe, Chantal, 1999, "Deliberative Democracy or Agonistic Pluralism?" *Social Research* 66 (3): 745–758. For a normative analysis of a "public right to hear" in journalism, see Ananny, *Networked Press Freedom*. For descriptive approaches of publics and of the overlap between publics and audiences, see Schudson, Michael, 1995, "Was There Ever a Public Sphere?" pp. 189–203 in *The Power of News*, Cambridge: Harvard University Press. In cultural studies, see Ang, Ien, 1991, *Desperately Seeking the Audience*, London: Routledge; Couldry, Nick, Sonia Livingstone, and Tim Markham, 2010, *Media Consumption and Public Engagement: Beyond the Presumption of Attention*, second edition, Basingstoke: Palgrave Macmillan; Hall, Stuart, 1980, "Encoding/Decoding," in *Culture, Media, Language*, edited by S. Hall, D. Hobson, A. Lowe, and P. Willis, 128–138, London: Hutchinson; Carey, James, 1992, *Communication as Culture: Essays on Media and Society*, New York: Routledge. Michael Warner adds an interesting dimension to this

discussion of publics and counter-publics by arguing that the idea of a public is also text-based. See Warner, Michael, 2002, *Publics and Counterpublics*, New York: Zone Books.

32. See, for instance, Gans, Herbert J., 2004 (1979), *Deciding What's News: A Study of CBS Evening News, NBC, Nightly News, Newsweek, and Time*, Evanston: Northwestern University Press; Darnton, Robert, 1975, "Writing News and Telling Stories," *Daedalus* 104 (2): 175–194; De Sola Pool, Ithiel, and Irwin Shulman, 1959, "Newsmen's Fantasies, Audiences, and Newswriting," *Public Opinion Quarterly* 23 (2): 145–158; Wahl-Jorgensen, Karin, 2002, "The Construction of the Public in Letters to the Editor. Deliberative Democracy and the Idiom of Insanity," *Journalism* 3 (2): 183–204.

33. See, for instance, Tandoc, Edson C., and R. J. Thomas, 2015, "The Ethics of Web Analytics: Implications of Using Audience Metrics in News Construction," *Digital Journalism* 3 (2): 243–258. In the words of journalism scholar Chris Anderson, "If the audiences' needs and wants are entirely knowable, then why should they not be catered to, particularly if catering to those wants can lead to the implementation of a highly successful business model?" Anderson, Chris, 2011, "Deliberative, Agonistic, and Algorithmic Audiences: Journalism's Vision of Its Public in an Age of Audience Transparency," *International Journal of Communication* 5: 529–547, 541.

34. For analyses of the uselessness of audience data in making predictions in other cultural industries, see Bielby, William T., and Denise D. Bielby, 1994, "All Hits Are Flukes: Institutionalized Decision Making and the Rhetoric of Network Prime-Time Program Development," *American Journal of Sociology* 99 (5): 1287–1313; Gitlin, Todd, 2000, *Inside Prime Time*, Berkeley: University of California Press; Napoli, Philip M., 2011, *Audience Evolution: New Technologies and the Transformation of Media Audiences*, New York: Columbia University Press. On the ambiguous aspect of audiences and publics in the case of music, see Baym, Nancy K., 2013, "Data Not Seen: The Uses and Shortcomings of Social Media Metrics," *First Monday* 18 (10). For recent research in digital on the co-construction of audiences and publics, see Baym, Nancy K., 2018, *Playing to the Crowd. Musicians, Audiences, and the Intimate Work of Connection*, New York: NYU Press; Anderson, "Web Metrics."

35. The concepts of publics and audiences are overlapping and have been defined in multiple ways in journalism studies, communication, and political theory. For instance, Ananny finds no fewer than ten possible definitions of the press's publics, ranging from "rational-information focused bodies" to "quantified aggregations," whereas Ryfe distinguishes between four key aspects of journalistic publics. See Ananny, *Networked Press Freedom*; Ryfe, *Journalism and the Public*, 23–25. Following Anderson's study, existing scholarship on audience metrics often relies on the concept of "algorithmic audience" to analyze the representation of readers through web analytics (Anderson, "Deliberative Audiences"). Yet I do not find that online readers are predictable entities for web journalists analyzing detailed analytics. Instead, I argue that algorithmic publics have the same unpredictable and yet civic nature as "imagined" (whether "deliberative" or "agonistic") publics in the print era. The concept of a "networked public sphere" is another

framework, pro-Habermassian and optimistic about the connective capabilities of digital technologies, developed in Benkler, Yochai, 2006, *The Wealth of Networks: How Social Production Transforms Markets and Freedom*, New Haven: Yale University Press. Compared to the "networked public sphere," the concept of "algorithmic public" developed here is primarily descriptive instead of normative. In this respect, my analysis bears more affinities with the idea of "networked publics" developed in Marwick, Alice E., and danah boyd, 2011, "I Tweet Honestly, I Tweet Passionately: Twitter Users, Context Collapse, and the Imagined Audience," *New Media & Society* 13 (1): 114–133. Yet I do not focus on mediated interactions between users on social media platforms but rather on the civic, commercial, and professional representations that web journalists and editors project onto algorithmic publics.

36. This understanding of commercialized publics in turn echoes the literature on "audiences," broadly defined as bodies of spectators or listeners, in media economics and marketing. See Napoli, *Audience Evolution*; Ettema, James S., and D. Charles Whitney, eds., 1994. *Audiencemaking: How the Media Create the Audience*, Thousand Oaks: Sage; Webster, James G., 1998, "The Audience," *Journal of Broadcasting & Electronic Media* 42 (2): 190–207. For an influential discussion of the "work" of audiences, see Smythe, Dallas W., 1981, "On the Audience Commodity and Its Work," pp. 22–51 in *Dependency Road: Communications, Capitalism, Consciousness, and Canada*, Norwood: Ablex.

37. For a discussion of the comparative benefits of interviews and observations in qualitative fieldwork, see Jerolmack, Colin, and Shamus Khan, 2014, "Talk Is Cheap: Ethnography and the Attitudinal Fallacy," *Sociological Methods & Research* 43 (2): 1–36.

38. On the challenges of anonymization in the age of Google, see Shklovski, Irina, and Janet Vertesi, 2013, "'Un-Googling' Publications: The Ethics and Problems of Anonymization," pp. 2169–2178 in *CHI '13 Extended Abstracts on Human Factors in Computing Systems*, New York: ACM.

39. This "bureaucratic" framework goes back to Max Weber's definition of the rationalization process (Weber, Max, 2013, *Economy and Society: An Outline of Interpretive Sociology*, Berkeley: University of California Press), whereas the "disciplinary" framework draws on Foucault's work (Foucault, *Discipline & Punish*). The contrast between bureaucratic and disciplinary ideal-types in turn has a long history in organizational sociology and the sociology of work, as we will see in chapters 5 and 6.

40. This framework, which is developed in chapter 1, draws on recent analyses of field dynamics at the transnational level, most importantly Benson, *Shaping Immigration News*; Benson and Neveu, *Bourdieu and the Journalistic Field*; Benson and Saguy, "Constructing Social Problems"; Powers, Matthew, and Sandra Vera Zambrano, 2016, "Explaining the Formation of Online News Startups in France and the United States: A Field Analysis," *Journal of Communication* 66 (5): 857–877.

41. This analysis of the French understanding of a unitary and political public owes a lot to Baker, Keith M., 2012, "Public Opinion as Political Invention," *Inventing the French Revolution. Essays on French Political Culture in the Eighteenth Century*, Cambridge, UK: Cambridge University Press, 167–200.

Chapter 1. From Circulation Numbers to Web Analytics

1. See Chin, "We Detox from Chartbeat"; Lepore, Jill, 2019, "Does Journalism Have a Future?" *The New Yorker*, January 21, retrieved: https://www.newyorker.com/magazine/2019/01/28/does-journalism-have-a-future; Abramson, Jill E., 2019, *Merchants of Truth. The Business of News and the Fight for Facts*, New York: Simon & Schuster, 244–248; Iftikhar, Bilal, 2014, "40 Under 40, Class of 2014—Tony Haile, 36," *Crain's New York Business*, retrieved: http://www.crainsnewyork.com/40under40/2014/Haile.

2. Foer, "When Silicon Valley Took Over Journalism."

3. Knorr-Cetina, Karin, and Urs Bruegger, 2002, "Inhabiting Technology: The Global Lifeform of Financial Markets," *Current Sociology* 50 (3): 389–405, 392. I will return to the question of how Chartbeat represents algorithmic publics in chapter 4.

4. This chapter explicitly connects the concept of the journalistic field and the question of the relationship between journalists and their readers. It is important to note, however, that the notion of democratic publics remains somewhat missing from Bourdieu's field theory. See Ananny, *Networked Press Freedom*, 50–56; Ryfe, *Journalism and the Public*, 47–74.

5. For vivid evocations of these respective perceptions, see Ferenczi, *Invention du journalisme*; Chalaby, Jean K., 1996, "Journalism as an Anglo-American Invention: A Comparison of the Development of French and Anglo-American Journalism, 1830s–1920s," *European Journal of Communication* 11 (3): 303–326.

6. Schudson, *Discovering the News*; Starr, *Creation of the Media*; Haveman, *Magazines and the Making of America*; Hamilton, *All the News*; Alexander, Jeffrey, 1981, "The Mass News Media in Systemic, Historical and Comparative Perspective," in *Mass Media and Social Change*, Sage Studies in International Sociology, edited by E. Katz and T. Szecskő, Thousand Oaks: Sage, 17–51. For more details on the mechanisms of journalism as a dual-product marketplace, see Hamilton, *All the News*; Napoli, Philip M., 2003, *Audience Economics: Media Institutions and the Audience Marketplace*, New York: Columbia University Press.

7. This involvement of elites in public affairs was not restricted to journalism. See Rodgers, Daniel T., 2000, *Atlantic Crossings. Social Politics in a Progressive Era*, Cambridge, MA: Harvard University Press. On the socialist political beliefs of many "muckrakers," see Evensen, Bruce J., 2017, "Journalism," pp. 178–189 in *A Companion to the Gilded Age and Progressive Era*, Wiley Blackwell Companions to American History, edited by C. M. Nichols and N. C. Unger, Malden: Wiley-Blackwell; Filler, Louis, 1993, *The Muckrakers*, Stanford: Stanford University Press. On the role of magazines in social reform movements, see Haveman, *Magazines and the Making of America*.

8. For instance, following the publication of muckraking investigative articles, laws were passed to regulate the meatpacking industry, the monopoly of Standard Oil, and the Trinity Church settlements. See Evensen, "Journalism." On the moral and often religious impetus behind the muckraking movement, see Filler, *Muckrakers*. Note that this may have been related to the social background of many of the muckrakers (often women, people of color, immigrants, and so on),

who may not have had access to more institutionalized markers of intellectual prestige. On the commercial success of muckraking, see Evensen, "Journalism," 181.

9. On the rise of the "yellow press" (most importantly William Randolph Hearst's *New York Journal* and Joseph Pulitzer's *New York World*) and its connection with muckraking journalism, see Campbell, W. Joseph, 2001, *Yellow Journalism. Puncturing the Myths, Defining the Legacies*, Westport: Praeger Publishers.

10. Schudson, *Discovering the News*, 99, 111.

11. The first journalism course opened at the University of Pennsylvania as early as 1893, the first journalism program was created at the University of Missouri-Columbia in 1908, and the Columbia Journalism School opened its doors in 1912. Professional awards (including the Pulitzer Prizes) soon followed. Journalists and editors also created press clubs and associations, cementing the idea that journalism was a respectable occupation with a distinct professional identity. Schudson, *Discovering the News*, 69, 122; Hohenberg, John, 1997, *The Pulitzer Diaries: Inside America's Greatest Prize*, Syracuse: Syracuse University Press.

12. See Ward, Douglas B., 1996, "The Reader as Consumer: Curtis Publishing Company and Its Audience, 1910–1930," *Journalism History* 22 (2): 47–55; Carey, James W., 1980, "Changing Communications Technology and the Nature of the Audience," *Journal of Advertising* 9 (2): 3–10; Napoli, *Audience Economics*.

13. These criticisms reached an apex during the 1912 presidential elections, when all candidates vehemently criticized the pro-business bias of the press. See Nadler, Anthony M., 2016, *Making the News Popular: Mobilizing U.S. News Audiences*, Urbana: University of Illinois Press, 39. See also the 1922 Lippman-Dewey debate on the responsibility of journalists towards the public: Lippmann, Walter, 1991 (1922), *Public Opinion*, Transaction Publishers; Dewey, John, 1922, "Review of Public Opinion," *New Republic* 30 (3): 338–344.

14. A more thorough analysis of the journalistic field in the United States and France would give a better sense of the variation and tensions taking place between publications and journalists as they struggled to impose a definition of what it meant to be a journalist. For instance, "yellow" newspapers and later the "tabloid" press maintained a different appreciation of circulation numbers. See, for instance, Schudson, *Discovering the News*; Haveman, *Magazines and the Making of America*; Campbell, *Yellow Journalism*.

15. Note that the history of French media began well before the late nineteenth century. Yet the development of a mass newspaper market truly started after the 1881 law, which reduced censorship and previous restrictions on the creation and daily operations of newspapers and magazines. See Charle, Christophe, 2004, *Le siècle de la presse, 1830–1939*, Paris: Seuil. In the words of Eugène Pelletan, the representative who promoted the legislation: "Having an affordable press is a tacit promise that the Republic makes towards universal suffrage. It isn't enough that every citizen has the right to vote; it is essential that they also understand their votes, and how would they do so if newspapers weren't available to every voter, from the wealthy to the poor, even in the most remote villages?" Delporte, Christian, Claire Blandin, and François Robinet, 2016, *Histoire de la presse en France, XXe–XXIe siècles*, Paris: Armand Colin, 13.

16. As sociologist Gabriel Tarde wrote in 1901, "Every morning, newspapers give to their public the conversation of the day" (*Tous les matins, les journaux servent à leur public la conversation de la journée*). See Delporte, Blandin, and Robinet, *Histoire*, 11. On the diversity of newspapers and magazines in nineteenth-century France, see Charle, *Siècle de la Presse*; De la Motte, Dean, and Jeannine M. Przyblyski, eds., 1999, *Making the News: Modernity and the Mass Press in Nineteenth-Century France*, Amherst: University of Massachusetts Press. On "imagined communities," see Anderson, Benedict R., 2006, *Imagined Communities: Reflections on the Origin and Spread of Nationalism*, London, New York: Verso.

17. On the overproduction of journalists, writers, and academics in late nineteenth-century Paris, see Charle, *Intellectuels*.

18. On the literary side, this was the case of Gaston Leroux, reporter for *Le Matin* and author of the popular detective novels *The Phantom of the Opera* and *The Mystery of the Yellow Room*. Well-known writers—including Emile Zola and Octave Mirbeau—also frequently wrote columns or "reportages" for newspapers. On the political side, one can take the example of Aristide Briand, who started his career as a journalist and later served eleven times as Prime Minister of the Third Republic. See Ferenczi, *Invention du journalisme*, 153, 157–160.

19. In the words of Fernand Xau, journalist and publisher of *Le Journal*, French journalists were "too refined to be satisfied with such dry reporting." Ferenczi, *Invention du journalisme*, 65.

20. In some cases, contentiousness was even the primary motivation of the publication: journalists often used their columns as an engine of social criticism. For instance, as early as 1868, the playwright and journalist Henri Rochefort opened up the first issue of his newspaper *La Lanterne* in the following way: "According to the Imperial Almanach, France counts thirty-six million subjects, not counting subjects of dispute." See Ferenczi, *Invention du journalisme*, 97. On the role of contentious position-takings in nineteenth century French literature, see Parkhurst Ferguson, Priscilla, 1991, *Literary France: The Making of a Culture*, Berkeley: University of California Press; Bourdieu, Pierre, 2006, *The Rules of Art: Genesis and Structure of the Literary Field*, Stanford: Stanford University Press.

21. *Le Soir* made Dreyfus's name public, while *L'éclair* published a document that had been kept from Dreyfus's defenders. *Le Figaro* counterattacked, publishing several pieces about another suspect. Charle, *Intellectuels*, 108; Delporte, Blandin, and Robinet, *Histoire*, 38.

22. Charle, *Intellectuels*. Yet Charle also reminds us that one should not overestimate the social, political, or intellectual unity of the *intellectuels*, who operated as a field rather than a coherent group. See also Eyal, Gil, and Larissa Buchholz, 2010, "From the Sociology of Intellectuals to the Sociology of Interventions," *Annual Review of Sociology* 36: 117–137.

23. On the professional struggle for jurisdictional control, see Abbott, Andrew D., 1988, *The System of Professions: An Essay on the Division of Expert Labor*, Chicago: University of Chicago Press; Larson, Magali Sarfatti, 1977, *The Rise of Professionalism: A Sociological Analysis*, Berkeley: University of California Press.

24. On journalistic unions, see Delporte, Blandin, and Robinet, *Histoire*, 38. On the "abominable venality" of the press and scandals that followed, see Martin, Marc, 2006, "Retour sur 'l'abominable vénalité de la presse française,'" *Le Temps des Médias* 1 (6): 22–33; Ferenczi, *Invention du journalisme*, 228–229; Parkhurst, *Literary France*, 94.

25. For instance, Eveno describes the reluctance of newspaper editors and managers to make their circulation figures public, which he analyzes as a key factor in the lesser development of the advertising market in the French media. At the same time, however, he notes that *Le Petit Journal* featured its circulations figures on its front page in 1869. Eveno, Patrick, 2015, "Mesurer l'audience de la presse, toute une histoire," INA, *La Revue des Médias*, retrieved: https://lare vuedesmedias.ina.fr/mesurer-laudience-de-la-presse-toute-une-histoire.

26. Hallin defines "high modernism" as "an era when ... it seemed possible for the journalist to be powerful and prosperous and at the same time independent, disinterested, public-spirited, and trusted and beloved by everyone, from the corridors of power around the world to the ordinary citizen and consumer." Hallin, Daniel C., 1992, "The Passing of the 'High Modernism' of American Journalism," *Journal of Communication* 42 (3): 14–25, 16. See also Schudson, *Discovering the News*, 164–165; McChesney, Robert W., 1993, *Telecommunications, Mass Media and Democracy: The Battle for Control of U.S. Broadcasting, 1928–1935*, New York: Oxford University Press.

27. Pickard, Victor, 2010, "Reopening the Postwar Settlement for U.S. Media: The Origins and Implications of the Social Contract between Media, the State, and the Polity," *Communication, Culture & Critique* 3 (2): 170–189. See also Nadler, *Making the News Popular*, 41. On modernism and its unintended social effects more broadly, see Scott, James C., 1999, *Seeing Like a State: How Certain Schemes to Improve the Human Condition Have Failed*, New Haven: Yale University Press.

28. Gans, *Deciding What's News*. Similarly, in his depiction of *The Washington Post* in the 1970s, Padioleau compared the newsroom to a "sanctuary" where profit concerns did not enter the picture. Padioleau, *Précepteurs et mousquetaires*, 161–179. See also Hallin, "High Modernism," 15.

29. On the role of audience measurements in the motion picture industry, see Napoli, *Audience Economics*; Zafirau, Stephen, 2009, "Imagined Audiences: Intuitive and Technical Knowledge in Hollywood," unpublished PhD dissertation, University of Southern California. On television, Gitlin, *Inside Prime Time*; Bielby and Bielby, "All Hits." In the case of radio, see Rossman, Gabriel, 2012, *Climbing the Charts. What Radio Airplay Tells Us about the Diffusion of Innovation*, Princeton: Princeton University Press. On the related role of Paul Lazarsfeld's Radio Research Project in shaping the field of public opinion research, see Napoli, *Audience Evolution*; Igo, *Averaged American*.

30. Gans, *Deciding What's News*, 230.

31. Darnton, "Writing News," 176. Pamela Shoemaker makes a related point when she writes that "When it comes to thinking about the kind of news most relevant to "the audience," newsmen exercise their news judgment rather than going out and seeking specific information about the composition, wants or tastes

of those who are being addressed." Shoemaker, Pamela J. and Elizabeth Kay, 1987, *Building a Theory of News Content: A Synthesis of Current Approaches*, Columbia: Journalism Monographs, Association for Education in Journalism and Mass Communication, 115–116.

32. See Gans, *Deciding What's News*; Darnton, "Writing News"; De Sola Pool and Shulman, "Newsmen's Fantasies." On how print journalists tend to dismiss their letter writing readers as "insane" and distance themselves from their public, see Wahl-Jorgensen, "The Construction of the Public"; Robinson, James G., 2019, "The Audience in the Mind's Eye: How Journalists Imagine Their Readers," *Tow Center for Digital Journalism*, Columbia School of Journalism, retrieved: https://www.cjr.org/tow_center_reports/how-journalists-imagine-their-readers.php ?mc_cid=389d4aee19.

33. Ryfe, *Can Journalism Survive*, 37 (numbers adjusted for inflation); Bagdikian, Ben, 2004, *The Media Monopoly*, Boston; Beacon Press; Downie Jr., Leonard, and Robert G. Kaiser, 2003, *The News about the News: American Journalism in Peril*, New York: Vintage Books.

34. Nadler, *Making the News Popular*; Ryfe, *Can Journalism Survive*; Putnam, Robert, 1996, "The Strange Disappearance of Civic America," *The American Prospect*, retrieved: http://prospect.org/article/strange-disappearance-civic-america.

35. See Turow, Joseph, 2005, "Audience Construction and Culture Production: Marketing Surveillance in the Digital Age," *The ANNALS of the American Academy of Political and Social Science* 597 (1): 103–121, 105; Nadler, *Making the News Popular*, 54; Napoli, Philip M., 2005, "Audience Measurement and Media Policy: Audience Economics, the Diversity Principle, and the Local People Meter," *Communication Law and Policy* 10 (4): 349–382; Napoli, *Audience Evolution*; McManus, John, 1994, *Market-Driven Journalism. Let the Citizen Beware?* Thousand Oaks: Sage; Klinenberg, Eric, 2007, *Fighting for Air: The Battle to Control America's Media*, New York: Metropolitan Books. On the invisible work that goes into making distribution reliable and consistent, offline and online, see Braun, Josh, 2015, *This Program Is Brought to You By … : Distributing Television News Online*, New Haven: Yale University Press.

36. This stood in sharp contrast to a vibrant set of newspapers and magazines that engaged in what came to be called "adversary culture." Many were run by minority communities (African-American, immigrant, socialist, LGBTQ), which covered these topics in depth. See Ostertag, Bob, 2007, *People's Movements, People's Press. The Journalism of Social Justice Movements*, New York: Beacon Press; Gonzalez, Juan, and Joseph Torres, 2012, *News for All the People. The Epic Story of Race and the American Media*, New York: Penguin Random House.

37. Cited in McCauley, Michael, B. Lee Artz, DeeDee Halleck, and Paul E. Peterson, eds., 2002, *Public Broadcasting and the Public Interest*, New York: Routledge; Nadler, *Making the News Popular*, 5, 58–64.

38. On "civic" or "public" journalism, see Glasser, Theodore L., ed., 1999. *The Idea of Public Journalism*, New York: Guilford; Anderson, "Deliberative Audiences." On race coverage and African-American journalism, see, for instance, Roberts, Gene, and Hank Klibanoff, 2007, *The Race Beat. The Press, the Civil Rights Struggle, and the Awakening of a Nation*, New York: Penguin Random House; Gonzalez and Torres, *News for All the People*; Ostertag, *People's Move-*

ments, People's Press. On "Gonzo" journalism, see Caron, James E., 1985, "Hunter S. Thompson's 'Gonzo' Journalism and the Tall Tale Tradition in America," *Studies in Popular Culture* 8 (1): 1–16. More generally, on "alternative journalism," see Atton, Chris, and James F. Hamilton, 2008, *Alternative Journalism,* London: Sage. For a fascinating analysis of how LGBTQ topics entered mainstream television through tabloid talk shows, see Gamson, Joshua, 1998, *Freaks Talk Back. Tabloid Talk Shows and Sexual Nonconformity,* Chicago: University of Chicago Press.

39. In the words of writer Albert Camus, "Appetite for money and indifference to truly important things worked together to create a press that, with few exceptions, had no other goal than increasing the power of a few and debasing the morality of all. Hence it was not difficult for newspapers to become what they were between 1940 and 1944, that is, the shame of the country." Delporte, Blandin, and Robinet, *Histoire,* 144. See also Kuhn, Raymond, 1995, *The Media in France,* London: Routledge, 54; Charon, Jean-Marie, 2003, *Les médias en France,* Paris: La Découverte, 14–17.

40. Delporte, Blandin, and Robinet, *Histoire,* 147; Padioleau, *Précepteurs et mousquetaires,* 18–19.

41. The 1935 Brachard Law granted important rights to professional journalists, including a national press identification card and the right to leave a publication with compensation in case of acquisition. See Delporte, Blandin, and Robinet, *Histoire.* In 1974, the Cressard Law extended some of these benefits to freelance journalists. See Charon, *Les médias;* we will return to this in chapter 6. Note also that several targeted subsidies were put in place in the 1970s for politically engaged newspapers in the name of the "defense of political pluralism." Benson, *Shaping Immigration News,* 38–39.

42. For instance, the newspaper *L'Humanité,* connected to the Communist Party, had the highest circulation figures after the Liberation. Similarly, *Combat,* a former Resistance newspaper, defined its mission as providing "critical journalism" that would "guide public opinion." Media analysts describe the French system as a case of "polarized pluralism," where political and ideological diversity are reached at the level of the newspaper field rather than at the level of each publication. Hallin and Mancini, *Comparing Media Systems.*

43. Although the first French journalism school had been created as early as 1899, it is only in the second half of the twentieth century that journalistic training became widespread in France. For instance, the *Centre de Formation des Journalistes* (CFJ), created in 1946, was launched by former Resistance members to prevent ethical failings such as the collaboration with the Nazis. See Lafarge, Géraud, and Dominique Marchetti, 2011, "Les portes fermées du journalisme," *Actes de la recherche en sciences sociales* 189 (4): 72–99; Bouron, Samuel, 2015, "Les écoles de journalisme face à l'expansion du marché. Stratégies d'internationalisation et transformations des curricula," *Cahiers de la recherche sur l'éducation et les savoirs* (14): 245–66; Fröhlich, Romy, and Christina Holtz-Bacha, eds., 2003, *Journalism Education in Europe and North America: An International Comparison,* Cresskill: Hampton Press.

44. Padioleau, *Précepteurs et mousquetaires,* 4, 62–75, 117. Delporte, Blandin, and Robinet, *Histoire,* 184.

45. Among other examples, take the case of Claude Julien, managing director of *Le Monde* in 1969. In one of Julien's speeches to the "Société des Rédacteurs du *Monde*," he pleaded: "I have been speaking as a manager so far, but am I allowed to speak now as a human being who decided a long time ago to become part of the splendid profession that is journalism? My greatest joy is not to cut operating costs.... Like you, I am a journalist. Like you, I like to write, and I prefer to read Garcia Marquez ... rather than analyze accounts." Padioleau, *Précepteurs et mousquetaires,* 63.

46. Padioleau, *Précepteurs et mousquetaires,* 83.

47. For similar findings based on a comparison of the specialization and work roles of British and German newsrooms, see Esser, Frank, 1998, "Editorial Structures and Work Principles in British and German Newsrooms," *European Journal of Communication* 13 (3): 375–405.

48. Padioleau, *Précepteurs et mousquetaires,* 96–97. In response to a survey distributed in the 1960s, young journalists claimed that they were doing this job in order to "serve the democratic ideal ... and educate, guide, and train the masses" (*à servir l'idéal démocratique ... ; à éduquer, à guider, à former les masses*). Martin, Marc, 1991, *Histoire et médias: Journalisme et journalistes français*, Paris: Albin Michel, 25.

49. Martin, Laurent, 2008, "La 'Nouvelle Presse' en France dans les années 1970 ou la réussite par l'échec," *Vingtième Siècle. Revue d'Histoire* 98 (2): 68–69.

50. On the privatization of television channels, see Dugowson, Maurice, and Marie-Eve Chamard, 1996, *Télévisions, Histoires Secrètes*, Gaumont Télévision—France 3. See also Delporte, Blandin, and Robinet, *Histoire*, 96–97; Bourdieu, *On Television*; Halimi, Serge, 1997, *Les nouveaux chiens de garde*, Paris: Raisons d'Agir; Duval, *Raison journalistique*.

51. Benson, *Shaping Immigration News*, 43; Krause, "Reporting," 98. On the financialization of the media, see Cranberg, Gilbert, Randall P. Bezanson, and John Soloski, 2001, *Taking Stock: Journalism and the Publicly Traded Newspaper Company*, New York: Wiley.

52. On "shovelware" and the slow transition to interactivity in online news, see Boczkowski, *Digitizing the News*; Nadler, *Making the News Popular*, 129. About interactivity and readers' feedback in online news, see Deuze, Mark, 2006, "Participation, Remediation, Bricolage: Considering Principal Components of a Digital Culture," *The Information Society* 22: 63–75; Domingo, David, 2008, "Interactivity in the Daily Routines of Online Newsrooms. Dealing with an Uncomfortable Myth," *Journal of Computer Mediated Communication* 13 (3): 680–704; Lewis, Seth C., 2012, "The Tension between Professional Control and Open Participation: Journalism and Its Boundaries," *Information, Communication & Society*, 15 (6), 836–866; Singer, Jane B., David Domingo, Ari Heinonen, Alfred Hermida, Steve Paulussen, Quandt Thorsten, Zvi Reich, and Marina Vujnovic, eds., 2011, *Participatory Journalism: Guarding Open Gates at Online Newspapers*, Malden: Wiley-Blackwell.

53. On the evolution of U.S. newspapers' advertising revenues, see Kaiser, Robert G., 2014, "The Bad News about the News," *The Brookings Essays*, October 16, 2014, retrieved: http://csweb.brookings.edu/content/research/essays/2014/bad-news.html. On U.S. circulation revenues, see Barthel, Michael, 2018, "News-

papers Fact Sheet," Pew Research Center, Journalism & Media. June 1, 2018, retrieved: http://www.journalism.org/fact-sheet/newspapers/. On the evolution of full-time newsroom employees, see American Society of News Editors, 2018, "ASNE Newsroom Employment Survey," retrieved: http://asne.org/content.asp ?contentid=144. On editorial budget and staff cuts as a way to maximize shareholder value and investors' demands, see McChesney and Pickard, eds., *Will the Last Reporter Please Turn out the Lights*. On the losses in magazine jobs, see Jurkowitz, Mark, 2014, "*State of the News Media 2014: The Growth in Digital Reporting: What It Means for Journalism and News Consumers*," March 26, retrieved: http://www.journalism.org/2014/03/26/the-losses-in-legacy/. See also Hamilton, James T., 2016, *Democracy's Detectives. The Economics of Investigative Journalism*, Cambridge, MA: Harvard University Press, 280. For the French figures, see Ministère de la Culture et de la Communication, 2013, "Chiffres Clés 2012: Presse," retrieved: http://www.culturecommunication.gouv.fr/Disciplines-et -secteurs/Presse/Chiffres-statistiques.

54. Angwin, *Dragnet Nation*. For an overview, see Zuboff, *Surveillance Capitalism*.

55. Turow, Joseph, 2013, *The Daily You: How the New Advertising Industry Is Defining Your Identity and Your Worth*, New Haven: Yale University Press, 37; Napoli, *Audience Evolution*; Crain, Matthew, 2014, "Financial Markets and On-line Advertising Demand: Reevaluating the Dotcom Investment Bubble," *Information, Communication, and Society* 17 (3): 371–394; Carlson, Matt, 2015, "When News Sites Go Native: Redefining the Advertising-Editorial Divide in Response to Native Advertising," *Journalism* 15 (7): 849–865; Ouakrat, Alan, Jean-Samuel Beuscart, and Kevin Mellet, 2010, "Les régies publicitaires de la presse en ligne," *Réseaux* 160–161 (2): 133–161.

56. Zuboff, *Surveillance Capitalism*, p. viii; Geertz, Clifford, 1978. "The Bazaar Economy: Information and Search in Peasant Marketing." *American Economic Review* 68 (2): 28–32.

57. Graves, Lucas, John Kelly, and Marissa Gluck, 2010, *Confusion Online: Faulty Metrics and the Future of Digital Journalism*," Tow Center for Digital Journalism, Columbia Journalism School, 6, retrieved: https://towcenter.org/research /confusion-online-faulty-metrics-and-the-future-of-digital-journalism/. For instance, in 2012, Nielsen and comScore, respectively, reported 58.8 million and 86 million monthly unique visitors for Yahoo! News. The difference between the two estimates was a non-negligible 27 million readers per month. See Pew Research Center's Project for Excellence in Journalism, 2013, *State of the News Media 2013*, retrieved: http://stateofthemedia.org/.

58. Given that news websites' traffic typically peaks during the workday and subsides at night, panel-based measures thus tend to systematically underestimate news sites' numbers of unique visitors compared to websites that are visited at night, such as video on-demand platforms like Netflix. See Boczkowski, *Digitizing the News*.

59. For an analysis of the overwhelming amount of "fake" traffic, see Read, Max, 2018, "How Much of the Internet Is Fake? Turns Out, A Lot of It, Actually," *New York Magazine*, Intelligencer, Dec. 26, 2018, retrieved: http://nymag.com /intelligencer/2018/12/how-much-of-the-internet-is-fake.html. Note that users can

also engage in various "obfuscation" strategies, deleting cookies and caches on their computers in order to avoid online tracking. Brunton, Finn, and Helen Nissenbaum, 2015, *Obfuscation. A User's Guide for Privacy and Protest*, Cambridge: MIT Press.

60. The information and quotes in this paragraph were retrieved on the company's website on April 9, 2014 (https://chartbeat.com/). See also Petre, "Engineering Consent."

61. This information was retrieved on the company's website on September 1, 2015: https://chartbeat.com/.

62. See Robinson, "The Audience in the Mind's Eye"; Anderson, "Deliberative Audiences"; Tandoc and Thomas, "Ethics of Web Analytics"; Christin, "Counting Clicks."

63. See quotes and analyses in Usher, "Al Jazeera English Online"; Petre, "Traffic Factories"; Zamith, Rodrigo, 2018, "Quantified Audiences in News Production. A Synthesis and Research Agenda," *Digital Journalism* 6 (4): 418–435; Blanchett Nehell, Nicole, 2018, "News by Numbers: The Evolution of Analytics in Journalism," *Digital Journalism* 6 (8): 1041–1051; Ferrer-Conill, Raul, and Edson C. Tandoc Jr., 2018, "The Audience-Oriented Editor: Making Sense of the Audience in the newsroom," *Digital Journalism* 6 (4): 436–453; Hanusch, Folker, 2017, "Web Analytics and the Functional Differentiation of Journalism Cultures: Individual, Organizational and Platform-Specific Influences on Newswork," *Information, Communication & Society* 20 (10): 1571–1586; Belair-Gagnon, Valerie, and Avery E. Holton, 2018, "Boundary Work, Interloper Media, and Analytics in Newsrooms," *Digital Journalism* 6 (8): 492–508; Welbers, Kasper, Wouter van Atteveldt, Jan Kleinnijenhuis, Nel Ruigrok, and Joep Schaper, 2015, "News Selection Criteria in the Digital Age: Professional Norms versus Online Audience Metrics," *Journalism* 17 (8): 1037–1053; Bunce, Mel, 2017, "Management and Resistance in the Digital Newsroom," *Journalism* 20 (8): 890–905.

64. On the "fragmentation" of online audiences and the difference with "civic" conceptions of the public, see Napoli, *Audience Evolution*; Anderson, "Deliberative Audiences"; Tandoc and Thomas, "Ethics of Web Analytics," 243–258.

Chapter 2. Utopian Beginnings

1. On the early days of techno-utopianism, see Turner, Fred, 2006, *From Counterculture to Cyberculture: Stewart Brand, the Whole Earth Network, and the Rise of Digital Utopianism*, Chicago: University of Chicago Press. For critical analyses of digital conglomerates, see Wu, Tim, 2010, *The Master Switch: The Rise and Fall of Information Empires*, New York: Random House; Vaidhyanathan, Siva, 2011, *The Googlization of Everything (And Why We Should Worry)*, Berkeley: University of California Press.

2. For critical studies of the ideology of the "New Frontier" in the early days of cyberculture, see Eubanks, Virginia, 1999, "The Mythography of the 'New' Frontier," working paper, Media in Transition Conference, Massachusetts Institute

of Technology, retrieved: http://web.mit.edu/m-i-t/articles/index_eubanks.html; Turner, Fred, 1999, "Cyberspace as the New Frontier? Mapping the Shifting Boundaries of the Network Society," paper presented to the Annual Meeting of the International Communication Association, retrieved: https://fredturner.stanford .edu/wp-content/uploads/turner-cyberspace-as-the-new-frontier.pdf. Regarding the territorial metaphor of the internet, William Gibson is often credited as having coined the term "cyberspace" in the novel *Neuromancer*. See Gibson, William, 1984, *Neuromancer*, New York: Ace Book. For a literary analysis of the role of *Neuromancer* in the cyberpunk culture, see Punday, Daniel, 2000, "The Narrative Construction of Cyberspace: Reading *Neuromancer*, Reading Cyberspace Debates," *College English* 2: 194–213.

3. Shirky, Clay, 2008, *Here Comes Everybody: The Power of Organizing without Organizations*, New York: Penguin, 98. For an analysis of the ideology and limits of "peer production," see Kreiss, Daniel, Megan Finn, and Fred Turner, 2011, "The Limits of Peer Production: Some Reminders from Max Weber for the Network Society," *New Media & Society*, 13 (2): 243–259.

4. Rosen, Jay, 2006, "The People Formerly Known as the Audience," *PressThink*, June 26, 2006, retrieved: http://archive.pressthink.org/2006/06/27/ppl _frmr.html; Benkler, *Wealth of Networks*. For an overview of the debate between Habermassian and post-Habermassian scholars about whether the internet is a positive or parasitic development for the public sphere, see Geiger, R. Stuart, 2009, "Does Habermas Understand the Internet? The Algorithmic Construction of the Blogo/Public Sphere," *Gnovis* 10 (1): 1–29.

5. Rosen, "The People"; see also Jenkins, Henry, 2006, *Convergence Culture. Where Old and New Media Collide*, New York: NYU Press.

6. Shirky, *Here Comes Everybody*, 70. In the words of journalism scholar and consultant Jeff Jarvis, the internet would reset "the journalistic relationship with the community, making the news organization less a producer and more an open platform for the public to share what it knows." Cited in Starkman, Dean, 2011, "Confidence Game. The Limited Visions of the New Gurus," *Columbia Journalism Review*, November 2011, retrieved: https://archives.cjr.org/essay/confidence _game.php. For an analytical perspective, see Deuze, Mark, 2008, "The Changing Context of News Work: Liquid Journalism and Monitorial Citizenship," *International Journal of Communication* 2: 848–865.

7. Turner, *From Counterculture to Cyberculture*. In France, an anti-commercial and anti-globalization repertoire explicitly shaped the online debate. Early bloggers and programmers established strong distinctions between the "independent web" (*web indépendant*), sometimes compared to a "resurrection of the Athenian agora," and the "commercial web" (*web marchant*), where "money-netizens" (*friconautes*) would betray the ideals of the networked public sphere. See Siles, Ignacio, 2017, *Networked Selves. Trajectories of Blogging in the United States and France*, New York: Peter Lang. The expression *friconautes* comes from Mauriac, Laurent, 2002, *Les flingueurs du net. Comment la finance a tué la nouvelle économie*, Paris: Calmann-Lévy.

8. Extract from an interview. [Name redacted], *Nieman Journalism Lab*. 2013. "Interview with John [founder of *TheNotebook*]."

9. "Interview," *Nieman Journalism Lab*.

10. Extract from an interview with John, founder of *TheNotebook*, 2006 [Name redacted], *My History of TheNotebook*.

11. Abbate, Janet, 1999, *Inventing the Internet*, Cambridge, MA: MIT Press, 106–109.

12. "Interview," *Nieman Journalism Lab*. In analytic terms, note that this "constant struggle" is a good instantiation of articulation work: computer programmers and journalists had to reach a consensus about what could be done to adjust the website to the needs of the journalistic team. Corbin, Juliet, and Anselm Strauss, 1993, "The Articulation of Work through Interaction," *The Sociological Quarterly* 34 (1): 71–83.

13. Unfootnoted quotes come from my own interviews.

14. Boczkowski, *Digitizing the News*.

15. In the words of a long-time writer for *TheNotebook*: "For years I consciously avoided the comments sections, fearing they were filled with nitpickers and stone-throwers there to tell me that my writing is bad, and that I should feel bad. I don't enjoy feeling bad, so I stayed away." [Name redacted], 2002, "Farewell to the [Commenting System]," *TheNotebook*, June 28, 2002. Many studies document the limitations and problems that followed the implementation of participatory structures in online news. See, for instance, Lewis, "Journalism and Its Boundaries"; Boczkowski, *Digitizing the News*. On trolling and online harassment more generally, see Reagle, Joseph R., 2015, *Reading the Comments: Likers, Haters, and Manipulators at the Bottom of the Web*, Cambridge: MIT Press; Citron, Danielle, 2014, *Hate Crimes in Cyberspace*, Cambridge: Harvard University Press.

16. For further analysis of the relationship between economic structures and editorial autonomy in online news, see Christin, Angèle, 2018, "Les sites d'information en ligne entre indépendance et course au clic: Une comparaison franco-américaine," *Sociétés contemporaines* 111 (3): 71–96.

17. See Benkler, *Wealth of Networks*; Rosen, "The People." For nuanced analyses of the connection between digital media, peer production, and the public sphere, see Papacharissi, Zizi, 2008, "The Virtual Sphere 2.0: The Internet, The Public Sphere, and Beyond," pp. 230–245 in the *Routledge Handbook of Internet Politics*, edited by A. Chadwick and P. Howard, New York: Routledge; Zuckerman, Ethan, 2016, "Ben Franklin, the Post Office, and the Digital Public Sphere," retrieved: http://www.ethanzuckerman.com/blog/2016/02/26/ben-franklin-the-post-office-and-the-digital-public-sphere/.

18. All the translations from French to English are mine.

19. Note that this type of criticism of the "lack of modernity" of the home country turns out to be a staple of transnational entrepreneurialism. See Irani, *Chasing Innovation*.

20. For further analysis of this asymmetry, see Christin, "Transnational Field."

21. Dezalay, Yves, and Bryant G. Garth, 2002, *The Internationalization of Palace Wars: Lawyers, Economists, and the Contest to Transform Latin American States*, Chicago: University of Chicago Press, 5–7; Hauchecorne, Mathieu, 2009, "Le 'professeur Rawls' et le 'Nobel des pauvres,' " *Actes de la recherche en sciences sociales*, 176–177 (1): 94–113; Czarniawska, Barbara, and Guje Sevón, 2005,

Global Ideas: How Ideas, Objects and Practices Travel in the Global Economy, Copenhagen: Copenhagen Business School Press; Molnár, Virág, 2005, "Cultural Politics and Modernist Architecture: The Tulip Debate in Post-war Hungary," *American Sociological Review* 70 (1): 111–135; Westney, Eleanor D., 1987, *Imitation and Innovation: The Transfer of Western Organizational Patterns to Meiji Japan*, Cambridge, MA: Harvard University Press.

22. Such subsidies, incidentally, are one of the major economic benefits of French journalists, who have the right to quit and receive an unemployment package whenever their news organization is acquired by a new media group. For an overview of the *clause de session*, see Charon, *Les médias*.

23. Syndicat de la Presse Indépendante d'Information en Ligne, 2009, "Qui sommes-nous?" retrieved: https://www.spiil.org/qui-sommes-nous.

24. Collins defines "emotional energy" as the "feeling of confidence, elation, strength, enthusiasm, and initiative in taking action" taking place within social groups. See Collins, Randall, 2004, *Interaction Ritual Chains*, Princeton: Princeton University Press, 49. See also Prenger, Mirjam, and Mark Deuze, 2017, "A History of Innovation and Entrepreneurialism in Journalism," in P. Boczkowski and C. W. Anderson, eds., *Remaking the News: Essays on the Future of Journalism in the Digital Age*, Cambridge: MIT Press, 235–250.

25. More broadly, on cultures of entrepreneurialism, see Saxenian, AnnaLee, 1994, *Regional Advantage: Culture and Competition in Silicon Valley and Route 128*, Harvard University Press; Neff, Gina, and David Stark, 2003, in "Permanently Beta: Responsive Organization in the Internet Era," *Society Online: The Internet in Context*, edited by P. Howard and S. Jones, New York: Sage, 173–188; Turner, Fred, 2009, "Burning Man at Google: A Cultural Infrastructure for New Media Production," *New Media & Society* 11 (1–2), 73–94; Neff, *Venture Labor*. Note that this kind of organizational culture is not specific to technology companies. For instance, in her analysis of music genres, Lena examines two phases— "avant-garde" and "scene-based" stages—that mirror the informal structuring and experimentation described here. See Lena, Jennifer C., 2012, *Banding Together: How Communities Create Genres in Popular Music*, Princeton: Princeton University Press.

Chapter 3. Entering the Chase for Clicks

1. See, for instance, Orlikowski, Wanda J., and Susan V. Scott, 2014, "What Happens When Evaluation Goes Online? Exploring Apparatuses of Valuation in the Travel Sector," *Organization Science* 25 (3), 868–891; Espeland, Wendy Nelson, and Michael Sauder, 2016, *Engines of Anxiety: Academic Rankings, Reputation, and Accountability*, New York: Russell Sage Foundation; Sharkey, Amanda J., and Patricia Bromley, 2015, "Can Ratings Have Indirect Effects? Evidence from the Organizational Response to Peers' Environmental Ratings," *American Sociological Review* 80 (1): 63–91; Lom, Stacy E. 2015, "Changing Rules, Changing Practices: The Direct and Indirect Effects of Tight Coupling in Figure Skating," *Organization Science* 27 (1): 36–52; Fligstein, Neil, 1985, "The Spread of the

Multidivisional Form Among Large Firms, 1919–1979," *American Sociological Review* 50 (3): 377–391.

2. Taylor, Catharine, 2010, "Newspapers Online Traffic Is Strong, So Why Are Ad Rates Weak?" *CBS News*, June 29, retrieved: http://www.cbsnews.com/news/newspapers-online-traffic-is-strong-so-why-are-ad-rates-weak/. For an account of how newspapers advertising revenues changed with the internet, see Waldman, Steven, 2011, "The Information of Communication. The Changing Media Landscape in a Broadband Age," *Federal Communications Commission*, 126–141, retrieved: https://transition.fcc.gov/osp/inc-report/The_Information_Needs_of_Communities.pdf. For an analysis of why digital advertising rates have remained low, see Turow, *Daily You*. On the dotcom bubble and crash, see Smith, Andrew, 2012, *Totally Wired. On the Trail of the Great Dotcom Swindle*, New York: Simon & Schuster.

3. Statista, 2017, "Number of Monthly Active Facebook Users Worldwide as of 4th Quarter 2016 (in millions)," retrieved: http://www.statista.com/statistics/264810/number-of-monthly-active-facebook-users-worldwide/; Statista, 2017, "Number of Monthly Active Twitter Users Worldwide From 1st Quarter 2010 to 3rd 2016 (in millions)," retrieved: http://www.statista.com/statistics/282087/number-of-monthly-active-twitter-users/; Pew Research Center, 2018, "News Use Across Social Media Platforms 2018," retrieved: https://www.journalism.org/2018/09/10/news-use-across-social-media-platforms-2018/.

4. On "trending," see Gillespie, Tarleton, 2016, "#Trendingistrending: When Algorithms Become Culture," in *Algorithmic Cultures: Essays on Meaning, Performance and New Technologies*, edited by S. Robert and J. Roberge, New York: Routledge; Wu, Tim, 2016, *The Attention Merchants: The Epic Scramble to Get Inside Our Heads*, New York: Penguin.

5. The term "organic" is often used to distinguish "naturally" occurring traffic from "paid" traffic, including advertisements and referrals. See Baye, Michael R., Babur De Los Santos, and Matthijs R. Wildenbeest, 2016, "Search Engine Optimization: What Drives Organic Traffic to Retail Sites?" *Journal of Economics and Management Strategy* 25 (1): 6–31.

6. Duffy, Brooke Erin, 2017, *(Not) Getting Paid to Do What You Love: Gender, Social Media, and Aspirational Work,* New Haven: Yale University Press. See also Ziewitz, "Rethinking Gaming"; Stuart, Forrest, 2020, *Ballad of the Bullet. Gangs, Drill Music, and the Power of Online Infamy*. Princeton: Princeton University Press.

7. On personal branding, fans, and followers, see Marwick, *Status Update*; Marwick and boyd, "I Tweet"; Baym, *Playing to the Crowd*. On the extension of this logic to other types of workers and forms of employment, see Gershon, Ilana, 2017, *Down and Out in the New Economy. How People Find (or Don't Find) Work Today*, Chicago: University of Chicago Press; Vallas, Steven P., and Angèle Christin, 2018, "Work and Identity in an Era of Precarious Employment: How Workers Respond to 'Personal Branding' Discourse," *Work & Occupation* 45 (1): 3–37.

8. See Roberts, Sarah T., 2018, *Behind the Screen. Content Moderation in the Shadows of Social Media*, New Haven: Yale University Press. See also Gray, Mary L., and Siddarth Suri, 2019, *Ghost Work. How to Stop Silicon Valley from*

Building a New Global Underclass, New York: Houghton Mifflin Harcourt. On the concept of "invisible work," first developed to analyze women's work and later used to emphasize infrastructural work, see Daniels, Arlene Kaplan, 1987, "Invisible Work," *Social Problems* 34 (5): 403–415; Star, Susan L., and Anselm Strauss, 1999, "Layers of Silence, Arenas of Voice: The Ecology of Visible and Invisible Work," *Computer Supported Cooperative Work* 8: 9–30.

9. Wu, *Master Switch*.

10. Hicks, Marie, 2017, *Programmed Inequality: How Britain Discarded Women Technologists and Lost Its Edge*, Cambridge: MIT Press. In 2013, the share of women in computing was a mere 26%. See West, Sarah Myers, Meredith Whittaker, and Kate Crawford, 2019, *Discriminating Systems. Gender, Race, and Power in AI*, AI Now Institute, 10–11, retrieved: https://ainowinstitute.org/dis criminatingsystems.pdf. More broadly, technological innovation often affects the distribution of power and expertise within organizations, along gendered but also status lines. See Star, Susan Leigh, 1999, "The Ethnography of Infrastructure," *American Behavioral Scientist* 43 (3): 377–391; Suchman, Lucy, Jeanette Blomberg, Julian E. Orr, and Randall Trigg, 1999, "Reconstructing Technologies as Social Practice," *American Behavioral Scientist* 43 (3), 392–408; Barley, Stephen R., 1986, "Technology as an Occasion for Structuring: Evidence from Observations of CT Scanners and the Social Order of Radiology Departments," *Administrative Science Quarterly* 31 (1): 78–108"; Bechky, Beth A., 2003, "Object Lessons: Workplace Artifacts as Representations of Occupational Jurisdiction," *American Journal of Sociology* 109 (3): 720–752; Zuboff, *Smart Machine*. For an analysis of the "fetishism" of algorithms as enabling the misrecognition of status and organizational displacements, see Thomas, Suzanne L., Dawn Nafus, and Jamie Sherman, 2018, "Algorithms as Fetish: Faith and Possibility in Algorithmic Work," *Big Data & Society*, 1–11. As data science becomes more legitimate—it was labelled "the sexiest job of the twenty-first century" by the Harvard Business Review in 2012—women run the risk of being downgraded to menial positions whereas men take over large-scale data initiatives, in online news and elsewhere. See Davenport, Thomas H., and D. J. Patil, 2012, "Data Scientist: The Sexiest Job of the 21st Century," *Harvard Business Review*, retrieved: https://hbr.org/2012 /10/data-scientist-the-sexiest-job-of-the-21st-century. As examples, see the gender breakdown of several high-level initiatives designed to improve newsroom metrics, such as the "Audience Explorer Dashboard" (https://medium.com/centerfor cooperativemedia/introducing-the-audience-explorer-dashboard-for-small-pub lishers-9fbff748c47) and "Metrics for News" (https://www.metricsfornews.com).

11. Weber, *Economy and Society*. For a case study of the routinization of charisma, see Bosk, Charles L., 1979, "The Routinization of Charisma: The Case of the Zaddik," *Sociological Inquiry* 49 (2–3): 150–167.

12. See Dupuy, Camille, 2014, "Repenser les acteurs et la négociation collective au travail. Le cas des sociétés de journalistes dans les entreprises de presse," *Négociations* 21 (1): 51–64.

13. For a comparable analysis, see Raviola, Elena, 2017, "Meetings Between Frames: Negotiating Worth Between Journalism and Management," *European Management Journal* 35: 737–744.

14. Note that the distinction between "short blog posts" and "other articles" in figure 3.1 is based on the distinct editorial formats in place at *TheNotebook* and *LaPlace*, not on the number of words of news articles published on the two websites. For *TheNotebook*, the darker bars ("short blog posts") are all the articles published in the section devoted to breaking news. For *LaPlace*, the darker bars count all the articles published in the aggregation-based section, also called "HuffPos" (see chapter 5).

15. In figures 2 and 4, the trendline was produced using the linear model function on R (http://stat.ethz.ch/R-manual/R-devel/library/stats/html/lm.html).

16. DiMaggio, Paul J., and Walter W. Powell, 1983, "The Iron Cage Revisited: Institutional Isomorphism and Collective Rationality in Organizational Fields," *American Sociological Review* 48 (2): 147–160; Meyer, John W., and Brian Rowan, 1977, "Institutionalized Organizations: Formal Structure as Myth and Ceremony," *American Journal of Sociology* 83 (2): 340–363.

17. For a similar application of the concept of isomorphism to the case of Facebook, see Caplan, Robyn, and danah boyd, 2018, "Isomorphism through Algorithms: Institutional Dependencies in the Case of Facebook," *Big Data & Society*, January-June: 1-12.

18. For an overview of the concepts and approaches in terms of "valuation/ evaluation," see Lamont, "Evaluation"; Boltanski and Thévenot, *On Justification*; Stark, *Sense of Dissonance*; Vatin, *Evaluer*.

19. As the next chapters will make clear, this synthetic overview of the two modes of evaluation simplifies a reality which is much more complex. On ideal types, see Weber, *Economy and Society*.

20. Note, however, that Schudson's distinction between the "news as information" and "news as stories" paradigms presented in chapter 1 does not perfectly match the modes of evaluation presented here, in the sense that U.S. elite journalism became increasingly narrative-driven over time (Benson, *Shaping Immigration News*). Along similar lines, Maria Luengo compares the "professional codes" of web journalists and the "unprofessional threats" of digital production. See Luengo, Maria, 2016, "When Codes Collide: Journalists Push Back Against Digital Desecration," pp. 119–134 in Alexander, Breese, and Luengo, *The Crisis of Journalism Reconsidered*, 127.

21. For additional references on the concept of "institutional logic," see Friedland, Roger, and Robert R. Alford, 1991, "Bringing Society Back In: Symbols, Practices, and Institutional Contradictions," pp. 232–263 in *The New Institutionalism in Organizational Analysis*, edited by P. J. DiMaggio and W. W. Powell, Chicago: University of Chicago Press; Thornton, Ocasio, and Lounsbury, "Institutional Logics." Yet, as Fligstein and McAdam underline, "The use of the term 'institutional logics' tends to imply way too much consensus in the field about what is going on and why and way too little concern over actors' positions." See Fligstein, Neil, and Doug McAdam, 2012, *A Theory of Fields*, New York: Oxford University Press, 11.

22. These findings on convergence resonate with previous studies showing that news websites are more likely than print newspapers to imitate each other's front pages and feature similar types of stories (namely, sensationalistic stories, "light" news, and opinion pieces), which may result in relative homogenization of

the news both within and between countries. See Boczkowski, Pablo J., 2010, *News at Work: Imitation in an Age of Information Abundance*, Chicago: University of Chicago Press; Benson, Rodney, Mark Blach-Ørsten, Matthew Powers, Ida Willig, and Sandra Vera Zambrano, 2012, "Media Systems Online and Off: Comparing the Form of News in the United States, Denmark, and France," *Journal of Communication* 62 (1): 21–38."

Chapter 4. The Multiple Meanings of Clicks

1. For further analysis of the concept of "hostile worlds" and how it informs the categories and repertoires people use to make sense of market and monetary forces in cases of problematic commodities, see Zelizer, Viviana, 2007, *The Purchase of Intimacy*, Princeton: Princeton University Press; Zelizer, Viviana, 2010, *Economic Lives: How Culture Shapes the Economy*, Princeton: Princeton University Press.

2. These shifting status hierarchies in turn shaped how I was received in web newsrooms. As a female ethnographer and graduate student asking questions about the "dirty" topic of traffic, I was often treated with condescension by senior male journalists scoring high on the editorial scale, whereas younger and lower-status journalists showed more interest in my project (see the methodological appendix). Similar gender dynamics were at the center of the so-called "LOL League" scandal in French web journalism, revealed in 2019. See Chrisafis, Angelique, 2019, "French Media in Crisis as They Face Their Own #MeToo Moment," *The Guardian*, Feb. 15, retrieved: https://www.theguardian.com/world/2019/feb/15/french-media-crisis-faces-own-metoo-moment-ligue-du-lol?CMP=share_btn_link.

3. Interestingly, writing about pre-internet media, James Carey analyzed a similar process in the construction of audience data for news organizations, and its representation for journalists: "The public, deconstituted into private readers, was now reconstituted as an audience: a group that did not interact with one another but were informed on events of significance as shaped, selected, indeed as constructed by a new professional guild: the journalist as reporter. Private reading cultivated private consciousness of individual members of the audience.... What was called public opinion was transvalued into the strategical aggregation of private opinions." Carey, "Nature of the Audience," 8.

4. For discussions of the distinction between "publics" and "audiences," see Webster, "Audience"; Napoli, *Audience Evolution*; Ettema and Whitney, *Audiencemaking*; Ang, *Desperately Seeking the Audience*; Couldry, Livingstone, and Markham, *Media Consumption*; Habermas, *Public Sphere*; Fraser, "Rethinking the Public Sphere"; Mouffe, "Deliberative Democracy"; Warner, *Publics and Counterpublics*; Benkler, *Wealth of Networks*; Geiger, "Habermas"; Marwick and boyd, "I Tweet." For the sake of this analysis, I use the term "public" broadly and descriptively in order to refer to the community of online news readers as considered by web journalists. Compared to the term "audience," "publics" retain a collective aspect and remain open to civic interpretations. For a similar distinction between "audiences" and "publics," although in a different historical context,

see Crow, Thomas E., 1985, *Painters and Public Life in Eighteenth Century Paris*, New Haven: Yale University Press.

5. "Media Kit: Advertise in *TheNotebook*, Find PR Contacts, etc.," *TheNotebook*, August 14, 2002 (names redacted).

6. As we will see in the next chapter, these writers were also among the "slow" (and expensive) ones. Hence, the decision to fire them was probably driven by several considerations at once.

7. Sean's assertion about traffic-based bonuses was directly confirmed by only one person. I asked several editors and staff writers working at *TheNotebook* about it. Some of them had recently started working for the website and did not know about the policy; others vaguely remembered that such bonuses used to exist but could not (or would not) tell me more about it.

8. See Petre, "Traffic Factories," for an analysis of Gawker's use of analytics, as well as Ananny, *Networked Press Freedom*, 137–142, for an overview of how analytics are used in major U.S. newsrooms.

9. Porter, *Trust in Numbers*, 8.

10. This metaphor of the random "fluke" or piece of luck when talking about the determinants of popularity in turn is not new in U.S. cultural industries. See Bielby and Bielby, "All Hits."

11. As Colin Jerolmack and Shamus Khan have argued, when it comes to people's description of their activities, "talk is cheap." Staff writers at *TheNotebook* could well be saying that they do not care about traffic while in fact obsessively tracking how many clicks their articles get. It could also be the case that staff writers refrained from talking about traffic because of my presence—a problem known as "reactivity" in qualitative research. To address the problem of reactivity, I triangulated my data carefully, relying not only on direct observations and interviews with current staff members but also on interviews with top editors, former staff members, administrative staff, etc. In particular, I tried to get the perspective of people who did not have the same incentives as current staff writers to misrepresent the use of analytics in the newsroom. See Jerolmack and Khan, "Talk Is Cheap."

12. When I asked *LaPlace*'s founders about this decision to display metrics on the homepage, they always answered with one word: "transparency." As André once put it, "We wanted to be clear and transparent. It's the same principle with edits: we always make our edits public. Also, I think it's a good idea for journalists to know their readers. We wanted everybody to be involved. People want to be part of the conversation.... If I see that three hundred people commented on an article, I'm going to read it, it's likely to be interesting." That said, most websites do not make their traffic numbers public. For instance, with a couple of well-orchestrated exceptions, *TheNotebook*'s traffic numbers remained out of public sight. One could find the numbers of likes, tweets, and comments when one clicked on the articles, but these metrics were not shown on the homepage.

13. Bourdieu, *Rules of Art*, 27. Cited in Childress, Clayton C., 2012, "Decision-Making, Market Logic and the Rating Mindset: Negotiating BookScan in the Field of US Trade Publishing," *European Journal of Cultural Studies* 15 (5): 604–620.

14. [Name redacted], 2013, "[title redacted]," *TheNotebook*, June 6; [Name redacted], 2013, "[title redacted]," *Chartbeat*, Press section. Drawing on Chart-

beat data about *TheNotebook*'s readers, the same writer found that 38% of the readers "bounced" at the top of each page, not even scrolling down the articles. Only 50% of the remaining readers made it to the midway point of any article published on the website.

15. [Name redacted], 2002, "Farewell," *TheNotebook*, June 28. Similarly, *TheNotebook*'s editor-in-chief made the following comment about the website's audience: "So our readers go low with us, and they go high with us, and, like Pharrell, we're happy either way." [Name redacted], 2014, "On *TheNotebook*," *Nieman Lab*, March 4.

16. After this episode, *LaPlace*'s editors abandoned their project to use quantitative performance measurements but maintained the goal to increase the amount of content published on the website.

Chapter 5. The Fast and the Slow

1. Tuchman, Gaye, 1973, "Making News by Doing Work: Routinizing the Unexpected," *American Journal of Sociology* 79 (1): 110–131. See also Esser, "Editorial Structures," for a similar analysis of the organizational structures of newsrooms.

2. Gans, *Deciding What's News*, 84–93; Hamilton, *Democracy's Detectives*, 13.

3. Usher, *Making News*. See also Klinenberg, Eric, 2005, "Convergence: News Production in a Digital Age," *The Annals of the American Academy of Political and Social Science* 597 (1): 48–64; Boczkowski, *News at Work*. For a historical perspective on the immediacy imperative, see Pettegree, Andrew, 2014, *The Invention of News: How the World Came to Know About Itself*, New Haven: Yale University Press.

4. Madrigal, Alexis, 2013, "A Day in the Life of a Digital Editor, 2013," *The Atlantic*, March 6, retrieved: https://www.theatlantic.com/technology/archive/2013/03/a-day-in-the-life-of-a-digital-editor-2013/273763/.

5. See Starkman, "The Hamster Wheel"; Usher, *Making News*, 89, 109; Boczkowski, *News at Work*. For an analysis of online news and publics in terms of "fast" and "slow," see Ananny, Mike, 2016, "Networked News Time: How Slow—or Fast—Do Publics Need News to Be?" *Digital Journalism*, 4 (4): 414–431.

6. In its original form, a blog—the word is a contraction of "web log"—consists of discrete entries posted in reverse chronological order. Blogs are usually associated with a more casual writing style, short and frequent posts, and an interactive component involving the readers. As this chapter and the next will make clear, however, the meaning of the term varies widely depending on the news website under consideration.

7. Though the borrowing and sharing of news is as old as journalism itself—colonial newspapers and telegraph companies frequently stole content from each other—such mimetic strategies reached a new magnitude of importance in online news. Hamilton, *Democracy's Detectives*, 179; Starr, *Creation of the Media*. For early debates about content aggregation, see Singel, Ryan, 2008, "The Huffington

Post Slammed for Content Theft," *Wired*, December 19, 2008, retrieved: https://
www.wired.com/2008/12/huffpo-slammed/; Grueskin, Bill, Ava Seave, and Lucas
Graves, 2011, "Chapter Six: Aggregation, 'Shameless'—and Essential," *Columbia Journalism Review*, May 10, retrieved: http://archives.cjr.org/the_business_of
_digital_journalism/chapter_six_aggregation.php.

8. Gans, *Deciding What's News*, 84–93, 95.

9. Gieryn, Thomas, 1983, "Boundary-Work and the Demarcation of Science
from Non-Science: Strains and Interests in Professional Ideologies of Scientists,"
American Sociological Review 48 (6): 781–95, 782. Michèle Lamont and Virág
Molnár define symbolic boundaries as "conceptual distinctions made by social ac-
tors to categorize objects, people, practices, and even time and space" to "creat(e),
maintain, contest ... institutionalized social differences." Lamont, Michèle, and
Virág Molnár, 2002, "The Study of Boundaries in the Social Sciences," *Annual
Review of Sociology* 28: 167–95, 168.

10. Saval, Nikil, 2014, *Cubed. A Secret History of the Workplace*, New York:
Doubleday.

11. I took a screenshot of *TheNotebook*'s homepage on April 18, 2014 at
11:14 a.m. and reproduced an anonymized version of it in figure 5.2. Note that
the articles featured on the homepage change every hour or so. Thus, figure 5.2
only represents one of the many homepages of *TheNotebook* that day.

12. The relevant metric for measuring the length of articles is different between the United States and France: French journalists use the number of letters,
or *signes*, as their main metric, whereas American journalists count the number
of words.

13. Another term for "HuffPo" used at *LaPlace* is "Lookout" (*vigie*). For the
sake of clarity, I only use the word "HuffPo" here.

14. This finding is based on a statistical analysis of the content of *LaPlace*'s
website performed on a data set gathered through a web crawl of all the articles
published on the French website between 2007 and 2013. See Christin, Angèle,
2015, "'Sex, Scandal, and Celebrities'? Exploring the Determinants of Success in
Online News," *About Journalism* 4 (2): 28–47.

15. This difference in how much *TheNotebook* and *LaPlace* relied on participatory content mirrors some of the findings of Anderson and Boczkowski. Both
found that there is a large amount of variation in the space and priority given to
user-generated content depending on the news organization under consideration.
Anderson, *Rebuilding the News*; Boczkowski, *Digitizing the News*.

16. See Christin, "Sex, Scandal, and Celebrities."

17. For similar feelings of exhaustion and critiques of the "relentlessness" of
the work rhythm among "new media" freelancers and entrepreneurs, see Neff,
Venture Labor; Barley, Stephen R., and Gideon Kunda, 2004, *Gurus, Hired Guns,
and Warm Bodies: Itinerant Experts in a Knowledge Economy*, Princeton: Princeton University Press. See also Raviola, "Meetings Between Frames," 737–744, for
a comparable analysis.

18. See Gouldner, Alvin Ward, 1954, *Patterns of Industrial Bureaucracy*, Glencoe: Free Press; Etzioni, Amitai, 1961, *A Comparative Analysis of Complex Organizations*, New York: The Free Press; Weber, *Economy and Society*; Burawoy, Michael,
1979, *Manufacturing Consent: Changes in the Labor Process under Monopoly
Capitalism*, Chicago: University of Chicago Press; Edwards, Richard, 1979, *Con-*

tested Terrain: The Transformation of the Workplace in the Twentieth Century, New York: Basic Books; Jacoby, Sanford M., 1985, *Employing Bureaucracy. Managers, Unions, and the Transformation of Work in the 20th Century*, New York: Columbia University Press. For a discussion of Gouldner's "indulgency" and "bureaucratic" patterns, see Burawoy, Michael, 1982, "The Written and the Repressed in Gouldner's Industrial Sociology," *Theory and Society* 11 (6): 831–851.

19. Kunda, Gideon, 2006, *Engineering Culture: Control and Commitment in a High-Tech Corporation*, revised edition, Philadelphia: Temple University Press; Sewell, "Discipline of Teams"; Foucault, *Discipline and Punish*; Etzioni, *Complex Organizations*. Note that these studies do not necessarily draw on the term "disciplinary" to describe these organizational dynamics; nor do they always systematically contrast bureaucratic and disciplinary forms of power. On the alternative concept of "post-bureaucracy," see, for instance, Heckscher, Charles C., 1994, "Defining the Post-Bureaucratic Type," in *The Post-Bureaucratic Organization: New Perspectives on Organizational Change*, edited by A. Donnellon and C. C. Heckscher, Thousand Oaks: Sage Publications, 14–62. Here my use of the term "disciplinary" refers to Sauder and Espeland's analysis of rankings as a form of discipline in the Foucauldian sense. See Sauder and Espeland, "The Discipline of Rankings"; Christin, "Counting Clicks." For a comparison of organizations with distinct cultures that echoes the one developed here, see Vertesi, Janet, forthcoming, *The Social Life of Spacecraft. How Organizations Shape Science on NASA's Robotic Team*, Chicago: University of Chicago Press.

20. For a recent example of these mixtures of bureaucratic and disciplinary systems, see Turco, Catherine J., 2018, *The Conversational Firm. Rethinking Bureaucracy in the Age of Social Media*, New York: Columbia University Press. See also Burawoy, *Manufacturing Consent*; Gouldner, *Patterns of Industrial Bureaucracy*; Edwards, *Contested Terrain*. Disciplinary power may operate on top of or in the cracks of bureaucratic structures. One can also distinguish between "rational" and "normative" forms of control, which complicate the comparison between bureaucratic and disciplinary ideal-types. See Barley, Stephen R., and Gideon Kunda, 1992, "Design and Devotion: Surges of Rational and Normative Ideologies of Control in Managerial Discourse," *Administrative Science Quarterly* 37 (3): 363–399. For a discussion, see Kellogg, Katherine C., Melissa Valentine, and Angèle Christin, 2020, "Algorithms at Work: The New Contested Terrain of Control," *Academy of Management Annals* 14(1): 366–410.

21. For analyses of the dialectical relationship between metrics and organizational dynamics in cases when platforms amended their metrics and ended up with unintended consequences that went against desired outcomes, see Rosenblat, *Uberland*; Rahman, Hatim A., 2019, "From Iron Cages to Invisible Cages: Algorithmic Evaluations in Online Labor Markets," unpublished manuscript.

Chapter 6. Between Exposure and Unpaid Work

1. Thayer, Nate, 2013, "A Day in the Life of a Freelance Journalist, 2013," March 4, retrieved: http://www.nate-thayer.com/a-day-in-the-life-of-a-freelance-journalist-2013/.

2. Coates, Ta-Nehisi, 2013, "'Lucrative Work-for-Free Opportunity.'" *The Atlantic.com*, March 9, retrieved: http://www.theatlantic.com/national/archive /2013/03/lucrative-work-for-freeopportunity/273846/.

3. Coscarelli, Joe, 2013, "Nate Thayer vs. The Atlantic: 'Exposure Doesn't Feed My F*cking Children!'" *New York Magazine, The Intelligencer*, March 5, retrieved: http://nymag.com/intelligencer/2013/03/nate-thayer-vs-the-atlantic-writing -for-free.html.

4. Gans, *Deciding What's News*; Tuchman, "Making News"; Whyte, William H., 1956, *The Organization Man*, New York: Simon & Schuster.

5. There is no national data about the proportion of freelance journalists in the United States, but small-scale evidence indicates that the number of journalists who freelance or have temporary or part-time positions is increasing. See Weaver, David H., Randal A. Beam, Bonnie J. Brownlee, Paul S. Voakes, and G. Cleveland Wilhoit, eds., 2007, *The American Journalist in the 21st Century: U.S. News People at the Dawn of a New Millennium*, Mahwah: L. Erlbaum Associates, 3; Cohen, Nicole S., 2016, *Writers' Rights: Freelance Journalism in a Digital Age*, Montreal: McGill-Queen's University Press; Salmon, Felix, 2013, "The Problem with Online Freelance Journalism," *Reuters Blogs*, March 5, retrieved: http://blogs .reuters.com/felix-salmon/2013/03/05/the-problem-with-online-freelance-jour nalism/. The data is also limited in France, but according to the official figures of the Observatoire des Métiers de la Presse, 63% of journalists under age 26 were freelancers or temporary workers in 2011 compared to 50% in 2009. Among the journalists who were between 26 and 34 years old, 33% were freelancers or temporary workers, a proportion that was increasing. Observatoire des Métiers de la Presse, 2013, "Les journalistes détenteurs de la carte de journaliste professionnel 2012," retrieved: http://www.metiers-presse.org/.

6. Freelance journalists have joined the growing ranks of workers, in Silicon Valley and elsewhere, who have to engage in "micro-celebrity" and "personal branding." See Marwick, *Status Update*; Vallas and Christin, "Work and Identity"; Vallas, Steven P., and Emily R. Cummins, 2015, "Personal Branding and Identity Norms in the Popular Business Press: Enterprise Culture in an Age of Precarity," *Organization Studies* 36 (3): 293–319. On entrepreneurialism and its history in journalism, see Prenger and Deuze, "Entrepreneurialism."

7. For statistical analyses of the number of self-employed workers in the United States, see Bureau of Labor Statistics, 2005, "Contingent and Alternative Employment Arrangements," July 27, retrieved: https://www.bls.gov/news.release /pdf/conemp.pdf. Bureau of Labor Statistics, 2017, "Selected Employment Indicators," May 5, retrieved: https://www.bls.gov/news.release/empsit.t09.htm. For a predictive study of the number of contingent workers in 2020, see Intuit, 2010, "Intuit 2020 Report," October, retrieved: http://http-download.intuit.com /http.intuit/CMO/intuit/futureofsmallbusiness/intuit_2020_report.pdf; Schrader, Brandon, 2015, "Here's Why the Freelancer Economy Is on the Rise," *Fast Company*, August 10, retrieved: https://www.fastcompany.com/3049532/the-future -of-work/heres-why-the-freelancer-economy-is-on-the-rise. For further analysis of contingent and "gig" or "ghost" work, see Pedulla, David, forthcoming, *Making the Cut. Hiring and Exclusion in the New Economy*, Princeton: Princeton University Press; Gray and Suri, *Ghost Work*; Roberts, *Behind the Screen*; Kalleberg,

Arne L., 2011, *Good Jobs, Bad Jobs: The Rise of Polarized and Precarious Employment Systems in the United States, 1970s to 2000s*, New York: Russell Sage Foundation.

8. For qualitative studies of the career strategies of freelance and precarious workers, see Neff, *Venture Labor*; Neff, Gina, Elizabeth Wissinger, and Sharon Zukin, 2005, "Entrepreneurial Labor among Cultural Producers: 'Cool' Jobs in 'Hot' Industries," *Social Semiotics* 15 (3): 307–34; Barley and Kunda, *Gurus*; Pilmis, Olivier, 2007, "Des 'employeurs multiples' au 'noyau dur' d'employeurs: Relations d'emploi et concurrence sur le marché des comédiens intermittents," *Sociologie du Travail* 49 (3): 297–315; Cohen, *Writers' Rights*; Zukin, Sharon, and Max Papadantonakis, 2017, "Hackathons as Co-optation Rituals: Socializing Workers and Institutionalizing Innovation in the 'New' Economy," pp. 157–181 in *Precarious Work* (Research in the Sociology of Work, Vol. 31), edited by A. L. Kalleberg and S. P. Vallas, Bingley: Emerald Publishing Limited.

9. As Jens Beckert and Patrik Aspers emphasize, "valuations according to different scales may lead to conflict over the assessment of the value of a good or an activity." Beckert and Aspers, *Worth of Goods*, 6. Yet to date there is little analysis of compensation as a form of evaluation, in spite of repeated calls for further work on the topic. See Zelizer, Viviana, 1996, "Payments and Social Ties," *Sociological Forum* 11 (3): 481–495.

10. A more complete analysis should also include the compensation of full-time employees, but I was not able to gather enough information about the salaries of *TheNotebook*'s employees to provide an accurate overview.

11. See Rosenkranz, Tim, 2018, "From Contract to Speculation: New Relations of Work and Production in the Field of Travel Journalism," *Work, Employment & Society* 33 (4): 613–630.

12. A more structural explanation, beyond the scope of the qualitative material analyzed in this article, should mobilize the literature on gender bias and the motherhood penalty in compensation and hiring decisions. At the time of the interview, Margaret had a young child. That was part of the reason why she had left her full-time job at the prestigious print publication and turned to freelancing in New York, where her husband was working. As she put it: "I became pregnant so I started looking around to see where I could go.... My husband got a job in New York, so I left, and I didn't have a job for a while, and then I had a baby and then I didn't work for about nine months and then I started freelancing again." She made it clear towards the end of the interview that her household primarily relied on her husband's salary—he was a programmer in the news business. See Correll, Shelley J., Stephen Benard, and In Paik, 2007, "Getting a Job: Is There a Motherhood Penalty?" *American Journal of Sociology* 112 (5): 1297–1339.

13. Average pay for *feuillets* ranges between 50 and 80 euros per page in France. The unit of payment for freelance pieces is different in the United States, where freelancers are paid by the word (typically 26–50 cents per word, according to the National Writers Union) or by the hour (typically $40–$50 per hour). For an overview of average rates in the two countries, see Syndicat National des Journalistes, 2015, "Barème de piges," retrieved: http://www.snj.fr/article/un-bareme-minimal-de-pige-en-presse-magazine-enfin; Editorial Freelancers Association, n.d., "Editorial Rates," retrieved: https://www.the-efa.org/rates/.

14. Note that these figures are based on what multiple journalists told me: I was not granted access to *LaPlace*'s payroll, so it is possible that journalists were mistaken about how much other people were paid in the newsroom.

15. *LaPlace*'s editors eventually agreed to compensate bloggers towards the end of my fieldwork at the Parisian website. About *The Huffington Post*'s case, see Gustin, Sam, 2011, "Unpaid Blogger Hits 'Slave Owner' Huffington with $105M Class Action Lawsuit," *Wired*, April 12, retrieved: https://www.wired.com /2011/04/tasini-sues-arianna/. U.S. District Judge John Koeltl ruled, "The principles of equity and good conscience do not justify giving the plaintiffs a piece of the purchase price when they never expected to be paid, repeatedly agreed to the same bargain, and went into the arrangement with eyes wide open." See Stempel, Jonathan, 2012, "Unpaid Bloggers' Lawsuit Versus Huffington Tossed," *Reuters*, March 30, retrieved: http://www.reuters.com/article/us-aol-huffingtonpost-bloggers -idUSBRE82T17L20120330.

16. For further analysis of code-switching, see Gumperz, John J., 1982, *Discourse Strategies*, Cambridge: Cambridge University Press; Bernstein, Basil B., 1975, *Class, Codes, and Control. Theoretical Studies towards a Sociology of Language*, New York: Schocken Books.

17. See Darnton, Robert, 1985, *The Literary Underground of the Old Regime*, Cambridge, MA: Harvard University Press; Lewis, "Journalism and Its Boundaries"; Boczkowski, *Digitizing the News*.

18. For similar findings, see Cohen, *Writers' Rights*, 113–140.

19. For similar findings regarding freelance programmers, see Barley and Kunda, *Gurus*.

20. Foucault, *Birth of Biopolitics*, 226.

21. Note that journalism is not the only sector where highly prestigious firms do not always pay their workers. For similar findings in the fashion industry, see Mears, Ashley, 2011, *Pricing Beauty: The Making of a Fashion Model*, Berkeley: University of California Press.

22. Bourdieu, *Field of Cultural Production*; Becker, Howard S., 1982, *Art Worlds*, University of California Press. See also Zuckerman, Ezra W., and Tai-Young Kim, 2003, "The Critical Trade-Off: Identity Assignment and Box-Office Success in the Feature Film Industry," *Industrial and Corporate Change* 12 (1): 27–67, for an example. Note that in the case of journalism, Bourdieu and others also define the heteronomous logic as being potentially based on political approval. Bourdieu, *On Television*; Champagne, "Double dépendance."

23. For similar findings about "micro-celebrity" strategies and "context collapse" on social media platforms, see Marwick, *Status Update*; Marwick and boyd, "I Tweet."

24. Interestingly, as of 2020, Patricia's Twitter account had reached 19,000 followers.

25. See Cohen, *Writers' Rights*; Pilmis, "Relations d'emploi."

26. See Aubert, Clémence, 2011, *La figure du pigiste comme forme de mobilisation de la main d'oeuvre: Le cas de la presse écrite française*, Sarrebruck: Éditions Universitaires Européennes; Charon, *Les médias*. It should be noted that from a legal standpoint, French *pigistes* are in fact tenured salaried employees (*salariés en contrat à durée indéterminée*) rather than independent contractors.

This legal status explains why *pigistes* benefit from the same advantages as tenured salaried employees in the press sector. In addition, in cases of legal disputes between news organization and *pigistes*, the burden of proof regarding the employment relationship is on the side of the employer. Yet most of the *pigistes* I met were not aware of this legal distinction (e.g., that they are salaried employees and not freelancers). Hence, I translate *pigiste* into English as "freelance journalist" for the sake of simplicity. A complete description of the French system would also include a comparative discussion of the status and benefits of performing artists (*intermittents du spectacle*). See Menger, Pierre, 2011, *Les intermittents du spectacle: Sociologie du travail flexible*, Paris: Éditions de l'École des Hautes Etudes en Sciences Sociales; Grégoire, Mathieu, 2009, "La clôture comme seule protection? Syndicats du spectacle et marché du travail dans l'Entre-Deux-Guerres (1919–1937)," *Sociologie du Travail* 51 (1): 1–24; Pilmis, Olivier, 2010, "Protection sociale, structures marchandes et temporalité de l'activité. Pigistes et comédiens face à l'Assurance-Chômage," *Sociologie* 2 (1): 215–233. Most of the French freelancers I interviewed, however, did not know about or did not claim the benefits associated with their status as "professional journalists." People who wrote occasionally for online publications were often not aware of the benefits associated with the *pigiste* status. The ones who knew about it often explained that they did not qualify because less than half of their income came from their writing. Finally, even the journalists who qualified rarely claimed the benefits. For instance, Marie told me: "When you're a *pigiste* and you have a bad month, Pôle Emploi helps you out.... But I've decided to stop, it's almost a full-time job to apply for the benefits.... For me it was a luxury, a couple of hundred euros here and there, but only for one or two months per year, so I stopped because it was not worth it."

27. See Vallas and Christin, "Work and Identity."

28. For further analysis of the different types of communication that occur in situations of context collapse on Twitter, see Marwick and boyd, "I Tweet." For complementary findings on how journalists use Twitter in the United States and France, see Powers, Matthew, and Sandra Vera Zambrano, 2017, "How Journalists Use Social Media in France and the United States: Analyzing Technology Use Across Journalistic Fields," *New Media & Society* 20 (8): 2728–2744; Molyneux, Logan, Avery Holton, and Seth Lewis, 2018, "How Journalists Engage in Branding on Twitter: Individual, Organizational and Institutional Levels," *Information, Communication & Society* 21 (10): 1386–1401.

29. Specifically, Lamont and Thévenot define "national cultural repertoires" as "relatively stable schemas of evaluation that are used in varying proportion across national contexts." Lamont and Thévenot, *Rethinking Comparative Cultural Sociology*, 8. Yet Lamont and Thévenot primarily focus on discourses rather than practices: the use of different repertoires of justification does not necessarily entail that individuals in fact behave differently. Lamont, Michèle, and Ann Swidler, 2014, "Methodological Pluralism and the Possibilities and Limits of Interviewing, *Qualitative Sociology* 37 (2): 153–171.

30. On the concept of decoupling at the organizational level, see Meyer and Rowan, "Institutionalized Organizations." On the decoupling that takes place at the individual level between discourses and practices, see Jerolmack and Khan, "Talk Is Cheap."

31. For further analysis of the contradictions between commercial and civic values on the French side, especially with respect to entrepreneurialism, see Vallas and Christin, "Work and Identity"; Abdelnour, Sarah, and Anne Lambert, 2014, "L'entreprise de soi, un nouveau mode de gestion politique des classes populaires?" *Genèses* 2 (95): 27–48.

Conclusion

1. Benkler, Yochai, Robert Faris, and Hal Roberts, 2018, *Network Propaganda: Manipulation, Disinformation, and Radicalization in American Politics*, New York: Oxford University Press.

2. See the analysis in Englehardt, Steven, and Arvind Narayanan, 2019, "Online Tracking: A 1-million-site Measurement and Analysis," retrieved: https://web transparency.cs.princeton.edu/webcensus/.

3. Zuboff, Shoshana, 2015, "Big Other: Surveillance Capitalism and the Prospects of an Information Civilization," *Journal of Information Technology* 30: 75–89; Zuboff, *Surveillance Capitalism*. See also Eubanks, Virginia, 2017, *Automating Inequality: How High-Tech Tools Profile, Police, and Punish the Poor*, New York: St Martin's Press; O'Neil, *Weapons of Math Destruction*.

4. See Turner, *From Counterculture to Cyberculture*, for a similar process.

5. See Kellogg, Valentine, and Christin, 2020, "Algorithms at Work." To develop the comparison between bureaucratic and disciplinary control, one can discuss the cases of policing, healthcare, trucking, ride-sharing, and criminal justice. Sarah Brayne's study of data-driven policing at the Los Angele Police Department describes a bureaucratic use of data. In contrast, Adam Reich's analysis of the uses of electronic data in hospitals bears closer affinities with the disciplinary model, as does Karen Levy's work on the remote surveillance of truckers. In Alex Rosenblat's study of Uber drivers, a mixed model emerges in which the demands and rewards of the bureaucratic system interact with the opacity and internalization of the disciplinary system. In the case of criminal justice, which I have studied, the use of metrics is primarily bureaucratic. See Brayne, Sarah, and Angèle Christin, forthcoming, "Technologies of Crime Prediction: The Reception of Algorithms in Policing and Courts," *Social Problems*; Reich, Adam, 2012, "Disciplined Doctors: The Electronic Medical Record and Physicians' Changing Relationship to Medical Knowledge," *Social Science & Medicine* 74 (7): 1021–1028; Levy, Karen, in preparation, *Data-Driven. Truckers and the New Workplace Surveillance*; Rosenblat, *Uberland*; Christin, "Algorithms in Practice."

6. See the additional information gathered for this project about legacy news organizations and digital native websites in New York and Paris in the methodological appendix. For supporting analysis of the uses of metrics in these two types of organizations, see Petre, "Traffic Factories"; Zamith, "Quantified Audiences"; Robinson, "The Audience in the Mind's Eye"; Nehell, "News by Number."

7. See, for instance, Schmidt, "Newsroom Culture," as well as the "Metrics for News" initiative (https://www.metricsfornews.com). Note that a more complete analysis should also take into account alternative metrics, for instance, existing

indicators about "impact" that are often promoted by nonprofit foundations. Benson, Rodney, 2017, "Can Foundations Solve the Journalism Crisis?" *Journalism* 19 (8): 1059–1077.

8. A promising path is charted by Karen Ho in her ethnographic study of traders. Ho analyzes how the precariousness and competitivity of financial careers shapes the worldview, justifications, and moral accounts of traders, which they then put to use when justifying their role in maximizing shareholder value, usually at the expense of workers. See Ho, Karen, 2009, *Liquidated. An Ethnography of Wall Street,* Durham and London: Duke University Press. One could similarly ask—more directly than I have done in this book—how the precarious careers and quantified definitions of value experienced by web journalists shape their understanding of the social world and is reflected in the articles they publish. Such an analysis would need to rely on a systematic statistical analysis of the content published by news organizations, before and after their adoption of metrics—an enterprise beyond the scope of the comparative qualitative project undertaken here.

9. See Turkle, Sherry, 2015, *Reclaiming Conversation. The Power of Talk in a Digital Age*, New York: Penguin Books; Vaidhyanathan, Siva, 2018, *Antisocial Media: How Facebook Disconnects Us and Undermines Democracy*, New York: Oxford University Press.

10. boyd, *It's Complicated.*

11. For a wonderful evocation of the power of livestreaming platforms in bringing together the desires and expectations of large flows of online viewers in China, see Wu, Hao, 2018, *People's Republic of Desire*, documentary, 1h35m. See also Taylor, T. L., 2018, *Watch Me Play. Twitch and the Rise of Game Live Streaming*, Princeton: Princeton University Press.

12. Weigel, Moira, 2016, *Labor of Love: The Invention of Dating*, New York: FSG.

13. Baym, *Playing to the Crowd*; Duffy, *(Not) Getting Paid.*

14. Weber, Max, 1919 (1946), "Science as a Vocation," in *From Max Weber: Essays in Sociology*, edited by H. H. Gerth and C. Wright Mills, New York: Oxford University Press, 129–156.

15. See Muller, *Tyranny of Metrics*; Espeland and Sauder, *Engines of Anxiety*; Gingras, Yves, 2016, *Bibliometrics and Research Evaluation: Uses and Abuses*, Cambridge: MIT Press; Strathern, Marilyn, ed., 2000, *Audit Cultures: Anthropological Studies in Accountability, Ethics, and the Academy*, Abingdon: Routledge.

16. For recent studies of these new occupations, see Duffy, *(Not) Being Paid*; Marwick, *Status Update*; Benkler, Faris, and Roberts, *Network Propaganda*; Lewis, Seth C., and Nikki Usher, 2016, "Trading Zones, Boundary Objects, and the Pursuit of News Innovation: A Case Study of Journalists and Programmers," *Convergence: The International Journal of Research into New Media Technologies* 22 (5): 543–560; Ananny, Mike, and Kate Crawford, 2015, "A Liminal Press: Situating News App Designers within a Field of Networked News Production," *Digital Journalism* 3 (2): 192–208; Lewis, Rebecca, 2018, "Alternative Influence. Broadcasting the Reactionary Right on YouTube," *Data & Society Institute*, research report, retrieved: https://datasociety.net/output/alternative-influence/; Marwick, Alice, and Rebecca Lewis, 2017, "Media Manipulation and Disinformation

Online," *Data & Society Institute*, report, retrieved: https://datasociety.net/pubs
/oh/DataAndSociety_MediaManipulationAndDisinformationOnline.pdf; Shestakofsky, "Working Algorithms"; Geiger, R. Stuart, 2017, "Beyond Opening Up the
Black Box: Investigating the Role of Algorithmic Systems in Wikipedian Organizational Culture," *Big Data & Society*, 1–14; Zukin and Papadantonakis, "Hackathons as Co-optation Ritual." For recent analyses of the complex collectives of
actors involved in the production of information and content across organizational and industry boundaries, before and after the development of these algorithmic and platform-based ecosystems, see Williams, Bruce A., and Michael X.
Delli Carpini, 2011, *After Broadcast News: Media Regimes, Democracy, and the
New Information Environment*, New York: Cambridge University Press; van Dijck,
José, 2013, *The Culture of Connectivity. A Critical History of Social Media*, Oxford: Oxford University Press.

Appendix. A Fly on the Screen

1. The proposal I submitted to the Princeton Institutional Review Board (IRB)
stipulated that I would anonymize individuals and organizations. This decision
to anonymize individuals is standard practice in ethnographic research, as is the
anonymization of firms and institutions in organizational studies. See, for instance,
Kunda, *Engineering Culture*; Barley, "Technology as an Occasion for Structuring"; Gouldner, *Patterns of Industrial Bureaucracy*; Bechky, "Object Lessons";
Reich, Adam, 2014, *Selling Our Souls: The Commodification of Hospital Care in
the United States*, Princeton: Princeton University Press; Kellogg, Katherine C.,
2011, *Challenging Operations. Medical Reform and Resistance in Surgery*, Chicago: University of Chicago Press. In contrast, scholars in journalism studies tend
not to anonymize the news organizations they study. See Boczkowski, *Digitizing
the News*; Anderson, *Rebuilding the News*; Usher, *Making News*.
2. Jerolmack and Khan, "Talk Is Cheap."
3. As Lise emailed me, "Philippe said: 'no worries.' Just let us know when
you're coming."
4. For a similar design based on built-in convergence and the comparison of
divergence, see Sallaz, Jeffrey J., 2009, *The Labor of Luck: Casino Capitalism
in the United States and South Africa*, Berkeley: University of California Press;
Sallaz, Jeffrey J., 2012, "Politics of Organizational Adornment Lessons from Las
Vegas and Beyond," *American Sociological Review* 77 (1): 99–119. Note that the
relative size of the two teams always differed. As of March 2014, when I was
finishing writing my dissertation, *TheNotebook* had 56 employees (including 41
writers and editors) and *LaPlace* had 30 employees (including 21 writers and
editors).
5. See Timmermans, Stefan, and Iddo Tavory, 2012, "Theory Construction in
Qualitative Research: From Grounded Theory to Abductive Analysis," *Sociological Theory* 30 (3): 167–186.
6. On theoretical sampling and the "grounded theory" approach more generally, see Glaser, Barney G., and Anselm L. Strauss, 1967, *The Discovery of*

Grounded Theory: Strategies for Qualitative Research, Chicago: Aldine; Charmaz, Kathy, 2006, *Constructing Grounded Theory: A Practical Guide Through Qualitative Analysis*; Tavory, Iddo, and Stefan Timmermans, 2009, "Two Cases of Ethnography: Grounded Theory and Extended Case Method," *Ethnography* 10 (3): 243–263.

7. In Paris, I conducted observations and four interviews at one of *LaPlace*'s main rivals, also a stand-alone news website, but one that relied on subscriptions rather than advertising as its main source of revenues. This fieldwork was part of a collective workshop organized by Cyril Lemieux and Eric Lagneau at the EHESS in the Winter of 2012 on the role of the media in the French presidential elections. I also conducted five interviews and several days of observation at another stand-alone website that had a partnership with a digital-native U.S. website and blogging platform. Last but not least, I studied a large Parisian web newsroom, the online version of a major print newspaper, where I conducted a week of observation and interviewed eight journalists. In New York, I complemented my study of *TheNotebook* in a similar way. First, I spent two days in the newsroom of one of *TheNotebook*'s main competitors—one that relied on aggressive traffic maximization techniques—and two days in the newsroom of a smaller website located in Brooklyn. As part of the research work I did for a French documentary on the future of journalism (Kieffer, Philippe, and Marie-Eve Chamard, 2014, *Presse: Vers un monde sans papier*, director: Pierre-Olivier François. Arte France, Extro), I also observed the offices of a major analytics company.

8. The percentages of women and individuals with journalism degrees in my sample of interviewees are consistent with the broader socio-demographic features of the journalistic workforce in the two countries at the time. See Weaver et al., *American Journalist*; Observatoire des Métiers de la Presse, "Les journalistes." Note, however, that one should not treat these two groups as representative samples. First, the journalists were recruited through snowball sampling, based on the websites they were working for, not in a representative manner. Second, the number of qualitative interviews that I conducted for this project is too low to engage in statistical analysis. On the risks associated with treating interviews as a statistical sample, see Small, Mario, 2009, "How Many Cases Do I Need? On Science and the Logic of Case Selection in Field-Based Research," *Ethnography* 10 (1): 5–38.

9. Maradan, Isabelle, 2014, "Interview: Course à l'audience, uniformisation, le journalisme web tiré vers le bas," *L'Express* 5 juillet, retrieved: https://www.lexpress.fr/actualite/medias/course-a-l-audience-uniformisation-le-journalisme-web-tire-vers-le-bas_1556491.html.

10. When the editors or journalists asked, I usually offered to present my findings to the newsroom in person.

11. See Bourdieu, Pierre, 1999b, "Understanding," *The Weight of the World: Social Suffering in Contemporary Society*, Stanford: Stanford University Press, 607–626; Venkatesh, Sudhir, 2002, "'Doin' the Hustle': Constructing the Ethnographer in the American Ghetto," *Ethnography* 3: 91–111.

12. On the overlapping networks of the French elite, see Bourdieu, Pierre, 1996, *The State Nobility: Elite Schools in the Field of Power*, Cambridge, UK: Polity Press; Champagne, "Double dépendance." On the symbolic violence that

comes with interviewing members of the elite, see Chamboredon, Hélène, Fabienne Pavis, Muriel Surdez, and Laurent Willemez, 1994, "S'imposer aux imposants. À propos de quelques obstacles rencontrés par des sociologues débutants dans la pratique et l'usage de l'entretien," *Genèses* 16 (1): 114–132.

13. Over the years, I stayed in touch with several researchers who studied *LaPlace* before me. We compared our observations and findings.

14. On the role of gender and feminization in French journalism, see Neveu, Erik, 2000, "Le genre du journalisme. Des ambivalences de la féminisation d'une profession," *Politix* 51: 179–212. More recently, see Chrisalis, "LOL League."

15. Note, however, that this type of behavior certainly exists in the United States. For a recent example, see Donegan, Moira, 2018, "I Started the Media Men List. My Name is Moira Donegan," *The Cut*, retrieved: https://www.thecut.com /2018/01/moira-donegan-i-started-the-media-men-list.html.

16. On the related concept of "screenwork," see Boyer, Dominic. 2013. *The Life Informatic: Newsmaking in the Digital Era*, Ithaca: Cornell University Press.

17. About the "fly on the wall" approach in urban ethnography, see, for instance, Goffman, Alice, 2014, "Appendix: A Methodological Note," in *On the Run: Fugitive Life in an American City*, Chicago: University of Chicago Press. For an analysis of the limitations of the representation of the ethnographer's role in the field as transparent and passive, see Venkatesh, "'Doin' the Hustle.'"

18. See, for instance, Knorr Cetina, Karin, 1999, *Epistemic Cultures: How the Sciences Make Knowledge*, Cambridge, MA: Harvard University Press; Morrill, Calvin, and Gary Alan Fine, 1997, "Ethnographic Contributions to Organizational Sociology," *Sociological Methods & Research* 25 (4): 424–451; Bechky, Beth, A., 2006, "Talking about Machines, Thick Description, and Knowledge Work," *Organization Studies* 27: 1757–1768; Comaroff, Jean, and John Comaroff, 2003, "Ethnography on an Awkward Scale: Postcolonial Anthropology and the Violence of Abstraction," *Ethnography* 4: 147–1381; Comaroff, John, and Jean Comaroff, 1992, *Ethnography and the Historical Imagination*, Boulder: Westview Press.

19. These tactics in turn draw on recent work in "digital," "virtual," "networked," and "trace" ethnography. See Coleman, E. Gabriella, 2010, "Ethnographic Approaches to Digital Media," *Annual Review of Anthropology* 39: 487–505; boyd, danah, 2015, "Making Sense of Teen Life: Strategies for Capturing Ethnographic Data in a Network Era," in *Digital Research Confidential: The Secrets of Studying Behavior Online*, edited by E. Hargittai and C. Sandvig, Cambridge, MA: MIT Press, 79–102; Howard, Philip N., 2002, "Network Ethnography and the Hypermedia Organization: New Media, New Organizations," *New Methods in New Media and Society* 4: 550–574; Burrell, Jenna, 2009, "The Field Site as a Network: A Strategy for Locating Ethnographic Research," *Field Methods* 21 (2): 181–199; Geiger, R. Stuart and David Ribes, "Trace Ethnography: Following Coordination through Documentary Practices," *HICSS '11 Proceedings of the 2011 44th Hawaii International Conference on System Sciences*, 1–10; Boellstorff, Tom, Bonnie Nardi, Celia Pearce, and T. L. Taylor, eds., 2012, *Ethnography and Virtual Worlds: A Handbook of Method*, Princeton: Princeton University Press; Takhatev, *Coding Places*; Seaver, "Algorithms as Culture."

20. On shadowing as a privileged strategy for witnessing how people move between settings and situations, see Trouille, David, and Iddo Tavory, 2019, "Shadowing: Warrants for Intersituational Variation in Ethnography," *Sociological Methods and Research* 48 (3): 534–560.

21. For instance, Yeykelis, Cummings, and Reeves found that switches between content on personal computers occurred every 19 seconds. Yeykelis, Leo, James J. Cummings, and Byron Reeves, 2014, "Multitasking on a Single Device: Arousal and the Frequency, Anticipation, and Prediction of Switching Between Media Content on a Computer," *Journal of Communication* 64 (1): 167–192.

22. Whenever I had an interview scheduled with a web journalist or an editor, I would start by looking them up online and downloading their resume or biographic sketch. I read several of their articles and wrote down the websites they had worked for.

23. See Christin, "Transnational Field," for a more complete analysis of this ethnographic vignette.

24. For elaborations, see Knox, Hannah, and Dawn Nafus, eds., 2018, *Ethnography for a Data-Saturated World*, Manchester: Manchester University Press; Murthy, Dhiraj, 2008, "Digital Ethnography: An Examination of the Use of New Technologies for Social Research," *Sociology* 42: 837.

25. Snow, David, 1980 "The Disengagement Process: A Neglected Problem in Participant Observation Research," *Qualitative Sociology* 3: 100–122.

26. See Christin, "Sex, Scandals, and Celebrities."

27. We also considered the possibility that our data collection missed some of the articles counted by *TheNotebook*'s servers and internal data team.

28. See Lane, *The Digital Street* (Appendix), for an example of a similar mixed-method approach.

29. See boyd, danah, 2016b, "Untangling Research and Practice: What Facebook's 'Emotional Contagion' Study Teaches Us," *Research Ethics* 12 (1): 4–13; Marwick, Alice E., and danah boyd, 2014, "Networked Privacy: How Teenagers Negotiate Context in Social Media," *New Media & Society*, 16 (7): 1051–1067.

BIBLIOGRAPHY

Abbate, Janet. 1999. *Inventing the Internet*. Cambridge, MA: MIT Press.

Abbott, Andrew D. 1988. *The System of Professions: An Essay on the Division of Expert Labor*. Chicago: University of Chicago Press

Abdelnour, Sarah, and Anne Lambert. 2014. "L'entreprise de soi, un nouveau mode de gestion politique des classes populaires?" *Genèses* 2(95):27–48.

Abramson, Jill E. 2019. *Merchants of Truth. The Business of News and the Fight for Facts*. New York: Simon & Schuster.

Adler-Bell, Sam. 2019. "Surviving Amazon." *Logic*, Bodies. 8. Retrieved: https://logicmag.io/bodies/surviving-amazon/.

Alexander, Jeffrey C. 1981. "The Mass News Media in Systemic, Historical, and Comparative Perspective." In *Mass Media and Social Change*, Sage Studies in International Sociology, edited by E. Katz and T. Szecskő. Beverly Hills: Sage Publications.

Alexander, Jeffrey C., Elizabeth Butler Breese, and Maria Luengo, eds. 2016. *The Crisis of Journalism Reconsidered*. New York: Cambridge University Press.

American Society of News Editors. 2018. *ASNE Newsroom Employment Diversity Survey*. Retrieved: https://www.asne.org/diversity-survey-2018.

Ames, Morgan G. 2019. *The Charisma Machine. The Life, Death, and Legacy of One Laptop Per Child*. 2019. Cambridge, MA: MIT Press

Ananny, Mike. 2016. "Networked News Time: How Slow—or Fast—Do Publics Need News To Be?" *Digital Journalism* 4(4):414–431.

Ananny, Mike. 2018. *Networked Press Freedom: Creating Infrastructures for a Public Right to Hear*. Cambridge, MA: MIT Press.

Ananny, Mike, and Kate Crawford. 2015. "A Liminal Press: Situating News App Designers within a Field of Networked News Production." *Digital Journalism* 3(2):192–208.

Anderson, Benedict R. 2006. *Imagined Communities: Reflections on the Origin and Spread of Nationalism*. London: Verso.

Anderson, Chris. 2008. "The End of Theory: The Data Deluge Makes the Scientific Method Obsolete." *Wired*, June 23. Retrieved: https://www.wired.com/2008/06/pb-theory/.

Anderson, Chris W. 2011. "Between Creative and Quantified Audiences: Web Metrics and Changing Patterns of Newswork in Local US Newsrooms." *Journalism* 12(5):550–566.

Anderson, Chris W. 2011. "Deliberative, Agonistic, and Algorithmic Audiences: Journalism's Vision of Its Public in an Age of Audience Transparency." *International Journal of Communication* 5:519–547.

Anderson, Chris W. 2013. *Rebuilding the News: Metropolitan Journalism in the Digital Age*. Philadelphia: Temple University Press.

Anderson, Chris W. 2018. *Apostles of Certainty: Data Journalism and the Politics of Doubt*. Oxford: Oxford University Press.

Ang, Ien. 1991. *Desperately Seeking the Audience*. London: Routledge.

Angwin, Julia. 2014. *Dragnet Nation: A Quest for Privacy, Security, and Freedom in a World of Relentless Surveillance*. New York: Times Books, Henry Holt and Company.

Anteby, Michel. 2008. *Moral Gray Zones: Side Productions, Identity, and Regulation in an Aeronautic Plant*. Princeton: Princeton University Press.

Anteby, Michel, Curtis Chan, and Julia DiBenigno. 2016. "Three Lenses on Occupations and Professions in Organizations: Becoming, Doing, and Relating." *Academy of Management Annals* 10(1):183–244.

Appaduraï, Arjun. 1996. *Modernity at Large: Cultural Dimensions of Globalization*. Minneapolis: University of Minnesota Press.

Atton, Chris, and James F. Hamilton. 2008. *Alternative Journalism*. London: Sage.

Aubert, Clémence. 2011. *La figure du pigiste comme forme de mobilisation de la main d'oeuvre: Le cas de la presse écrite française*. Sarrebruck: Éditions Universitaires Européennes.

Bagdikian, Ben H. 2004. *The New Media Monopoly*. Boston: Beacon Press.

Baker, Keith M. 2012. "Public Opinion as Political Invention." *Inventing the French Revolution. Essays on French Political Culture in the Eighteenth Century*. Cambridge: Cambridge University Press, 167–200.

Bakshy, Eytan, Solomon Messing, and Lada A. Adamic. 2015. "Exposure to Ideologically Diverse News and Opinion on Facebook." *Science* 348(6239):1130–1132.

Barley, Stephen R. 1986. "Technology as an Occasion for Structuring: Evidence from Observations of CT Scanners and the Social Order of Radiology Departments." *Administrative Science Quarterly* 31(1):78–108.

Barley, Stephen R., and Gideon Kunda. 1992. "Design and Devotion: Surges of Rational and Normative Ideologies of Control in Managerial Discourse." *Administrative Science Quarterly* 37(3):363–399.

Barley, Stephen R., and Gideon Kunda. 2014. *Gurus, Hired Guns, and Warm Bodies: Itinerant Experts in a Knowledge Economy*. Princeton: Princeton University Press.

Barocas, Solon, Alex Rosenblat, danah boyd, Seeta Pena Gangdharan, and Corrine Yu. 2014. "Data & Civil Rights: Technology Primer." *Data & Civil Rights Conference*, October. Retrieved: https://papers.ssrn.com/sol3/papers.cfm?abstract_id=2536579.

Barocas, Solon, and Andrew Selbst. 2016. "Big Data's Disparate Impact." *California Law Review* 104(3):671–732.

Barthel, Michael. 2018. *Newspapers Fact Sheet*. Pew Research Center. Retrieved: http://www.journalism.org/fact-sheet/newspapers/.

Baye, Michael R., Babur De Los Santos, and Matthijs R. Wildenbeest. 2016. "Search Engine Optimization: What Drives Organic Traffic to Retail Sites?" *Journal of Economics & Management Strategy* 25(1):6–31.

Baym, Nancy K. 2013. "Data Not Seen: The Uses and Shortcomings of Social Media Metrics." *First Monday* 18(10).

Baym, Nancy K. 2018. *Playing to the Crowd: Musicians, Audiences, and the Intimate Work of Connection*. New York: New York University Press.

Bechky, Beth A. 2003. "Object Lessons: Workplace Artifacts as Representations of Occupational Jurisdiction." *American Journal of Sociology* 109(3):720–752.

Bechky, Beth A. 2006. "Talking about Machines, Thick Description, and Knowledge Work." *Organization Studies* 27(12):1757–1768.

Becker, Howard Saul. 1982. *Art Worlds*. Berkeley: University of California Press.

Beckert, Jens, and Patrik Aspers, eds. 2011. *The Worth of Goods: Valuation and Pricing in the Economy*. New York: Oxford University Press.

Beer, David. 2016. *Metric Power*. London: Palgrave Macmillan.

Belair-Gagnon, Valerie, and Avery E. Holton. 2018. "Boundary Work, Interloper Media, and Analytics in Newsrooms." *Digital Journalism* 6(8):492–508.

Benjamin, Ruha. 2019. *Race after Technology*. New York: Polity Press.

Benkler, Yochai. 2006. *The Wealth of Networks: How Social Production Transforms Markets and Freedom*. New Haven: Yale University Press.

Benkler, Yochai, Robert Faris, and Hal Roberts. 2018. *Network Propaganda: Manipulation, Disinformation, and Radicalization in American Politics*. New York: Oxford University Press.

Benson, Rodney. 2013. *Shaping Immigration News: A French-American Comparison*. Cambridge: Cambridge University Press.

Benson, Rodney. 2017. "Can Foundations Solve the Journalism Crisis?" *Journalism* 19(8):1059–1077.

Benson, Rodney, Mark Blach-Ørsten, Matthew Powers, Ida Willig, and Sandra Vera Zambrano. 2012. "Media Systems Online and Off: Comparing the Form of News in the United States, Denmark, and France." *Journal of Communication* 62(1):21–38.

Benson, Rodney, and Erik Neveu. 2005. *Bourdieu and the Journalistic Field*. Cambridge: Polity.

Benson, Rodney, and Abigail C. Saguy. 2005. "Constructing Social Problems in an Age of Globalization: A French-American Comparison." *American Sociological Review* 70(2):233–259.

Bernstein, Basil B. 1975. *Class, Codes, and Control: Theoretical Studies towards a Sociology of Language*. New York: Schocken Books.

Bielby, William T., and Denise D. Bielby. 1994. "'All Hits Are Flukes': Institutionalized Decision Making and the Rhetoric of Network Prime-Time Program Development." *American Journal of Sociology* 99(5):1287–1313.

Blanchett Nehell, Nicole. 2018. "News by Numbers: The Evolution of Analytics in Journalism." *Digital Journalism* 6(8):1041–1051.

Boczkowski, Pablo J. 2005. *Digitizing the News: Innovation in Online Newspapers*. Cambridge, MA: MIT Press.

Boczkowski, Pablo J. 2010. *News at Work: Imitation in an Age of Information Abundance*. Chicago: University of Chicago Press.

Boczkowski, Pablo Javier, and Ignacio Siles. 2014. "Steps toward Cosmopolitanism in the Study of Media Technologies." *Information, Communication & Society* 17(5):560–571.

Boellstorff, Tom, Bonnie Nardi, Celia Pearce, and T. L. Taylor, eds. 2012. *Ethnography and Virtual Worlds: A Handbook of Method*. Princeton: Princeton University Press.

Boltanski, Luc, and Laurent Thévenot. 2006. *On Justification: Economies of Worth*. Princeton: Princeton University Press.

Bosk, Charles L. 1979. "The Routinization of Charisma: The Case of the Zaddik." *Sociological Inquiry* 49(2–3):150–167.

Bouk, Daniel B. 2018. *How Our Days Became Numbered: Risk and the Rise of the Statistical Individual*. Chicago: University of Chicago Press.

Bourdieu, Pierre. 1993. *The Field of Cultural Production: Essays on Art and Literature*, edited by R. Johnson. New York: Columbia University Press.

Bourdieu, Pierre. 1996. *The State Nobility: Elite Schools in the Field of Power*. Stanford: Stanford University Press.

Bourdieu, Pierre. 1999a. *On Television*. New York: New Press.

Bourdieu, Pierre. 1999b. "Understanding." In *The Weight of the World: Social Suffering in Contemporary Society*, edited by P. Bourdieu and A. Accardo. Cambridge: Polity Press.

Bourdieu, Pierre. 2005. "The Political Field, the Social Science Field, and the Journalistic Field." In *Bourdieu and the Journalistic Field*, edited by R. Benson and E. Neveu. Cambridge: Polity Press.

Bourdieu, Pierre. 2006. *The Rules of Art: Genesis and Structure of the Literary Field*. Stanford: Stanford University Press.

Bourdieu, Pierre, and Loïc J. D. Wacquant. 1992. *An Invitation to Reflexive Sociology*. Chicago: University of Chicago Press.

Bouron, Samuel. 2015. "Les écoles de journalisme face à l'expansion du marché. Stratégies d'internationalisation et transformations des curricula." *Cahiers de la recherche sur l'éducation et les savoirs* (14):245–266.

boyd, danah. 2014. *It's Complicated: The Social Lives of Networked Teens*. New Haven: Yale University Press.

boyd, danah. 2015. "Making Sense of Teen Life: Strategies for Capturing Ethnographic Data in a Networked Era." In *Digital Research Confidential: The Secrets of Studying Behavior Online*, edited by E. Hargittai and C. Sandvig. Cambridge, MA: MIT Press.

boyd, danah. 2016a. "Reality Check: I Blame the Media." *Data & Society: Points*. Retrieved: https://points.datasociety.net/reality-check-de447f2131a3.

boyd, danah. 2016b. "Untangling Research and Practice: What Facebook's 'Emotional Contagion' Study Teaches Us." *Research Ethics* 12(1):4–13.

boyd, danah, and Kate Crawford. 2012. "Critical Questions for Big Data: Provocations for a Cultural, Technological, and Scholarly Phenomenon." *Information, Communication & Society* 15(5):662–679.

Boyer, Dominic. 2013. *The Life Informatic: Newsmaking in the Digital Era*. Ithaca: Cornell University Press.

Braun, Josh. 2015. *This Program Is Brought to You by: Distributing Television News Online*. New Haven: Yale University Press.

Brayne, Sarah. 2017. "Big Data Surveillance: The Case of Policing." *American Sociological Review* 82(5):977–1008.

Brayne, Sarah, and Angèle Christin. Forthcoming. "Technologies of Crime Prediction: Comparing the Reception of Algorithms in Policing and Criminal Justice." *Social Problems*.

Broussard, Meredith. 2018. *Artificial Unintelligence. How Computers Misunderstand the World*. Cambridge, MA: MIT Press.

Browne, Simone. 2015. *Dark Matters. On the Surveillance of Blackness*. Durham: Duke University Press.

Brubaker, Rogers. 1984. *The Limits of Rationality: An Essay on the Social and Moral Thought of Max Weber*. London: Allen & Unwin.

Brunton, Finn, and Helen Nissenbaum. 2015. *Obfuscation: A User's Guide for Privacy and Protest*. Cambridge, MA: MIT Press.

Bucher, Taina. 2017. "The Algorithmic Imaginary: Exploring the Ordinary Affects of Facebook Algorithms." *Information, Communication & Society* 20(1): 30–44.

Bucher, Taina. 2018. *If … Then: Algorithmic Power and Politics*. New York: Oxford University Press.

Bunce, Mel. 2017. "Management and Resistance in the Digital Newsroom." *Journalism* 20(8):890–905.

Burawoy, Michael. 1979. *Manufacturing Consent: Changes in the Labor Process under Monopoly Capitalism*. Chicago: University of Chicago Press.

Burawoy, Michael. 1982. "The Written and the Repressed in Gouldner's Industrial Sociology." *Theory and Society* 11(6):831–851.

Bureau of Labor Statistics. 2005. "Contingent and Alternative Employment Arrangements." Retrieved: https://www.bls.gov/news.release/History/conemp.txt.

Bureau of Labor Statistics. 2019. "Selected Employment Indicators." Retrieved: https://www.bls.gov/news.release/empsit.t09.htm.

Burrell, Jenna. 2009. "The Field Site as a Network: A Strategy for Locating Ethnographic Research." *Field Methods* 21(2):181–199.

Burrell, Jenna. 2012. *Invisible Users: Youth in the Internet Cafés of Urban Ghana*. Cambridge, MA: MIT Press.

Cagé, Julia. 2015. *Sauver les médias. Capitalisme, financement participatif et démocratie*. Paris: Le Seuil, La République des idées.

Campbell, W. Joseph. 2001. *Yellow Journalism: Puncturing the Myths, Defining the Legacies*. Westport: Praeger.

Caplan, Robyn, and danah boyd. 2018. "Isomorphism through Algorithms: Institutional Dependencies in the Case of Facebook." *Big Data & Society*. January–June: 1–12.

Carey, James W. 1980. "Changing Communications Technology and the Nature of the Audience." *Journal of Advertising* 9(2):3–43.

Carey, James W. 1992. *Communication as Culture: Essays on Media and Society*. New York: Routledge.

Carlson, Matt. 2014. "The Robotic Reporter. Automated Journalism and the Redefinition of Labor, Compositional Forms, and Journalistic Authority." *Digital Journalism* 3(3):416–431.

Carlson, Matt. 2015. "When News Sites Go Native: Redefining the Advertising–Editorial Divide in Response to Native Advertising." *Journalism: Theory, Practice & Criticism* 16(7):849–865.

Caron, James E. 1985. "Hunter S. Thompson's "Gonzo" Journalism and the Tall Tale Tradition in America." *Studies in Popular Culture* 8(1):1–16.

Carruthers, Bruce G., and Wendy Nelson Espeland. 1991. "Accounting for Rationality: Double-Entry Bookkeeping and the Rhetoric of Economic Rationality." *American Journal of Sociology* 97(1):31–69.

Chalaby, Jean K. 1996. "Journalism as an Anglo-American Invention: A Comparison of the Development of French and Anglo-American Journalism, 1830s–1920s." *European Journal of Communication* 11(3):303–326.

Chamboredon, Hélène, Fabienne Pavis, Muriel Surdez, and Laurent Willemez. 1994. "S'imposer aux imposants. A propos de quelques obstacles rencontrés par des sociologues débutants dans la pratique et l'usage de l'entretien." *Genèses. Sciences sociales et histoire* 16(1):114–132.

Champagne, Patrick. 1995. "La double dépendance. Quelques remarques sur les rapports entre les champs politique, économique et journalistique." *Hermès* 17–18:215–229.

Champagne, Patrick, and Dominique Marchetti. 2005. "The Contaminated Blood Scandal: Reframing Medical News." In *Bourdieu and the Journalistic Field*, edited by R. D. Benson and E. Neveu. Cambridge: Polity.

Charle, Christophe. 1990. *Naissance des "Intellectuels": 1880–1900*. Paris: Éd. de Minuit.

Charle, Christophe. 2004. *Le siècle de la presse, 1830–1939*. Paris: Seuil.

Charmaz, Kathy. 2006. *Constructing Grounded Theory*. Thousand Oaks: Sage Publications.

Charon, Jean-Marie. 2003. *Les médias en France*. Paris: La Découverte.

Chartbeat.com. Retrieved April 9, 2014 and September 1, 2015: https://chartbeat .com/.

Chen, Julie Yujie. 2018. "Thrown under the Bus and Outrunning It! The Logic of Didi and Taxi Drivers' Labour and Activism in the On-Demand Economy." *New Media & Society* 20(8):2691–2711.

Childress, C. Clayton. 2012. "Decision-Making, Market Logic and the Rating Mindset: Negotiating BookScan in the Field of US Trade Publishing." *European Journal of Cultural Studies* 15(5):604–620.

Childress, C. Clayton. 2017. *Under the Cover: The Creation, Production, and Reception of a Novel*. Princeton: Princeton University Press.

Chin, Jeff. 2018. "We Detox from Chartbeat." *NiemanLab*, Predictions of Journalism 2019. Retrieved: https://www.niemanlab.org/2018/12/we-detox-from -chartbeat/.

Chrisafis, Angelique. 2019. "French Media in Crisis as They Face Their Own #MeToo Moment." *The Guardian*, Feb. 15, 2019. Retrieved: https://www.the guardian.com/world/2019/feb/15/french-media-crisis-faces-own-metoo -moment-ligue-du-lol?CMP=share_btn_link.

Chong, Phillipa K. 2020. *Inside the Critics' Circle: Book Reviewing in Uncertain Times*. Princeton: Princeton University Press.

Christin, Angèle. 2015. "'Sex, Scandals, and Celebrities'? Exploring the Determinants of Popularity in Online News." *About Journalism* 4(2):28–47.

Christin, Angèle. 2016. "Is Journalism a Transnational Field? Asymmetrical Relations and Symbolic Domination in Online News." *Sociological Review* 64(2): 212–234.

Christin, Angèle. 2017. "Algorithms in Practice: Comparing Web Journalism and Criminal Justice." *Big Data & Society* 4(2):1–14.

Christin, Angèle. 2018. "Counting Clicks: Quantification and Variation in Web Journalism in the United States and France." *American Journal of Sociology* 123(5):1382–1415.

Christin, Angèle. 2018. "Les sites d'information en ligne entre indépendance et course au clic: Une comparaison franco-américaine." *Sociétés contemporaines* 111(3):71–96.

Citron, Danielle Keats. 2014. *Hate Crimes in Cyberspace*. Cambridge, MA: Harvard University Press.

Coates, Ta-Nehisi. 2013. "'Lucrative Work-for-Free Opportunity.'" *The Atlantic*, March 9. Retrieved: https://www.theatlantic.com/national/archive/2013/03/lucrative-work-for-free-opportunity/273846/.

Cohen, Nicole S. 2016. *Writers' Rights: Freelance Journalism in a Digital Age*. Montreal: McGill-Queen's University Press.

Coleman, E. Gabriella. 2010. "Ethnographic Approaches to Digital Media." *Annual Review of Anthropology* 39(1):487–505.

Collins, Randall. 2004. *Interaction Ritual Chains* Princeton: Princeton University Press.

Comaroff, Jean, and John Comaroff. 2003. "Ethnography on an Awkward Scale: Postcolonial Anthropology and the Violence of Abstraction." *Ethnography* 4(2):147–179.

Comaroff, John L., and Jean Comaroff. 1992. *Ethnography and the Historical Imagination*. Boulder: Westview Press.

Coopmans, Catelijne, Janet Vertesi, Michael E. Lynch, and Steve Woolgar, eds. 2014. *Representation in Scientific Practice Revisited*. Cambridge, MA: MIT Press.

Corbin, Juliet M., and Anselm L. Strauss. 1993. "The Articulation of Work through Interaction." *The Sociological Quarterly* 34(1):71–83.

Correll, Shelley J., Stephen Benard, and In Paik. 2007. "Getting a Job. Is There a Motherhood Penalty?" *American Journal of Sociology* 112(5):1297–1339.

Coscarelli, Joe. 2013. "Nate Thayer vs. The Atlantic: 'Exposure Doesn't Feed My F*cking Children!'" *New York Magazine*, The Intelligencer. Retrieved: http://nymag.com/intelligencer/2013/03/nate-thayer-vs-the-atlantic-writing-for-free.html.

Cottom, Tressie McMillan. 2017. "Black CyberFeminism: Intersectionality, Institutions, and Digital Sociology." In *Digital Sociologies*, edited by J. Daniels, K. Gregory, and T. McMillan Cottom. Bristol, UK: Policy Press, 211–232.

Couldry, Nick, and Ulises A. Mejias. 2019. *The Costs of Connection. How Data Is Colonizing Human Life and Appropriating It for Capitalism*. Stanford: Stanford University Press.

Couldry, Nick, Sonia M. Livingstone, and Tim Markham. 2010. *Media Consumption and Public Engagement: Beyond the Presumption of Attention*. Basingstoke: Palgrave Macmillan.

Crain, Matthew. 2014. "Financial Markets and Online Advertising: Reevaluating the Dotcom Investment Bubble." *Information, Communication & Society* 17(3):371–384.

Cranberg, Gilbert, Randall P. Bezanson, and John Soloski. 2001. *Taking Stock: Journalism and the Publicly Traded Newspaper Company*. New York: Wiley.

Crow, Thomas E. 1985. *Painters and Public Life in Eighteenth Century Paris*. New Haven: Yale University Press.

Czarniawska, Barbara, and Guje Sevón, eds. 2005. *Global Ideas: How Ideas, Objects and Practices Travel in the Global Economy*. Copenhagen: Liber & Copenhagen Business School Press.

Daniels, Arlene Kaplan. 1987. "Invisible Work." *Social Problems* 34(5):403–415.

Darnton, Robert. 1975. "Writing News and Telling Stories." *Daedalus* 104(2):175–194.

Darnton, Robert. 1985. *The Literary Underground of the Old Regime*. Cambridge, MA: Harvard University Press.

Daston, Lorraine, and Peter Galison. 2007. *Objectivity*. New York: Zone Books.

Davenport, Thomas H., and D. J. Patil. 2012. "Data Scientist: The Sexiest Job of the 21st Century." Harvard Business Review. Retrieved: https://hbr.org/2012/10/data-scientist-the-sexiest-job-of-the-21st-century.

De la Motte, Dean, and Jeannene M. Przyblyski, eds. 1999. *Making the News: Modernity & the Mass Press in Nineteenth-Century France*. Amherst: University of Massachusetts Press.

De Sola Pool, Ithiel, and Irwin Shulman. 1959. "Newsmen's Fantasies, Audiences, and Newswriting." *Public Opinion Quarterly* 23(2):145–158.

Delporte, Christian, Claire Blandin, and François Robinet. 2016. *Histoire de la presse en France: XXe–XXIe siècles*. Malakoff: Armand Colin.

Deringer, William. 2018. *Calculated Values: Finance, Politics, and the Quantitative Age*. Cambridge, MA: Harvard University Press.

Desmond, Matthew. 2019. "If You Want to Understand the Brutality of American Capitalism, You Have to Start on the Plantation." *New York Times*, Aug. 14, 2019. Retrieved: https://www.nytimes.com/interactive/2019/08/14/magazine/slavery-capitalism.html.

Desrosieres, Alain. 2000. *La politique des grands nombres: Histoire de la raison statistique*. Paris: La Découverte.

Deuze, Mark. 2006. "Participation, Remediation, Bricolage: Considering Principal Components of a Digital Culture." *The Information Society* 22(2):63–75.

Deuze, Mark. 2008. "The Changing Context of News Work: Liquid Journalism and Monitorial Citizenship." *International Journal of Communication* 2:848–865.

Dewey, John. 1922. "Review of Public Opinion." *New Republic* 30(387):286–288.

Dezalay, Yves, and Bryant G. Garth. 2002. *The Internationalization of Palace Wars: Lawyers, Economists, and the Contest to Transform Latin American States*. Chicago: University of Chicago Press.

Diakopoulos, Nicholas. 2019. *Automating the News: How Algorithms Are Rewriting the Media*. Cambridge, MA: Harvard University Press.

DiMaggio, Paul J., and Walter W. Powell. 1983. "The Iron Cage Revisited: Institutional Isomorphism and Collective Rationality in Organizational Fields." *American Sociological Review* 48(2):147–160.

Domingo, David. 2008. "Interactivity in the Daily Routines of Online Newsrooms: Dealing with an Uncomfortable Myth." *Journal of Computer-Mediated Communication* 13(3):680–704.

Donegan, Moira. 2018. "I Started the Media Men List. My Name Is Moira Donegan." *The Cut*, January 10. Retrieved: https://www.thecut.com/2018/01/moira-donegan-i-started-the-media-men-list.html.

Downie Jr., Leonard, and Robert G. Kaiser. 2003. *The News about the News: American Journalism in Peril*. New York: Vintage Books.

Downie Jr., Leonard, and Michael Schudson. 2009. "The Reconstruction of American Journalism." *Columbia Journalism Review*. October 19. Retrieved: https://archives.cjr.org/reconstruction/the_reconstruction_of_american.php.

Duffy, Brooke Erin. 2017. *(Not) Getting Paid to Do What You Love: Gender, Social Media, and Aspirational Work*. New Haven: Yale University Press.

Duffy, Brooke Erin, and Emily Hund. 2015. "'Having it All' on Social Media: Entrepreneurial Femininity and Self Branding Among Fashion Bloggers." *Social Media + Society*: 1–15.

Dugowson, Maurice, and Marie-Eve Chamard. 1996. *Télévisions, histoires secrètes*, Gaumont Télévision—France 3.

Dupuy, Camille. 2014. "Repenser les acteurs et la négociation collective au travail. Le cas des sociétés de journalistes dans les entreprises de presse." *Négociations* 21(1):51–64.

Duval, Julien. 2004. *Critique de la raison journalistique: Les transformations de la presse économique en France*. Paris: Seuil.

Editorial Freelancers Association. n.d. "Editorial Rates." Retrieved: https://www.the-efa.org/rates/.

Edmonds, Rick. 2014. "Time to Ditch Uniques and Page Views for Engagement in Measuring Digital Audiences." *Poynter*, March 17, 2014. Retrieved: https://www.poynter.org/reporting-editing/2014/time-to-ditch-uniques-and-page-views-for-engagement-in-measuring-digital-audiences/.

Edwards, Richard. 1979. *Contested Terrain: The Transformation of the Workplace in the Twentieth Century*. New York: Basic Book.

Englehardt, Steven, and Arvind Narayanan. 2019. "Online Tracking: A 1-million-site Measurement and Analysis." Retrieved: https://webtransparency.cs.princeton.edu/webcensus/.

Espeland, Wendy Nelson, and Michael Sauder. 2007. "Rankings and Reactivity: How Public Measures Recreate Social Worlds." *American Journal of Sociology* 113(1):1–40.

Espeland, Wendy Nelson, and Michael Sauder. 2016. *Engines of Anxiety: Academic Rankings, Reputation, and Accountability*. New York, New York: Russell Sage Foundation.

Espeland, Wendy Nelson, and Mitchell L. Stevens. 1998. "Commensuration as a Social Process." *Annual Review of Sociology* 24(1):313–343.

Esser, Frank. 1998. "Editorial Structures and Work Principles in British and German Newsrooms." *European Journal of Communication* 13(3):375–405.

Ettema, James S., and D. Charles Whitney, eds. 1994. *Audiencemaking: How the Media Create the Audience*. Thousand Oaks: Sage Publications.

Etzioni, Amitai. 1961. *A Comparative Analysis of Complex Organizations on Power, Involvement, and Their Correlates*. New York: Free Press of Glencoe.

Eubanks, Virginia. 1999. "The Mythography of the 'New' Frontier." MIT Communication Forum. Retrieved: http://web.mit.edu/comm-forum/legacy/papers/eubanks.html.

Eubanks, Virginia. 2017. *Automating Inequality: How High-Tech Tools Profile, Police, and Punish the Poor*. New York: St Martin's Press.

Eveno, Patrick. 2015. "Mesurer l'audience de la presse, toute une histoire." INA, La Revue des Médias. Retrieved: https://larevuedesmedias.ina.fr/mesurer-laudience-de-la-presse-toute-une-histoire.

Evensen, Bruce J. 2017. "Journalism." In *A Companion to the Gilded Age and Progressive Era*, Wiley Blackwell Companions to American History, edited by C. M. Nichols and N. C. Unger. Malden: Wiley-Blackwell.

Eyal, Gil, and Larissa Buchholz. 2010. "From the Sociology of Intellectuals to the Sociology of Interventions." *Annual Review of Sociology* 36(1):117–137.

Ferenczi, Thomas. 1993. *L'invention du journalisme en France: Naissance de la presse moderne à la fin du XIXe siècle*. Paris: Plon.

Ferrer-Conill, Raul, and Edson C. Tandoc Jr. 2018. "The Audience-Oriented Editor: Making Sense of the Audience in the Newsroom." *Digital Journalism* 6(4):436–453.

Filler, Louis. 1993. *The Muckrakers*. Stanford: Stanford University Press.

Fligstein, Neil. 1985. "The Spread of the Multidivisional Form Among Large Firms, 1919–1979." *American Sociological Review* 50(3):377–391.

Fligstein, Neil, and Doug McAdam. 2012. *A Theory of Fields*. New York: Oxford University Press.

Foer, Franklin. 2017. "When Silicon Valley Took over Journalism." *The Atlantic*, September 2017. Retrieved: https://www.theatlantic.com/magazine/archive/2017/09/when-silicon-valley-took-over-journalism/534195/.

Foucault, Michel. 1995. *Discipline and Punish: The Birth of the Prison*. New York: Vintage Books.

Foucault, Michel. 2010. *The Birth of Biopolitics: Lectures at the Collège de France, 1978–79*, edited by M. Senellart. New York: Picador.

Fourcade, Marion. 2010. *Economists and Societies: Discipline and Profession in the United States, Britain, and France, 1890s to 1990s*. Princeton: Princeton University Press.

Fourcade, Marion. 2011. "Cents and Sensibility: Economic Valuation and the Nature of 'Nature.'" *American Journal of Sociology* 116(6):1721–1777.

Fraser, Nancy. 1990. "Rethinking the Public Sphere: A Contribution to the Critique of Actually Existing Democracy." *Social Text* (25/26):56.

Friedland, Roger, and Robert R. Alford. 1991. "Bringing Society Back In: Symbols, Practices, and Institutional Contradictions." In *The New Institutionalism in Organizational Analysis*, edited by P. J. DiMaggio and W. W. Powell. Chicago: University of Chicago Press.

Fröhlich, Romy, and Christina Holtz-Bacha, eds. 2003. *Journalism Education in Europe and North America: An International Comparison*. Cresskill: Hampton Press.

Gamson, Joshua. 1998. *Freaks Talk Back. Tabloid Talk Shows and Sexual Nonconformity*. Chicago: University of Chicago Press.

Gans, Herbert J. 2004. *Deciding What's News: A Study of CBS Evening News, NBC Nightly News, Newsweek, and Time*. Evanston: Northwestern University Press.

Geertz, Clifford. 1978. "The Bazaar Economy: Information and Search in Peasant Marketing." *American Economic Review* 68(2):28–32.

Geiger, R. Stuart. 2009. "Does Habermas Understand the Internet? The Algorithmic Construction of the Blogo/Public Sphere." *Gnovis: A Journal of Communication, Culture, and Technology* 10(1):1–29.

Geiger, R. Stuart. 2017. "Beyond Opening Up the Black Box: Investigating the Role of Algorithmic Systems in Wikipedian Organizational Culture." *Big Data & Society*, 1–14.

Geiger, R. Stuart, and David Ribes. 2011. "Trace Ethnography: Following Coordination through Documentary Practices." In *HICSS 2011 44th Hawaii International Conference on System Sciences*. Kauai: IEEE.

Gerber, Alison. 2017. *The Work of Art. Value in Creative Careers*. Stanford: Stanford University Press.

Gershon, Ilana. 2017. *Down and Out in the New Economy: How People Find (or Don't Find) Work Today*. Chicago: University of Chicago Press.

Gibson, William. 1984. *Neuromancer*. New York: Ace Books.

Gieryn, Thomas F. 1983. "Boundary-Work and the Demarcation of Science from Non-Science: Strains and Interests in Professional Ideologies of Scientists." *American Sociological Review* 48(6):781–795.

Gillespie, Tarleton. 2010. "The Politics of 'Platforms.'" *New Media & Society* 12 (3):347–364.

Gillespie, Tarleton. 2016. "#Trendingistrending: When Algorithms Become Culture." In *Algorithmic Cultures: Essays on Meaning, Performance and New Technologies*, edited by R. Seyfert and J. Roberge. Abingdon: Routledge.

Gillespie, Tarleton. 2018. *Custodians of the Internet: Platforms, Content Moderation, and the Hidden Decisions That Shape Social Media*. New Haven: Yale University Press.

Gingras, Yves. 2016. *Bibliometrics and Research Evaluation: Uses and Abuses*. Cambridge, MA: MIT Press.

Gitlin, Todd. 2000. *Inside Prime Time*. Berkeley: University of California Press.

Glaser, Barney G., and Anselm L. Strauss. 1967. *The Discovery of Grounded Theory: Strategies for Qualitative Research*. New York: Aldine.

Glasser, Theodore Lewis, ed. 1999. *The Idea of Public Journalism*. New York: Guilford Press.

Goffman, Alice. 2014. *On the Run: Fugitive Life in an American City, Fieldwork Encounters and Discoveries*. Chicago: University of Chicago Press.

Gonzalez, Juan, and Joseph Torres. 2012. *News for All the People. The Epic Story of Race and the American Media*. New York: Penguin Random House.

Gouldner, Alvin Ward. 1954. *Patterns of Industrial Bureaucracy*. Glencoe: Free Press.

Graham, Mark, and Mohammad Amir Anwar. 2018. "Digital Labour." In *Digital Geographies*, edited by J. Ash, R. Kitchin, and Leszczynski. London: Sage.

Graves, Lucas, John Kelly, and Marissa Gluck. 2010. *Confusion Online: Faulty Metrics and the Future of Digital Journalism*. Tow Center for Digital Journalism.

Gray, Mary L., and Siddarth Suri. 2019. *Ghost Work. How to Stop Silicon Valley from Building a New Global Underclass*. New York: Houghton Mifflin Harcourt.

Grégoire, Mathieu. 2009. "La clôture comme seule protection? Syndicats du spectacle et marché du travail dans l'entre-deux-guerres (1919–1937)." *Sociologie du Travail* 51(1):1–24.

Grueskin, Bill, Ava Seave, and Lucas Graves. 2011. "Chapter Six: Aggregation." *Columbia Journalism Review*, May 10. Retrieved: https://archives.cjr.org/the_business_of_digital_journalism/chapter_six_aggregation.php.

Gumperz, John J. 1982. *Discourse Strategies*. Cambridge: Cambridge University Press.

Gustin, Sam. 2011. "Unpaid Blogger Hits 'Slave Owner' Huffington with $105M Class Action Lawsuit." *Wired*, April 12. Retrieved: https://www.wired.com /2011/04/tasini-sues-arianna/.

Habermas, Jürgen. 1989. *The Structural Transformation of the Public Sphere: An Inquiry into a Category of Bourgeois Society.* Cambridge, MA: MIT Press.

Hacking, Ian. 1990. *The Taming of Chance.* Cambridge: Cambridge University Press.

Halimi, Serge. 1997. *Les nouveaux chiens de garde.* Paris: Raisons d'Agir.

Hall, Stuart. 1980. "Encoding/Decoding." In *Culture, Media, Language*, edited by S. Hall, D. Hobson, A. Lowe, and P. Willis. London: Routledge.

Hallin, Daniel C. 1992. "The Passing of the 'High Modernism' of American Journalism." *Journal of Communication* 42(3):14–25.

Hallin, Daniel C., and Paolo Mancini. 2004. *Comparing Media Systems: Three Models of Media and Politics.* Cambridge: Cambridge University Press.

Hamilton, James. 2006. *All the News That's Fit to Sell: How the Market Transforms Information into News.* Princeton: Princeton University Press.

Hamilton, James. 2016. *Democracy's Detectives: The Economics of Investigative Journalism.* Cambridge, MA: Harvard University Press.

Hannerz, Ulf. 1997. "Scenarios for Peripheral Cultures." In *Culture, Globalization, and the World-System: Contemporary Conditions for the Representation of Identity*, edited by A. D. King. Minneapolis: University of Minnesota Press.

Hanusch, Folker. 2017. "Web Analytics and the Functional Differentiation of Journalism Cultures: Individual, Organizational and Platform-Specific Influences on Newswork." *Information, Communication & Society* 20(10):1571–1586.

Hauchecorne, Mathieu. 2009. "Le 'professeur Rawls' et le 'Nobel des pauvres'. La politisation différenciée des théories de la justice de John Rawls et d'Amartya Sen dans les années 1990 en France." *Actes de la recherche en sciences sociales* 176–177(1–2):94–113.

Haveman, Heather A. 2015. *Magazines and the Making of America: Modernization, Community, and Print Culture, 1741–1860.* Princeton: Princeton University Press

Healy, Kieran. 2018. *Data Visualization: A Practical Introduction.* Princeton: Princeton University Press.

Heckscher, Charles C. 1994. "Defining the Post-Bureaucratic Type." In *The Post-Bureaucratic Organization: New Perspectives on Organizational Change*, edited by A. Donnellon and C. C. Heckscher. Thousand Oaks: Sage Publications, 14–62.

Hicks, Marie. 2017. *Programmed Inequality: How Britain Discarded Women Technologists and Lost Its Edge.* Cambridge, MA: MIT Press.

Ho, Karen. 2009. *Liquidated. An Ethnography of Wall Street.* Durham: Duke University Press.

Hohenberg, John. 1997. *The Pulitzer Diaries: Inside America's Greatest Prize.* Syracuse: Syracuse University Press.

Howard, Philip N. 2002. "Network Ethnography and the Hypermedia Organization: New Media, New Organizations, New Methods." *New Media & Society* 4(4):550–574.

Ibsen, Henrik. 1882. *An Enemy of the People*. Retrieved: https://www.gutenberg.org/files/2446/2446-h/2446-h.htm.

Iftikhar, Bilal. 2014. "40 Under 40, Class of 2014—Tony Haile, 36." *Crain's New York Business*. Retrieved: https://www.crainsnewyork.com/node/300641.

Igo, Sarah Elizabeth. 2008. *The Averaged American: Surveys, Citizens, and Making of Mass Public*. Cambridge, MA: Harvard University Press.

Intuit. 2010. "Intuit 2020 Report." Retrieved: https://http-download.intuit.com/http.intuit/CMO/intuit/futureofsmallbusiness/intuit_2020_report.pdf.

Irani, Lilly. 2019. *Chasing Innovation. Making Entrepreneurial Citizens in Modern India*. Princeton: Princeton University Press.

Jacoby, Sanford M. 1985. *Employing Bureaucracy. Managers, Unions, and the Transformation of Work in the 20th Century*. New York: Columbia University Press.

Jenkins, Henry. 2006. *Convergence Culture. Where Old and New Media Collide*. New York: NYU Press.

Jerolmack, Colin, and Shamus Khan. 2014. "Talk Is Cheap: Ethnography and the Attitudinal Fallacy." *Sociological Methods & Research* 43(2):178–209.

Jurkowitz, Mark. 2014. *State of the News Media 2014: The Growth in Digital Reporting: What It Means for Journalism and News Consumers*. Pew Research Center, March 26. Retrieved: http://www.journalism.org/2014/03/26/the-losses-in-legacy/.

Kaiser, Robert G. 2014. "The Bad News about the News." *The Brookings Essay*, October 16. Retrieved: http://csweb.brookings.edu/content/research/essays/2014/bad-news.html.

Kalleberg, Arne L. 2011. *Good Jobs, Bad Jobs: The Rise of Polarized and Precarious Employment Systems in the United States, 1970s to 2000s*. New York: Russell Sage Foundation.

Kellogg, Katherine C. 2011. *Challenging Operations. Medical Reform and Resistance in Surgery*. Chicago: University of Chicago Press.

Kellogg, Katherine C., Melissa Valentine, and Angèle Christin. 2020. "Algorithms at Work: The New Contested Terrain of Control." *Academy of Management Annals* 14(1): 366–410.

Kennedy, Helen, Rosemary Lucy Hill, Giorgia Aiello, and William Allen. 2016. "The Work that Visualisation Conventions Do." *Information, Communication & Society* 19(6):715–735.

Kieffer, Philippe, and Marie-Eve Chamard. 2014. *Presse: Vers un monde sans papier*. Documentary. 1h30mn. Direction: Pierre-Olivier François. Arte France, Extro.

Klinenberg, Eric. 2005. "Convergence: News Production in a Digital Age." *The ANNALS of the American Academy of Political and Social Science* 597(1): 48–64.

Klinenberg, Eric. 2007. *Fighting for Air: The Battle to Control America's Media*. New York: Metropolitan Books.

Knorr-Cetina, Karin. 1999. *Epistemic Cultures: How the Sciences Make Knowledge*. Cambridge, MA: Harvard University Press.

Knorr-Cetina, Karin. 2003. "From Pipes to Scopes: The Flow Architecture of Financial Markets." *Distinktion* 2:7–23.

Knorr-Cetina, Karin, and Urs Bruegger. 2002. "Inhabiting Technology: The Global Lifeform of Financial Markets." *Current Sociology* 50(3):389–405.

Knox, Hannah, and Dawn Nafus, eds. 2018. *Ethnography for a Data-Saturated World*. Manchester: Manchester University Press.

Kramer, Melody. 2019. "How to Build a Metrics-Savvy Newsroom." *American Press Institute*, March 13. Retrieved: https://www.americanpressinstitute.org/publications/how-to-build-a-metrics-savvy-newsroom/single-page/.

Krause, Monika. 2011. "Reporting and the Transformations of the Journalistic Field: US News Media, 1890–2000." *Media, Culture & Society* 33(1):89–104.

Kreiss, Daniel, Megan Finn, and Fred Turner. 2011. "The Limits of Peer Production: Some Reminders from Max Weber for the Network Society." *New Media & Society* 13(2):243–259.

Kuhn, Raymond. 1995. *The Media in France*. Reprinted. London: Routledge.

Kunda, Gideon. 2006. *Engineering Culture: Control and Commitment in a High-Tech Corporation*. Rev. ed. Philadelphia: Temple University Press.

Lafarge, Géraud, and Dominique Marchetti. 2011. "Les portes fermées du journalisme." *Actes de la recherche en sciences sociales* 189(4):72–99.

Lamont, Michèle. 1992. *Money, Morals, and Manners: The Culture of the French and American Upper-Middle Class*. Chicago: University of Chicago Press.

Lamont, Michèle. 2012. "Toward a Comparative Sociology of Valuation and Evaluation." *Annual Review of Sociology* 38(1):201–221.

Lamont, Michèle, Stefan Beljean, and Matthew Clair. 2014. "What is Missing? Cultural Pathways to Inequality." *Socio-Economic Review*, 1–36.

Lamont, Michèle, Gregoire Mallard, and Joshua Guetzkow. 2009. "Fairness as Appropriateness: Negotiating Epistemological Differences in Peer Review." *Science, Technology & Human Values* 34(5):573–606.

Lamont, Michèle, and Virág Molnár. 2002. "The Study of Boundaries in the Social Sciences." *Annual Review of Sociology* 28:167–195.

Lamont, Michèle, and Ann Swidler. 2014. "Methodological Pluralism and the Possibilities and Limits of Interviewing." *Qualitative Sociology* 37(2):153–171.

Lamont, Michèle, and Laurent Thévenot, eds. 2000. *Rethinking Comparative Cultural Sociology: Repertoires of Evaluation in France and the United States*. Cambridge: Cambridge University Press.

Lane, Jeffrey. 2018. *The Digital Street*. New York: Oxford University Press.

Larson, Magali Sarfatti. 1977. *The Rise of Professionalism: A Sociological Analysis*, Berkeley: University of California Press.

Lena, Jennifer C. 2012. *Banding Together: How Communities Create Genres in Popular Music*. Princeton: Princeton University Press.

Lena, Jennifer C. 2019. *Entitled: Discriminating Tastes and the Expansion of the Arts*. Princeton: Princeton University Press.

Lepore, Jill. 2019. "Does Journalism Have a Future?" *The New Yorker*, January 21, 2019. Retrieved: https://www.newyorker.com/magazine/2019/01/28/does-journalism-have-a-future.

Leschziner, Vanina. 2015. *At the Chef's Table. Culinary Creativity in Elite Restaurants*. Stanford: Stanford University Press.

Levy, Karen E. C. 2015. "The Contexts of Control: Information, Power, and Truck-Driving Work." *Information Society* 31 (2):160–174.

Levy, Karen E. C. n.d. "Data-Driven: Truckers and the New Workplace Surveillance." Manuscript in preparation.

Lewis, Rebecca. 2018. "Alternative Influence. Broadcasting the Reactionary Right on YouTube." *Data & Society Institute*. Research Report. Retrieved: https://datasociety.net/output/alternative-influence/.

Lewis, Seth C. 2012. "The Tension between Professional Control and Open Participation: Journalism and Its Boundaries." *Information, Communication & Society* 15(6):836–866.

Lewis, Seth C., and Nikki Usher. 2016. "Trading Zones, Boundary Objects, and the Pursuit of News Innovation: A Case Study of Journalists and Programmers." *Convergence: The International Journal of Research into New Media Technologies*, 22(5):543–560.

Lewis, Seth C., and Oscar Westlund. 2015. "Big Data and Journalism: Epistemology, Expertise, Economics, and Ethics." *Digital Journalism* 3(3):447–466.

Lippmann, Walter. 1991. *Public Opinion*. New Brunswick: Transaction Publishers.

Lippmann, Walter. 2011. *The Phantom Public*. New Brunswick: Transaction Publishers.

Lom, Stacy E. 2015. "Changing Rules, Changing Practices: The Direct and Indirect Effects of Tight Coupling in Figure Skating." *Organization Science* 27(1):36–52.

Luengo, Maria. 2016. "When Codes Collide: Journalists Push Back against Digital Desecration." In *The Crisis of Journalism Reconsidered*, edited by J. C. Alexander, E. B. Breese, and M. Luengo. New York: Cambridge University Press.

Madrigal, Alexis C. 2013. "A Day in the Life of a Digital Editor, 2013." *The Atlantic*, March 6. Retrieved: https://www.theatlantic.com/technology/archive/2013/03/a-day-in-the-life-of-a-digital-editor-2013/273763/.

Maradan, Isabelle. 2014. "Course à l'audience, uniformisation, le journalisme Web tiré vers le bas." *L'Express.fr*, July 10. Retrieved: https://www.lexpress.fr/actualite/medias/course-a-l-audience-uniformisation-le-journalisme-web-tire-vers-le-bas_1556491.html.

Marchetti, Dominique. 2011. "Les portes fermées du journalisme. L'espace social des étudiants des formations 'reconnues.'" *Actes de la recherche en sciences sociales* 189(4):72–99.

Marcus, Sharon. 2019. *The Drama of Celebrity*. Princeton: Princeton University Press.

Martin, Laurent. 2008. "La 'Nouvelle Presse' en France dans les années 1970 ou la réussite par l'échec." *Vingtième siècle. Revue d'histoire*. 98(2):68–69.

Martin, Marc, ed. 1991. *Histoire et médias: Journalisme et journalistes français*. Paris: Albin Michel.

Martin, Marc. 2006. "Retour sur 'l'abominable vénalité de la presse française.'" *Le Temps des médias* 6(1):22–33.

Marwick, Alice E. 2013. *Status Update: Celebrity, Publicity, and Branding in the Social Media Age*. New Haven: Yale University Press.

Marwick, Alice E., and danah boyd. 2011. "I Tweet Honestly, I Tweet Passionately: Twitter Users, Context Collapse, and the Imagined Audience." *New Media & Society* 13(1):114–133.

Marwick, Alice E., and danah boyd. 2014. "Networked Privacy: How Teenagers Negotiate Context in Social Media." *New Media & Society*, 16(7):1051–1067.

Marwick, Alice E., and Rebecca Lewis. 2017. "Media Manipulation and Disinformation Online." *Data & Society Institute*. Research report. Retrieved: https://datasociety.net/pubs/oh/DataAndSociety_MediaManipulationAnd DisinformationOnline.pdf.

Mau, Steffen. 2019. *The Metric Society: On the Quantification of the Social.* New York: Polity.

Mauriac, Laurent. 2002. *Les flingueurs du net: Comment la finance a tué la nouvelle économie.* Paris: Calmann-Lévy.

Mayer-Schönberger, Viktor, and Kenneth Cukier. 2013. *Big Data: A Revolution That Will Transform How We Live, Work, and Think.* Boston: Mariner Books, Houghton Mifflin Harcourt.

Mazzotti, Massimo. 2017. "Algorithmic Life." *Los Angeles Review of Books*, January 22. Retrieved: https://lareviewofbooks.org/article/algorithmic-life/.

McCauley, Michael, B. Lee Artz, DeeDee Halleck, and Paul E. Peterson, eds. 2002. *Public Broadcasting and the Public Interest.* New York: Routledge.

McChesney, Robert Waterman. 1993. *Telecommunications, Mass Media, and Democracy: The Battle for the Control of U.S. Broadcasting, 1928–1935.* New York: Oxford University Press.

McChesney, Robert W., and Victor W. Pickard, eds. 2011. *Will the Last Reporter Please Turn out the Lights: The Collapse of Journalism and What Can Be Done to Fix It.* New York: New Press.

McManus, John H. 1994. *Market-Driven Journalism: Let the Citizen Beware?* Thousand Oaks: Sage Publications.

Mears, Ashley. 2011. *Pricing Beauty: The Making of a Fashion Model.* Berkeley: University of California Press.

Menger, Pierre-Michel. 2011. *Les intermittents du spectacle: Sociologie du travail flexible.* Paris: Editions de l'Ecole des hautes études en sciences sociales.

Meyer, John W., and Brian Rowan. 1977. "Institutionalized Organizations: Formal Structure as Myth and Ceremony." *American Journal of Sociology* 83(2): 340–363.

Miller, Alex P. 2018. "Want Less-Biased Decisions? Use Algorithms." *Harvard Business Review*, July 26. Retrieved: https://hbr.org/2018/07/want-less-biased -decisions-use-algorithms.

Ministère de la Culture et de la Communication. 2013. *Chiffres clés 2012: Presse.* Retrieved: http://www.culture.gouv.fr/Thematiques/Etudes-et-statistiques/Pub lications/Collections-d-ouvrages/Chiffres-cles-statistiques-de-la-culture-2012 -2018/Chiffres-cles-2012.

Molnár, Virág. 2005. "Cultural Politics and Modernist Architecture: The Tulip Debate in Postwar Hungary." *American Sociological Review* 70(1):111–135.

Molyneux, Logan, Avery Holton, and Seth Lewis. 2018. "How Journalists Engage in Branding on Twitter: Individual, Organizational and Institutional Levels." *Information, Communication & Society* 21(10):1386–1401.

Moran, Chris. 2019. "You May Hate Metrics, But They're Making Journalism Better." *Columbia Journalism Review*, April 2. Retrieved: https://www.cjr.org /innovations/you-may-hate-metrics-guardian-audience-twitter-images.php.

Morrill, Calvin, and Gary Alan Fine. 1997. "Ethnographic Contributions to Organizational Sociology." *Sociological Methods & Research* 25(4):424–451.

Mouffe, Chantal. 1999. "Deliberative Democracy or Agonistic Pluralism?" *Social Research* 66(3):745–758.

Muller, Jerry Z. 2018. *The Tyranny of Metrics*. Princeton: Princeton University Press.

Murthy, Dhiraj. 2008. "Digital Ethnography: An Examination of the Use of New Technologies for Social Research." *Sociology* 42(5):837–855.

Nadler, Anthony M. 2016. *Making the News Popular: Mobilizing U.S. News Audiences*. Urbana: University of Illinois Press.

Napoli, Philip M. 2003. *Audience Economics: Media Institutions and the Audience Marketplace*. New York: Columbia University Press.

Napoli, Philip M. 2005. "Audience Measurement and Media Policy: Audience Economics, the Diversity Principle, and the Local People Meter." *Communication Law and Policy* 10(4):349–382.

Napoli, Philip M. 2011. *Audience Evolution: New Technologies and the Transformation of Media Audiences*. New York: Columbia University Press.

Neff, Gina. 2012. *Venture Labor: Work and the Burden of Risk in Innovative Industries*. Cambridge, MA: MIT Press.

Neff, Gina, and David Stark. 2003. "Permanently Beta: Responsive Organization in the Internet Era." In *Society Online: The Internet in Context*, edited by P. N. Howard and S. Jones. Thousand Oaks: Sage.

Neff, Gina, Elizabeth Wissinger, and Sharon Zukin. 2005. "Entrepreneurial Labor among Cultural Producers: 'Cool' Jobs in 'Hot' Industries." *Social Semiotics* 15(3):307–334.

Nelson, Alondra. 2016. *The Social Life of DNA: Race, Reparations, and Reconciliation after the Genome*. New York: Beacon Press.

Neveu, Érik. 2000. "Le genre du journalisme. Des ambivalences de la féminisation d'une profession." *Politix* 13(51):179–212.

Nielsen, Rasmus Kleis. 2016. "The Many Crises of Western Journalism: A Comparative Analysis of Economic Crises, Professional Crises, and Crises of Confidence." In *The Crisis of Journalism Reconsidered*, edited by J. C. Alexander, E. B. Breese, and M. Luengo. New York: Cambridge University Press.

Noble, David F. 1984. *Forces of Production: A Social History of Industrial Automation*. New York: Knopf.

Noble, Safiya U. 2018. *Algorithms of Oppression: How Search Engines Reinforce Racism*. New York: NYU Press.

Observatoire des métiers de la presse. 2018. "Les journalistes détenteurs de la carte de journaliste professionnel 2018." *Métiers presse*. Retrieved: https://metiers-presse.org/.

O'Neil, Cathy. 2016. *Weapons of Math Destruction: How Big Data Increases Inequality and Threatens Democracy*. New York: Crown.

Orlikowski, Wanda J., and Susan V. Scott. 2014. "What Happens When Evaluation Goes Online? Exploring Apparatuses of Valuation in the Travel Sector." *Organization Science* 25(3):868–891.

Ory, Pascal, and Jean-François Sirinelli. 1986. *Les intellectuels en France, de l'affaire Dreyfus à nos jours*. Paris: Armand Colin.

Ostertag, Bob. 2007. *People's Movements, People's Press. The Journalism of Social Justice Movements*. New York: Beacon Press.

Ouakrat, Alan, Jean-Samuel Beuscart, and Kevin Mellet. 2010. "Les régies publicitaires de la presse en ligne." *Réseaux* 160–161(2–3):133–161.

Padioleau, Jean G. 1985. *"Le Monde" et le "Washington Post": Précepteurs et mousquetaires*. Paris: Presse Universitaires de France.

Papacharissi, Zizi. 2008. "The Virtual Sphere 2.0: The Internet, the Public Sphere, and Beyond." In *Routledge Handbook of Internet Politics*, edited by A. Chadwick and P. N. Howard. London: Routledge.

Pariser, Eli. 2011. *The Filter Bubble: How the New Personalized Web Is Changing What We Read and How We Think*. London: Penguin Books.

Parkhurst Ferguson, Priscilla. 1991. *Literary France: The Making of a Culture*. Berkeley: University of California Press.

Pasquale, Frank. 2015. *The Black Box Society: The Secret Algorithms That Control Money and Information*. Cambridge, MA: Harvard University Press.

Pedulla, David. 2020. *Making the Cut. Hiring Decisions, Bias, and the Consequences of Nonstandard, Mismatched, and Precarious Employment*. Princeton: Princeton University Press.

Petre, Caitlin. 2015. "The Traffic Factories: Metrics at Chartbeat, Gawker Media, and The New York Times." Tow Center for Digital Journalism, Columbia School of Journalism. Retrieved: https://academiccommons.columbia.edu/doi/10.7916/D80293W1.

Petre, Caitlin. 2018. "Engineering Consent: How the Design and Marketing of Newsroom Analytics Tools Rationalize Journalists' Labor." *Digital Journalism* 6(4):509–527.

Pettegree, Andrew. 2014. *The Invention of News: How the World Came to Know about Itself*. New Haven: Yale University Press.

Pew Research Center. 2013. *State of the News Media 2013*. Retrieved: http://stateofthemedia.org.

Pew Research Center. 2016. *State of the News Media 2016*. Retrieved: http://www.pewresearch.org/topics/state-of-the-news-media/2016/.

Pew Research Center. 2018. "News Use Across Social Media Platforms 2018." Retrieved: https://www.journalism.org/2018/09/10/news-use-across-social-media-platforms-2018/.

Pickard, Victor. 2010. "Reopening the Postwar Settlement for U.S. Media: The Origins and Implications of the Social Contract Between Media, the State, and the Polity." *Communication, Culture & Critique* 3(2):170–189.

Pilmis, Olivier. 2007. "Des 'employeurs multiples' au 'noyau dur' d'employeurs: Relations d'emploi et concurrence sur le marché des comédiens intermittents." *Sociologie du travail* 49(3):297–315.

Pilmis, Olivier. 2010. "Protection sociale, structures marchandes et temporalité de l'activité. Pigistes et comédiens face à l'assurance-chômage." *Sociologie* 2(1).

Porter, Theodore M. 1996. *Trust in Numbers: The Pursuit of Objectivity in Science and Public Life*. Princeton: Princeton University Press.

Powers, Matthew, and Sandra Vera Zambrano. 2016. "Explaining the Formation of Online News Startups in France and the United States." *Journal of Communication* 66(5):857–877.

Powers, Matthew, and Sandra Vera Zambrano. 2017. "How Journalists Use So-cial Media in France and the United States: Analyzing Technology Use across Journalistic Fields." *New Media & Society* 20(8):2728–2744.

Prenger, Mirjam, and Mark Deuze. 2017. "A History of Innovation and Entrepre-neurialism in Journalism." In *Remaking the News: Essays on the Future of Journalism Scholarship in the Digital Age*, edited by P. J. Boczkowski and C. W. Anderson. Cambridge, MA: MIT Press.

Punday, Daniel. 2000. "The Narrative Construction of Cyberspace: Reading Neu-romancer, Reading Cyberspace Debates." *College English* 63(2):194–213.

Putnam, Robert. 1996. "The Strange Disappearance of Civic America." *The American Prospect*. Retrieved: https://prospect.org/article/strange-disappearance -civic-america.

"Qui Sommes-Nous?" 2009. *Syndicat de la presse indépendante d'information en ligne*. Retrieved: https://www.spiil.org/qui-sommes-nous.

Rahman, Hatim A. 2019. "From Iron Cages to Invisible Cages: Algorithmic Eval-uations in Online Labor Markets." Unpublished manuscript.

Raviola, Elena. 2017. "Meetings Between Frames: Negotiating Worth Between Journalism and Management. *European Management Journal* 35: 737–744.

Read, Max. 2018. "How Much of the Internet is Fake? Turns Out, A Lot of It, Actually." *New York Magazine*, Intelligencer, Dec. 26. Retrieved: http://nymag .com/intelligencer/2018/12/how-much-of-the-internet-is-fake.html.

Reagle, Joseph Michael. 2015. *Reading the Comments: Likers, Haters, and Ma-nipulators at the Bottom of the Web*. Cambridge, MA: MIT Press.

Reich, Adam D. 2012. "Disciplined Doctors: The Electronic Medical Record and Physicians' Changing Relationship to Medical Knowledge." *Social Science & Medicine* 74(7):1021–1028.

Reich, Adam D. 2014. *Selling Our Souls: The Commodification of Hospital Care in the United States*. Princeton: Princeton University Press.

Ritzer, George. 2011. *The McDonaldization of Society*. 6th ed. Los Angeles: Sage.

Roberts, Gene, and Hank Klibanoff. 2007. *The Race Beat. The Press, the Civil Rights Struggle, and the Awakening of a Nation*. New York: Penguin Random House.

Roberts, Sarah T. 2018. *Behind the Screen. Content Moderation in the Shadows of Social Media*. New Haven: Yale University Press.

Robinson, James G. 2019. "The Audience in the Mind's Eye: How Journalists Imagine Their Readers." *Tow Center for Digital Journalism*, Columbia School of Journalism. Retrieved: https://www.cjr.org/tow_center_reports/how-journal ists-imagine-their-readers.php?mc_cid=389d4aee19.

Rodgers, Daniel T. 2000. *Atlantic Crossings: Social Politics in a Progressive Age*. Cambridge, MA: Belknap Press.

Rosen, Jay. 2006. "The People Formerly Known as the Audience." *PressThink*. Retrieved: http://archive.pressthink.org/2006/06/27/ppl_frmr.html.

Rosenblat, Alex. 2018. *Uberland: How Algorithms Are Rewriting the Rules of Work*. Berkeley: University of California Press.

Rosenblat, Alex, Tamara Kneese, and danah boyd. 2014. "Workplace Surveil-lance." *SSRN Electronic Journal*. Retrieved: https://repository.usfca.edu/cgi/view content.cgi?article=1021&context=ms.

Rosenblat, Alex, and Luke Stark. 2016. "Algorithmic Labor and Information Asymmetries: A Case Study of Uber's Drivers." *International Journal of Communication* 10: 3758–3784.

Rosenkranz, Tim. 2018. "From Contract to Speculation: New Relations of Work and Production in Freelance Travel Journalism." *Work, Employment & Society* 33(4): 613–630.

Rossman, Gabriel. 2012. *Climbing the Charts: What Radio Airplay Tells Us about the Diffusion of Innovation*. Princeton: Princeton University Press.

Rottenburg, Richard, Sally E. Merry, Sung-Joon Park, and Johanna Mugler, eds. 2015. *The World of Indicators: The Making of Governmental Knowledge through Quantification*. Cambridge: Cambridge University Press.

Ryfe, David. 2012. *Can Journalism Survive? An Inside Look at American Newsrooms*. Cambridge: Polity Press.

Ryfe, David. 2016. *Journalism and the Public*. New York: Polity.

Sallaz, Jeffrey J. 2009. *The Labor of Luck: Casino Capitalism in the United States and South Africa*. Berkeley: University of California Press.

Sallaz, Jeffrey J. 2012. "Politics of Organizational Adornment: Lessons from Las Vegas and Beyond." *American Sociological Review* 77(1):99–119.

Salmon, Felix. 2013. "The Problem with Online Freelance Journalism." *Reuters Blogs*. Retrieved: http://blogs.reuters.com/felix-salmon/2013/03/05/the-problem-with-online-freelance-journalism/.

Sauder, Michael, and Wendy Nelson Espeland. 2009. "The Discipline of Rankings: Tight Coupling and Organizational Change." *American Sociological Review* 74(1):63–82.

Saval, Nikil. 2014. *Cubed: A Secret History of the Workplace*. New York: Doubleday.

Saxenian, AnnaLee. 1994. *Regional Advantage: Culture and Competition in Silicon Valley and Route 128*. Cambridge, MA: Harvard University Press.

Schmidt, Christine. 2019. "How to Build a Newsroom Culture that Cares about Metrics Beyond Pageviews." *NiemanLab*, March 13, 2019. Retrieved: https://www.niemanlab.org/2019/03/how-to-build-a-newsroom-culture-that-cares-about-metrics-beyond-pageviews/.

Scholz, Trebor, ed. 2012. *Digital Labor: The Internet as Playground and Factory*. New York: Routledge.

Schrader, Brendon. 2015. "Here's Why the Freelancer Economy Is on the Rise." *Fast Company*, August 10. Retrieved: https://www.fastcompany.com/3049532/heres-why-the-freelancer-economy-is-on-the-rise.

Schudson, Michael. 1978. *Discovering the News: A Social History of American Newspapers*. New York: Basic Books.

Schudson, Michael. 1995. "Was There Ever a Public Sphere?" In *The Power of News*. Cambridge, MA: Harvard University Press.

Schudson, Michael. 2005. "Autonomy from What?" In *Bourdieu and the Journalistic Field*, edited by R. D. Benson and E. Neveu. Cambridge: Polity.

Scott, James C. 1999. *Seeing like a State: How Certain Schemes to Improve the Human Condition Have Failed*. New Haven: Yale University Press.

Seaver, Nick. 2017. "Algorithms as Culture: Some Tactics for the Ethnography of Algorithmic Systems." *Big Data & Society* 4(2).

Sewell, Graham. 1998. "The Discipline of Teams: The Control of Team-Based Industrial Work Through Electronic and Peer Surveillance." *Administrative Science Quarterly* 43(2):397–428.

Sharkey, Amanda J., and Patricia Bromley. 2015. "Can Ratings Have Indirect Effects? Evidence from the Organizational Response to Peers' Environmental Ratings." *American Sociological Review* 80(1):63–91.

Shestakofsky, Benjamin. 2017. "Working Algorithms: Software Automation and the Future of Work." *Work and Occupations* 44(4):376–423.

Shirky, Clay. 2008. *Here Comes Everybody: The Power of Organizing without Organizations.* New York: Penguin Press.

Shklovski, Irina, and Janet Vertesi. 2013. "'Un-Googling' Publications: The Ethics and Problems of Anonymization." P. 2169 in *CHI '13 Extended Abstracts on Human Factors in Computing Systems on—CHI EA '13.* ACM Press.

Shoemaker, Pamela J., and Elizabeth Kay. Mayfield. 1987. *Building a Theory of News Content: A Synthesis of Current Approaches.* Columbia: Association for Education in Journalism and Mass Communication.

Siles, Ignacio. 2017. *Networked Selves: Trajectories of Blogging in the United States and France.* New York: Peter Lang.

Silverman, Craig. 2016. "This Analysis Shows How Viral Fake Election News Stories Outperformed Real News on Facebook." *Buzzfeed News,* November 16. Retrieved: https://www.buzzfeednews.com/article/craigsilverman/viral-fake-election-news-outperformed-real-news-on-facebook.

Simmel, Georg. 2011. *The Philosophy of Money.* Abingdon: Routledge.

Singel, Ryan. 2008. "The Huffington Post Slammed for Content Theft." *Wired,* December 19. Retrieved: https://www.wired.com/2008/12/huffpo-slammed/.

Singer, Jane B., David Domingo, Ari Heinonen, Alfred Hermida, Steve Paulussen, Quandt Thorsten, Zvi Reich, and Marina Vujnovic, eds. 2011. *Participatory Journalism: Guarding Open Gates at Online Newspapers.* Malden: Wiley-Blackwell.

Small, Mario Luis. 2009. "'How Many Cases Do I Need?': On Science and the Logic of Case Selection in Field-Based Research." *Ethnography* 10(1):5–38.

Smith, Andrew. 2012. *Totally Wired: The Wild Rise and Crazy Fall of the First Dotcom Dream.* London: Simon & Schuster.

Smythe, Dallas W. 1981. "On the Audience Commodity and Its Work." In *Dependency Road: Communications, Capitalism, Consciousness, and Canada.* Norwood, NJ: Ablex.

Snow, David A. 1980. "The Disengagement Process: A Neglected Problem in Participant Observation Research." *Qualitative Sociology* 3(2):100–122.

Sousa Santos, Boaventura. 2006. "The Heterogeneous State and Legal Pluralism in Mozambique." *Law & Society Review* 40(1):39–76.

Star, Susan Leigh. 1999. "The Ethnography of Infrastructure." *American Behavioral Scientist* 43(3):377–391.

Star, Susan Leigh, and Anselm Strauss. 1999. "Layers of Silence, Arenas of Voice: The Ecology of Visible and Invisible Work." *Computer Supported Cooperative Work (CSCW)* 8(1–2):9–30.

Stark, David. 2011. *The Sense of Dissonance: Accounts of Worth in Economic Life.* Princeton: Princeton University Press.

Starkman, Dean. 2010. "The Hamster Wheel: Why Running as Fast as We Can Is Getting Us Nowhere." *Columbia Journalism Review*, October. Retrieved: https://archives.cjr.org/cover_story/the_hamster_wheel.php.

Starkman, Dean. 2011. "Confidence Game: The Limited Vision of the News Gurus." *Columbia Journalism Review*, December. Retrieved: https://archives.cjr.org/essay/confidence_game.php.

Starr, Paul. 2005. *The Creation of the Media: Political Origins of Modern Communications*. New York: Basic Books.

Stempel, Jonathan. 2012. "Unpaid Bloggers' Lawsuit versus Huffington Post Tossed." *Reuters*, March 30. Retrieved: https://www.reuters.com/article/us-aol-huffingtonpost-bloggers/unpaid-bloggers-lawsuit-versus-huffington-post-tossed-idUSBRE82T17L20120330.

Strathern, Marilyn, ed. 2000. *Audit Cultures: Anthropological Studies in Accountability, Ethics, and the Academy*. Abingdon: Routledge.

Statista. 2016. "Number of Monthly Active Twitter Users Worldwide From 1st Quarter 2010 to 3rd 2016 (in Millions)." Retrieved: https://www.statista.com/statistics/282087/number-of-monthly-active-twitter-users/.

Statista. 2017. "Number of Monthly Active Facebook Users Worldwide as of 4th Quarter 2016 (in Millions)." Retrieved: https://www.statista.com/statistics/264810/number-of-monthly-active-facebook-users-worldwide/.

Stuart, Forrest. 2020. *Ballad of the Bullet. Gangs, Drill Music, and the Power of Online Infamy*. Princeton: Princeton University Press

Suchman, Lucy, Jeanette Blomberg, Julian E. Orr, and Randall Trigg. 1999. "Reconstructing Technologies as Social Practice." *American Behavioral Scientist* 43(3):392–408.

Swidler, Ann. 2003. *Talk of Love: How Culture Matters*. Chicago: University of Chicago Press.

Syndicat National des Journalistes. 2015. *Barêmes de piges*. Retrieved: http://www.snj.fr/?q=salaires.

Takhatev, Yuri. 2012. *Coding Places. Software Practice in a South American City*. Cambridge, MA: MIT Press.

Tandoc, Edson C., and Ryan J. Thomas. 2015. "The Ethics of Web Analytics: Implications of Using Audience Metrics in News Construction." *Digital Journalism* 3(2):243–258.

Tarnoff, Ben. 2017. "Silicon Valley Siphons Our Data Like Oil. But the Deepest Drilling Has Just Begun." *The Guardian*, August 23. Retrieved: https://www.theguardian.com/world/2017/aug/23/silicon-valley-big-data-extraction-amazon-whole-foods-facebook.

Tavory, Iddo, and Stefan Timmermans. 2009. "Two Cases of Ethnography: Grounded Theory and the Extended Case Method." *Ethnography* 10(3): 243–263.

Taylor, Catherine. 2010. "Newspapers Online Traffic Is Strong, So Why Are Ad Rates Weak?" *CBS News*. June 29. Retrieved: https://www.cbsnews.com/news/newspapers-online-traffic-is-strong-so-why-are-ad-rates-weak/.

Taylor, T. L. 2018. *Watch Me Play. Twitch and the Rise of Game Live Streaming*. Princeton: Princeton University Press.

Thayer, Nate. 2013. "A Day in the Life of a Freelance Journalist—2013." *Nate Thayer—Journalist. A Compilation of Current Reporting and Archived Published Work of Journalist Nate Thayer*. Retrieved: http://www.nate-thayer.com /a-day-in-the-life-of-a-freelance-journalist-2013/.

Thomas, Suzanne L., Dawn Nafus, and Jamie Sherman. 2018. "Algorithms as Fetish: Faith and Possibility in Algorithmic Work." *Big Data & Society*, 1–11.

Thornton, Patricia H., William Ocasio, and Michael Lounsbury. 2012. *The Institutional Logics Perspective: A New Approach to Culture, Structure, and Process*. Oxford: Oxford University Press.

Ticona, Julia, and Alexandra Mateescu. 2018. "Trusted Strangers: Cultural Entrepreneurship on Domestic Work Platforms in the On Demand Economy." *New Media & Society* 20(11):4384–4404.

Timmermans, Stefan, and Iddo Tavory. 2012. "Theory Construction in Qualitative Research: From Grounded Theory to Abductive Analysis." *Sociological Theory* 30(3):167–186.

Tocqueville, Alexis de. 2003. *Democracy in America and Two Essays on America*. London: Penguin.

Trouille, David, and Iddo Tavory. 2019. "Shadowing: Warrants for Intersituational Variation in Ethnography." *Sociological Methods and Research* 48(3):534–560.

Tuchman, Gaye. 1973. "Making News by Doing Work: Routinizing the Unexpected." *American Journal of Sociology* 79(1):110–131.

Turco, Catherine J. 2018. *The Conversational Firm. Rethinking Bureaucracy in the Age of Social Media*. New York: Columbia University Press.

Turkle, Sherry. 2015. *Reclaiming Conversation. The Power of Talk in a Digital Age*. New York: Penguin Books.

Turner, Fred. 1999. "Cyberspace as the New Frontier? Mapping the Shifting Boundaries of the Network Society." Red Rock Eater News Service. Retrieved: https://fredturner.stanford.edu/wp-content/uploads/turner cyberspace-as-the -new-frontier.pdf.

Turner, Fred. 2006. *From Counterculture to Cyberculture: Stewart Brand, the Whole Earth Network, and the Rise of Digital Utopianism*. Chicago: University of Chicago Press.

Turner, Fred. 2009. "Burning Man at Google: A Cultural Infrastructure for New Media Production." *New Media & Society* 11(1–2):73–94.

Turow, Joseph. 2005. "Audience Construction and Culture Production: Marketing Surveillance in the Digital Age." *The ANNALS of the American Academy of Political and Social Science* 597(1):103–121.

Turow, Joseph. 2013. *The Daily You: How the New Advertising Industry Is Defining Your Identity and Your Worth*. New Haven: Yale University Press.

Usher, Nikki. 2013. "Al Jazeera English Online." *Digital Journalism* 1(3):335–351.

Usher, Nikki. 2014. *Making News at The New York Times*. Ann Arbor: University of Michigan Press.

Vaidhyanathan, Siva. 2011. *The Googlization of Everything: And Why We Should Worry*. Berkeley: University of California Press.

Vaidhyanathan, Siva. 2018. *Antisocial Media: How Facebook Disconnects Us and Undermines Democracy*. New York: Oxford University Press.

Vallas, Steven P., and Angèle Christin. 2018. "Work and Identity in an Era of Precarious Employment: How Workers Respond to 'Personal Branding' Discourse." *Work and Occupations* 45(1):3–37.

Vallas, Steven P., and Emily R. Cummins. 2015. "Personal Branding and Identity Norms in the Popular Business Press: Enterprise Culture in an Age of Precarity." *Organization Studies* 36(3):293–319.

van Dijck, José. 2013. *The Culture of Connectivity. A Critical History of Social Media*. Oxford: Oxford University Press.

Vatin, François. 2009. *Evaluer et valoriser: une sociologie économique de la mesure*. Toulouse: Presses Universitaires du Mirail.

Venkatesh, Sudhir. 2002. "'Doin' the Hustle': Constructing the Ethnographer in the American Ghetto." *Ethnography* 3(1):91–111.

Vertesi, Janet. Forthcoming. *The Social Life of Spacecraft. How Organizations Shape Science on NASA's Robotic Team*. Chicago: University of Chicago Press.

Wahl-Jorgensen, Karin. 2002. "The Construction of the Public in Letters to the Editor: Deliberative Democracy and the Idiom of Insanity." *Journalism: Theory, Practice & Criticism* 3(2):183–204.

Waldman, Steven. 2011. *The Information Needs of Communities: The Changing Media Landscape in a Broadband Age*. Federal Communications Commission. Retrieved: https://transition.fcc.gov/osp/inc-report/The_Information_Needs_of_Communities.pdf.

Ward, Douglas B. 1996. "The Reader as Consumer: Curtis Publishing Company and Its Audience, 1910–1930." *Journalism History* 22(2):47.

Warner, Michael. 2002. *Publics and Counterpublics*. New York: Zone Books.

Weaver, David H., Randal A. Beam, Bonnie J. Brownlee, Paul S. Voakes, and G. Cleveland Wilhoit, eds. 2007. *The American Journalist in the 21st Century: U.S. News People at the Dawn of a New Millennium*. Mahwah: L. Erlbaum Associates.

Weber, Max. 1919 (1946). "Science as a Vocation." In *From Max Weber: Essays in Sociology*, edited by H. Gerth and C. Wright Mills. New York: Oxford University Press, 129–156.

Weber, Max. 2013. *Economy and Society: An Outline of Interpretive Sociology*. Berkeley: University of California Press.

Webster, James G. 1998. "The Audience." *Journal of Broadcasting & Electronic Media* 42(2):190–207.

Weigel, Moira. 2016. *Labor of Love: The Invention of Dating*. New York: FSG.

Welbers, Kasper, Wouter van Atteveldt, Jan Kleinnijenhuis, Nel Ruigrok, and Joep Schaper. 2015. "News Selection Criteria in the Digital Age: Professional Norms versus Online Audience Metrics." *Journalism* 17(8):1037–1053.

West, Sarah Myers, Meredith Whittaker, and Kate Crawford. 2019. *Discriminating Systems. Gender, Race, and Power in AI*. AI Now Institute. Retrieved: https://ainowinstitute.org/discriminatingsystems.pdf.

Westney, D. Eleanor. 1987. *Imitation and Innovation: The Transfer of Western Organizational Patterns to Meiji Japan*. Cambridge, MA: Harvard University Press.

Whyte, William H. 1956. *The Organization Man*. New York: Simon & Schuster.

Williams, Bruce A., and Michael X. Delli Carpini. 2011. *After Broadcast News: Media Regimes, Democracy, and the New Information Environment.* New York: Cambridge University Press.

Wimmer, Andreas, and Nina Glick Schiller. 2003. "Methodological Nationalism, the Social Sciences, and the Study of Migration: An Essay in Historical Epistemology." *The International Migration Review* 37(3):576–610.

Wood, Alex J., Vili Lehdonvirta, and Mark Graham. 2018. "Workers of the Internet Unite? Online Freelancer Organisation among Remote Gig Economy Workers in Six Asian and African Countries." *New Technology, Work and Employment* 33(2):95–112.

Wu, Hao. 2018. *People's Republic of Desire.* Documentary. 1h35m.

Wu, Tim. 2010. *The Master Switch: The Rise and Fall of Information Empires.* New York: Knopf.

Wu, Tim. 2016. *The Attention Merchants: The Epic Scramble to Get inside Our Heads.* New York: Knopf.

Yeykelis, Leo, James J. Cummings, and Byron Reeves. 2014. "Multitasking on a Single Device: Arousal and the Frequency, Anticipation, and Prediction of Switching Between Media Content on a Computer: Multitasking and Arousal." *Journal of Communication* 64(1):167–192.

Zafirau, Stephen. 2009. "Imagined Audiences: Intuitive and Technical Knowledge in Hollywood." Unpublished PhD dissertation, University of Southern California.

Zamith, Rodrigo. 2018. "Quantified Audiences in News Production. A Synthesis and Research Agenda." *Digital Journalism* 6(4):418–435.

Zelizer, Viviana A. 1994. *Pricing the Priceless Child: The Changing Social Value of Children.* Princeton: Princeton University Press.

Zelizer, Viviana A. 1996. "Payments and Social Ties." *Sociological Forum* 11(3): 481–95.

Zelizer, Viviana A. 1997. *The Social Meaning of Money.* Princeton: Princeton University Press.

Zelizer, Viviana A. 2007. *The Purchase of Intimacy.* Princeton: Princeton University Press.

Zelizer, Viviana A. 2010. *Economic Lives: How Culture Shapes the Economy.* Princeton: Princeton University Press.

Ziewitz, Malte. 2016. "Governing Algorithms: Myth, Mess, and Methods." *Science, Technology, & Human Values* 41(1):3–16.

Ziewitz, Malte. 2019. "Rethinking Gaming: The Ethical Work of Optimization in Web Search Engines." *Social Studies of Science*, 1–25.

Zuboff, Shoshana. 1988. *In the Age of the Smart Machine: The Future of Work and Power.* New York: Basic Books.

Zuboff, Shoshana. 2015. "Big Other: Surveillance Capitalism and the Prospects of an Information Civilization." *Journal of Information Technology* 30:75–89

Zuboff, Shoshana. 2019. *The Age of Surveillance Capitalism. The First for a Human Future at the New Frontier of Power.* New York: Public Affairs.

Zuckerman, Ethan. 2016. "Ben Franklin, the Post Office and the Digital Public Sphere." *My Heart's in Accra: Ethan Zuckerman's Online Home, since 2003.*

Retrieved: http://www.ethanzuckerman.com/blog/2016/02/26/ben-franklin-the-post-office-and-the-digital-public-sphere/.

Zuckerman, Ezra W., and Tai-Young Kim. 2003. "The Critical Trade-Off: Identity Assignment and Box-Office Success in the Feature Film Industry." *Industrial and Corporate Change* 12(1):27–67

Zukin, Sharon, and Max Papadantonakis. 2017. "Hackathons as Co-optation Rituals: Socializing Workers and Institutionalizing Innovation in the 'New' Economy." In *Precarious Work* (Research in the Sociology of Work, Vol. 31), edited by A. L. Kalleberg and S. P. Vallas. Bingley: Emerald Publishing Limited.

INDEX

· · · · · · · ·